The Psychology of Diversity

The Psychology of Diversity

Perceiving and Experiencing Social Difference

Bruce Evan Blaine

Hofstra University

MAYFIELD
PUBLISHING
COMPANY

Mountain View, California

London • Toronto

Library of Congress Cataloging-in-Publication Data

Blaine, Bruce Evan.
　The psychology of diversity: perceiving and experiencing social
　difference / Bruce Evan Blaine.
　　　p.　cm.
　Includes bibliographical references and index.
　ISBN 1-55934-938-7
　1. Prejudices. 2. Stereotype (Psychology) 3. Multiculturalism.
I. Title.
HM1091.B53 1999
303.3′85—dc21
　　　　　　　　　　　　　　　　　　　　　　　　　　　99-44172
　　　　　　　　　　　　　　　　　　　　　　　　　　　CIP

Manufactured in the United States of America
10　9　8　7　6　5　4　3　2　1

Mayfield Publishing Company
1280 Villa Street
Mountain View, CA 94041

Sponsoring editor, Franklin Graham; production editor, Melissa Williams Kreischer; manuscript editor, Elaine Kehoe; design manager, Glenda King; text and cover designer, Joan Greenfield; photo researcher, Brian Pecko; art editor, Rennie Evans; manufacturing manager, Randy Hurst. The text was set in 9/12 Stone Serif by ColorType, San Diego and printed on acid-free 45# Highland Plus by Malloy Lithographing, Inc.

Photo credits appear on page 179, which constitutes an extension of the copyright page.

♻ This book is printed on recycled paper.

CONTENTS

v

PREFACE

This book has grown out of my interest in teaching prejudice-related topics to undergraduate students, combined with the conviction that learning about the experience of prejudice is every bit as important as learning about the process of prejudice. Most books for undergraduate students that address the general topic of prejudice—either surveys of social psychology or more focused books on prejudice—emphasize topics on the "process" side. Check any social psychology textbook: The number of pages devoted to stereotyping and prejudice will far exceed the pages devoted to social stigma. This coverage, of course, partly reflects the research activity in the respective domains. However, the coverage also may reflect an attitude in students and teachers that the process of prejudice (for example, How and why does it occur?) is more important to grasp than the experience of prejudice (e.g., What are the social and psychological effects of being in a minority group?).

This book helps students appreciate the complementary perspectives of "perceiver" and "experiencer" of social difference. In that regard this book has drawn inspiration from Gordon Allport's *The Nature of Prejudice* (Addison-Wesley, 1954). These complementary viewpoints are reflected in the chapter content and organization. Chapters 2–7 present topics relevant to the perception of social difference and address the question, How does the individual help construct the diversity of our social world? Some highlights include material on how stereotypes operate directly to alter our social context (Chapter 3) and how television contributes to our perception of social difference (Chapter 7). The focus of the book shifts with Chapters 8–11, which present topics relevant to the experience of social difference and address the question, How does the diversity of the social world affect the individual? Highlights in these chapters include material on stigma management (Chapter 10) and an analysis of the experience of affirmative action (Chapter 11).

This book has a secondary pedagogical goal: As a social scientist I wanted to weigh in on the topic of "diversity." The academic study of diversity has become, in one guise or another, a mainstay of undergraduate curricula. Its emergence in college catalogs seems to reflect a broader societal concern about how to understand and cope with the increasing degree of social and cultural difference in our communities. Students can study diversity from many perspectives—college courses on diversity often reflect historical and sociological, as well as artistic and literary, voices and perspectives. However, if the study of diversity includes the need to understand the presence of, as well as the problems and issues associated with, social and cultural difference in our society, then psychology has much to offer. This book attempts to draw together a basic psychology of diversity for students in diversity-related courses that are taught outside of psychology departments and curricula.

Following these two pedagogical goals, the book is likely to be serviceable in two course environments: courses on prejudice taught within psychology departments, and courses on diversity that contribute to general education or core curricula. Here are some ideas on how the book might be used in these two environments. As a primary textbook in junior- or senior-level psychology courses on prejudice, the book's conceptual framework (the reciprocal relationship between the individual and his or her social context) might be emphasized across the class discussions and threaded through other reading, writing, and research assignments. Because I have striven to keep jargon and technical discourse to a minimum, instructors in these courses would likely supplement each chapter in this book with primary-source reading of an empirical or theoretical nature.

In using the book as a text in (nonpsychology) diversity courses, instructors might find a more topical approach helpful. Each of the chapters can be taken as a freestanding facet of a psychological perspective on diversity. Admittedly, the relatively abstract (but nonetheless essential) material in Chapters 2 and 3 will challenge nonpsychology students. However, the chapters are more than a routine survey of current and classic research; each of them strives to connect the surveyed research to a specific issue or problem. For example, in Chapter 4 a run-of-the-mill survey of prejudice concepts is exchanged for an analysis of how we evaluate people who are different from ourselves. Rather than being a general overview of theory and research on racism, Chapter 6 helps students learn to what extent racial/ethnic differences in intelligence and school achievement are constructed by ourselves—the social perceivers. In Chapters 9 and 10 the fundamentals of stigma and stigma management are enlivened by applying them to the experience of being overweight. In short, the book incorporates some social issues to help structure the nonpsychology student's learning of general social psychological concepts. Supplementary readings might, therefore, represent alternative perspectives on that particular social issue. Instructors of these types of courses might find that Virginia Cyrus's reader, *Experiencing Race, Class, and Gender in the United States* (Mayfield, 1997) makes a relevant companion text for diversity courses.

Two areas of controversy surfaced in the writing and reviewing of this book—the first surrounding the term "race" and the second about avoiding or adopting an ideological stance toward social difference. I'll briefly address each in turn. Racial stereotyping and discrimination are, obviously, important issues to confront in a book like this. However, most social scientists agree that the concept of race—as a marker for the (so-called) inherent qualities of a group of similar-looking people—is inaccurate and unworkable. Indeed, it is an important task for this book (in Chapter 6) to show students that the notion of race is constructed from cognitive and cultural elements and that this process is based on the erroneous assumption that people who look alike have similar essences. To avoid further reification of race constructs, I use the term *ethnicity* throughout the book when referring to the perception or experience of particular minority groups. Like race, ethnicity is another category label used by perceivers to identify "similar" people. However, unlike race, the term *ethnicity* acknowledges that people may share a history, culture, language, or religion and that these have implications for behavior. In sum, whereas race implies the presence of an unseen essence among "group" members, ethnicity implies the presence of common experience and values. Compared with the former, the latter is a less troublesome construct.

The second controversy concerns how to balance the analysis of and advocacy for issues related to diversity. In other words, when we analyze how people perceive and experience social difference, we confront the fact that social injustices exist. Too much emphasis on social injustices (such as where they originate or how they can be addressed) adds a political element to the book that may be troubling to instructors and students. Avoiding social injustices altogether, however, leads to a sterile, intellectual approach that has its own drawbacks in the classroom. I have chosen to avoid explicit (but probably, given my own social and political attitudes, not implicit) polemic regarding social injustice in the body of the book (Chapters 2–11). I have used Chapters 1 and 12 in bookend fashion as vehicles for addressing those issues. In doing so, I hope the book remains viable for "prejudice" courses in which a more intellectual approach is the norm while offering something to instructors of "diversity" courses who adopt a socially active approach to teaching. As always, ideological perspectives on the text material can be arranged through supplementary readings, videos, or class activities.

Though this book bears my name, it exists because of the contributions and support of many. Appropriately, I take sole responsibility for the book's shortcomings but share responsibility for its strengths with the following people. Frank Graham, my sponsoring editor at Mayfield, has been a patient and wise guide. As a role model for my writing and as a reviewer, Dave Myers's (Hope College) handprint is all over this book. Stephan Franzoi (Marquette University), Charles Behling (University of Michigan), and Charles Walker (St. Bonaventure University) each helped craft this book through their expert reviews and suggestions. I am also indebted to the following reviewers for their suggestions: Christine L. Allegretti, Queens College; John C. Brigham, Florida State University; Brenda S. Collins, Santa Rosa Junior College; Randi I Kim, Humboldt State University; Louis A. Penner, University of South Florida; and Theodore M. Singelis, California State University at Chico. Closer to home, my Hofstra University colleagues Charles Levinthal and Stavros Valenti have administered regular doses of affirmation. Finally, I thank Patti and Kate for their patience and inspiration.

Diversity and the Individual

CHAPTER OBJECTIVE
To introduce the term *diversity* and discuss its various common meanings; to set out the main ideas in a psychology of diversity while also contrasting them with other perspectives on the study of diversity; to give a brief and inviting overview of a psychology of diversity.

Each of us lives in a diverse social world. Although we are frequently unaware of it, our lives unfold within social contexts that are populated by people who are different—both from us and from each other. The people who populate our day-to-day lives may differ in many ways, such as in ethnic identity, sex, cultural background, economic status, political affiliation, or religious belief. The specific dimensions of difference do not matter nearly as much as the fact that we think, feel, and behave within diverse social contexts. Two important ideas follow from the fact that we as individuals are perpetually embedded in social difference.

First, because individuals are literally part of the social contexts in which they behave, those *situations cannot be understood independently of the people in them.* Have you ever been amazed that you perceived a situation, such as a job interview, much differently than a friend did? Perhaps you approached the interview with optimism and confidence, regarding it as a potentially positive step toward your career goals. Your friend, however, may have viewed the same scenario as threatening, bemoaning that it would never work out. This example illustrates how social situations are, in vital part, constructed and maintained by people. We project our own attitudes, feelings, expectations, and fears onto the situations we encounter. Applied to our social contexts, this principle says that the "differentness" we perceive between ourselves and other people, or among other people, may be inaccurate. As we will learn in subsequent chapters in this book, there are times when we project too much social difference onto our contexts and the people in them. At other times, however, we underestimate the diversity around us. So the diversity in our lives is partly a function of ourselves—of our individual ways of thinking and emotional needs.

1

Second, because people live and behave in diverse social contexts, *individuals cannot be understood independently of the situations in which they act and interact.* Do you sometimes behave like a "different person" or show a different side of yourself as your social setting changes? For example, do you display different table manners when eating with your friends at the local deli than during a holiday meal with the family? Do you think of yourself differently in those situations? If so, then you realize how we are in large part social beings. Our behavior and identity are constructed and maintained by the situations in which we act and live. Likewise, our thoughts and actions flex with the situational norms we encounter. If we are interested in explaining who we are and why we behave as we do, we must look to the social context for insight. The diversity of our social contexts is laden with informative clues to help us demystify our own behavior and confront our attitudes and beliefs.

In sum, if we are to fully understand the diversity of our community or nation, we must appreciate that diversity is more than statistics about ethnicity, religious preference, or cultural background. Diversity and the individual are inextricably linked; therefore, the study of one must include the other. This book examines how we can better understand diversity by studying how the individual constructs it and how we can better understand the individual by learning how she or he is defined and influenced by social diversity. These two principles of the psychology of diversity will be revisited and elaborated at the end of this chapter. First we must consider what diversity is and examine some of the common ways the term is used.

THE CONCEPT OF DIVERSITY

What is diversity? According to the dictionary, diversity indicates the mere presence of difference. However, the most common usages of *diversity* refer to social difference, or differences among people. In the paragraphs that follow, I briefly describe the range and a few of the dimensions of social differences in our nation and communities. Following that snapshot, we will consider some of the approaches to understanding this diversity.

How Do We Differ? Let's Count the Ways

Although it states the obvious to say that people differ, a picture of how different we are now—and how different we likely will become—is revealing. Let's begin with sex diversity. The American population is presently 49% male and 51% female (all statistics from the U.S. Bureau of the Census, 1996). Although this dimension of social difference is mundane and not likely to change much, it is striking to note how underrepresented women are in many situations and contexts. There are many other dimensions in which an already diverse population

Our social differences are many and varied and include our gender, racial and ethnic background, economic status, and religion.

is becoming more different. In 1997 83% of the U.S. population was White (or of European descent); Black, Asian, and all other ethnic groups combined contributed the remaining 17%. In 2025, however, ethnic minority individuals will make up 22% of the population. As our nation becomes more ethnically diverse, we observe more language diversity and interracial marriages. Indeed, there are now 27 languages spoken by 100,000 or more people in the United States. Imagine 27 large cities, in each of which all of the residents spoke a different language from that of all the other cities. Similarly, the rate of interracial marriages has doubled since 1980; mixed-ethnic unions now occur in 1 out of every 50 marriages.

A similar situation exists with regard to age diversity. Presently about 12% of the population is over 65 years of age. In 2025, however, "seniors" will make up 18% of our country. Much of this increasing age diversity can be attributed to the greater life expectancy for both men and women, which has risen by about 4 years since 1980. We are an increasingly diverse lot with regard to religion too. There are now 76 denominations with at least 60,000 practicing members in the United States. In addition to the variety of Christian and Jewish religious groups, the prevalence of so-called Eastern faiths has increased dramatically in the United States. Our population now includes over 4 million Orthodox believers, one-half million Muslims, 400,000 Buddhists, and about one-quarter million Hindus. Finally, there is a stunning range of economic diversity in our nation. In 1996 the median annual income for all individuals in the United States was about $41,000. However, the income figures for White ($43,000) and Asian ($46,000) Americans were much different from the average incomes for African American ($26,000) and Hispanic ($25,000) individuals. The official poverty level in 1996 was $15,500 for a family of four; according to that figure, 14% of the U.S. population lives in poverty.

These statistics offer a glimpse of the extent of social differences around us. If we are shaped by these differences, then it appears that there is a great potential for our social contexts to influence us. But how do we make sense of this diversity? What does it mean and how do we talk about social difference? Diversity can be approached from several intellectual perspectives, each using the term *diversity* within a different vocabulary. As these shades of meaning can be confusing, we should clarify what is meant by diversity from demographic, political, and ideological perspectives before going on to address the psychology of diversity.

Diversity as a Demographic Concern

A common meaning of diversity involves the range or proportion of social differences that are represented in a group of people, an organization, or a situation. When used in this way—often in concert with social statistics—the term reflects demographic concerns. To understand the nature of social differences and how they differ from individual differences, try this exercise. The next time you attend the class for which you are reading this book, look around and consider the many ways that the people in your class differ. Physically, they have different dimensions, such as weight and height, and characteristics, such as hair color and style. Psychologically, they have varying levels of self-confidence and anxiety. Intellectually, they differ in their verbal ability and intelligence. Finally, the students in your class probably differ in the social categories or groupings that they represent, such as sex, ethnicity, cultural background, and religion. Notice how the first three (physical, psychological, and intellectual) are examples of *individual* differences—each student probably differs from every other student on that dimension. Social differences, however, refer to groupings or categories of individuals—such as male or female; Catholic, Jewish, or Protestant; or single, divorced, or married. People are *socially* different when they associate with or are members of different social categories. Demographers, as scientists of vital and social statistics, study diversity using social categories.

Social categories are also useful and informative tools for a psychological study of diversity. They help us organize and remember other information about people, operating something like computer files in which social information is arranged and stored. As a result, when an individual's social category is brought to mind, that related information—such as our attitudes, beliefs, and expectations about people in that category—becomes very accessible. Try this free association task. What images or thoughts come to mind when you think of the social category *poor*? If you imagined a person who was lacking in intelligence or motivation to make something of him- or herself, dressed in shabby clothes, and living in the bad section of town, you begin to see how social categories are rich with information about a person's characteristics and behavior and how the concept of diversity is influenced by the kind of information we associate with dimensions of social difference.

Social categories are also useful for describing people; that is, we commonly identify others by their social characteristics. In describing a person to a friend, you might say, "you know, she's Hispanic, an engineering major, and a Sigma Tau." (How many social categories are employed in that description?) Compared with descriptions of others that cite individual differences, such as height, level of optimism, and grade point average, descriptions that involve social differences are more available and informative. Social identification is not limited to our thinking about other people; we also identify ourselves in social terms. If asked to describe yourself, you would likely use many social terms such as Asian American, female, Catholic, or Republican. Because we identify ourselves in social terms, we are conscious of the beliefs and assumptions that other people typically associate with those categories.

Psychologists and demographers, therefore, share a common interest in social categories. But whereas demographers analyze social statistics, psychologists are interested in how social differences are related to individual behavior. Clearly, dimensions of social difference play an integral role in thinking about ourselves and other people. The significance of social differences, however, goes beyond the mere fact that we think of people in terms of their social groups. Social categories are laden with a great deal of information that influences how we perceive and experience our social world.

Diversity as a Political Concern

Sometimes the term *diversity* refers to specific dimensions of social difference that typically include sex, race, ethnicity, and, to a lesser extent, physical disability. This meaning may stem from the 1978 Supreme Court *University of California v. Bakke* decision in which "diversity" was viewed as a goal that could justify admitting students to a university based on their race. If so, this meaning of diversity refers to particular social groups who have experienced disadvantage and discrimination (i.e., women, Blacks, Hispanics, and other ethnic minority groups). To have a diverse corporation or university, for example, is to include (or not exclude) members of historically disadvantaged social groups. This definition, however, fails to acknowledge that many social groups other than women and racial minorities have experienced injustice in our society, including gay men and lesbians, the poor, released convicts, Muslims and Jews, and the obese and physically unattractive.

This conceptualization—that diversity means the presence of people from historically disadvantaged social groups or categories—is limiting to a psychological study of diversity in two ways. First, recall that one of the principles of this book is that we construct diversity through our perceptions, beliefs, expectations, and behavior toward people based on social dimensions. But if the concept of diversity is linked predominantly to women and ethnic minorities, then the range of social difference (or *important* social difference) is preestablished for us. Although the motives for including members of historically disadvantaged groups in our schools and businesses are noble, this political meaning of diversity greatly restricts the actual diversity of our social environment.

Second, the political definition of diversity focuses too much attention on social differences that are visible. Although some social differences are visibly apparent, others are not so obvious. For example, can you tell which of your classmates is learning disabled? or Jewish? or gay? Perhaps you think you can based on their behavior or appearance, but, in fact, those judgments are probably not very accurate. From a psychological standpoint, diversity need not be limited to visible dimensions of social difference. Indeed, whether our social differences are visible or hidden from others is an important factor in understanding their influence on our psychological and social adjustment.

While understanding the need to correct historical and contemporary injustices, the psychological study of stigmatization goes beyond the current political definitions to include both the obvious dimensions of social difference and those that are less apparent or even unobservable. Psychological and political approaches to diversity, however, share an important feature—the recognition that there is a greater psychological burden associated with being a member of some social categories than others and that some of this burden is attributable to past oppression and injustice.

Diversity as an Ideological Concern

Thus far we have considered that the concept of diversity is both a demographic and a political concern. If social difference is a fact of life in our schools, communities, and nation, why is the concept of diversity such a controversial and divisive topic? The controversy that surrounds the term *diversity* is due to a third meaning that incorporates qualities that should be present in a socially diverse environment. The qualities that should accompany social diversity are subjective and, as a result, open to debate and controversy. Not surprisingly, people take different positions on why diversity is valuable or desirable. Two well-known ideologies feature, respectively, "melting-pot" and "multicultural" ideals.

THE MELTING POT   The most prominent and enduring set of values regarding diversity is summarized by the "melting-pot" ideal. For decades, the United States has nurtured the melting-pot ideal and taken great pride in that national identity and its symbol, the Statue of Liberty. People who use the term *diversity* in this way tend to believe that a diverse society should be one in which social differences are accepted and understood, in which people with social differences relate harmoniously. In the film *Manhattan Murder Mystery,* Larry (Woody Allen) refers to a serial killer who eats his victims as "pursuing an alternative lifestyle" and, when a gentlemanly neighbor is suspected of murdering his wife, Larry blithely quips, "So, New York is a melting pot." This parody of the melting-pot ideal is nevertheless instructive: Diversity is more than social difference; it is the acceptance of others' difference if they are (perceived to be) otherwise devoted to the majority group's values and goals, such as working hard and being a responsible citizen. This melting-pot view of diversity is reflected in an essay by Edgar Beckham (1997), who coordinates Wesleyan University's Campus Diversity Initiative: "How unfortunate, especially in a democracy, that we fail to note how insistently diversity also points to unity" (p. 58). Beckham argues that diversity requires a unifying context in which social differences among people can work together for the benefit of everyone. So the melting pot embodies a vision of a school, community, or nation in which differences among people—especially those that relate to ethnicity and cultural heritage—are blended into a single social and cultural product.

MULTICULTURALISM   Ideological uses of the term *diversity* are also associated with multiculturalism, a system of beliefs and values in which diversity plays a prominent role. Multiculturalism is the name given to beliefs or ideals that promote the recognition, appreciation, celebration, and preservation of social difference. People who espouse multiculturalism value the preservation of the separate voices and traditions that compose our communities and nation. A patchwork quilt, rather than a melting pot, provides a helpful metaphor for appreciating multiculturalism. "Patches" of people, each with a distinct cultural or national heritage, become sewn into a large social quilt. The patches are connected to each other, perhaps by a common commitment to some overarching value such as democracy or freedom. In the spirit of the metaphor and the values surrounding multiculturalism, the quilt preserves the uniqueness of social and cultural groups while at the same time uniting them for a superordinate purpose. In short, melting-pot ideals hold that social differences can and should be blended in a harmonious way. Multiculturalism also values unity, but in a way that preserves and even capitalizes on our social differences.

These two ideologies, which underlie the use of the term *diversity,* have much different implications for individuals from minority or disadvantaged social groups. In a melting-pot society, immigrant and ethnic minority groups gain acceptance by the majority group, but only to the extent that they adopt the majority-group identity and customs. In a multicultural society, minority groups' culture and customs are accepted and preserved by the majority group. Some researchers believe that these ideologies represent different steps in the evolution of attitudes toward minority groups (Kleinpenning & Hagendoorn, 1993). That is, the melting-pot ideal is itself a more progressive view of diversity than the racist, caste-based views of diversity that existed in pre–Civil War America. Yet a melting-pot society maintains (majority-defined) conditions for minority groups to receive equality and acceptance. This is perhaps not as fair and respectful of our social and cultural differences as is a multicultural ideal.

Regardless of whether we believe that multicultural ideals are possible or even desirable to achieve, we must acknowledge that the concept of diversity is often used in a manner that combines description (what *is*) and ideology (what *should be*). With regard to diversity, melting-pot and multicultural ideals are statements of what some people believe a socially diverse environment should be. A psychological study of diversity, therefore, seeks to separate the facts of social difference from their political and ideological components, insofar as that is possible. To discuss and study diversity does not mean that we must become embroiled in political and ideological debates. Thus we will think about social difference as neither good nor bad, neither desirable nor undesirable, but simply as an important characteristic of our social world.

Diversity and Social Justice

Diversity is also a concern of individuals who value and strive for social justice. Social justice exists when all the groups of people in a society are afforded the same rights and opportunities, and when their life outcomes are not unfairly constrained by prejudice and discrimination. As the diversity of a community increases, so does the potential for some groups of people to be disadvantaged relative to other groups. In a socially just community, the accomplishments and well-being of some people are not won at the expense of others.

In the towns and cities of America, is there social justice? Much data suggests that although all Americans enjoy similar rights and opportunities, not all realize comparable outcomes. Here are a few examples that highlight the divergent life outcomes of Whites compared with racial and ethnic minority individuals and of the wealthy compared with the poor (U.S. Bureau of the Census, 1996). All U.S. citizens are entitled to free public education through Grade 12, but not all of them get it: In 1996, 83% of Whites had earned a high school diploma, but only 74% of Blacks and 53% of Hispanics had done so. This inequity in education is reflected in the average annual earnings of White ($27,600), Black ($20,500), and Hispanic ($18,300) people.

In principle all people should have access to health care, if not from their employers then from a government health care program such as Medicaid. Practically, however, many people live with inadequate or no health care coverage. In 1996 14% of Whites were not covered by some form of health insurance, but 21% of Black and 33% of Hispanic individuals had no health insurance. Furthermore, not all of those citizens who rely on Medicaid for health care receive the same quality of treatment. In the period from 1985 to 1995, the U.S. government spent an annual average of $1,790 on Medicaid care for Whites, but spent only $1,060 per year on Black and Hispanic people. Similarly, the government spent an annual average of $2,420 on the richest Medicaid subscribers and $1,100 on the poorest.

In a socially just society, people will not be victimized because of their group membership. However, Black and Hispanic people are about 50% more likely to be crime victims and about three times more likely to be victims of robberies or hate crimes than Whites are. If you're poor, you're twice as likely to be victimized by crime and (amazingly) five times as likely to be robbed than if you're wealthy. Although in the U.S. population there is one Black individual for every six to seven Whites, Blacks are more likely than Whites to be arrested for a crime (one Black is arrested for every two Whites). Finally, although twice as many Whites as

Blacks are arrested for crimes, White and Black individuals are imprisoned in equal numbers.

These statistics paint an unsettling image. In a nation devoted to life, liberty, and pursuit of happiness for every citizen, racial and ethnic minorities and poor people have less chance of achieving these than White and wealthy people do. The facts show that diversity in America—particularly racial and economic diversity—is associated with gross social injustice. A psychological study of diversity must acknowledge the social injustices that people from some social groups face. Although understanding the psychology of social difference is an admirable goal in and of itself, understanding must also be a catalyst for addressing social injustice. This conviction is evident in much of the research reviewed in this book. Researchers want to understand how we perceive and experience social difference in part because they want to address problems such as racism, sexism, and discrimination against people based on their economic status. In this way, then, there is an ideological component to the psychology of diversity. However, unlike melting-pot and multicultural ideals, the ideal of a socially just society is much less controversial.

THE PSYCHOLOGY OF DIVERSITY

Although the study of diversity can be approached from demographic, political, ideological, and social justice perspectives, this book is about the *psychology* of diversity. As such, it considers how the behavior of the individual is related to the diverse social context in which it occurs. A psychological approach to diversity identifies principles that explain how individuals' thoughts, feelings, and behavior are intertwined with the social differences in their social environment. For instance, psychological theories and research provide insight into the conditions under which people feel goodwill or antipathy toward someone whose ethnicity differs from their own. At the beginning of this chapter I introduced two principles that frame a psychological study of diversity. First, social difference is constructed and maintained by individuals; and second, social difference exerts influence on individuals. Let us consider further the interdependence of the individual and his or her social context.

Diversity Is Socially Constructed

THE INDIVIDUAL IS A SOCIAL PERCEIVER   As individuals living in a social world, we confront and process volumes of social information each day. From others' skin color to facial characteristics, from their clothing preferences to political attitudes, we sift through, organize, and make sense of countless pieces of social information. Although we can be very fast and efficient in the way we process these data, psychological researchers have demonstrated that we commonly make mistakes and exhibit inaccuracies in our thinking about other people and our social world. These tendencies and errors have consequences for our conclusions and judgments about our social world and the people who compose it. For example, we tend to rely on information that is most available in our memory banks to help us make judgments about other people. This information leads us to make mistakes in judging the diversity of our social environments. You would probably underestimate how many physically disabled individuals are in your college or university because, typically, we tend to have rather infrequent interactions with disabled individuals. The set of accessible memories of our own interactions, then, is a biased basis for making that particular social judgment. In sum, the extent of diversity that we perceive in our dorms, organizations, and communities, then, is influenced by our natural limitations and biases in dealing with an overwhelming amount of social information.

The way we organize information also influences our perceptions of diversity. Our attention to and memory for social information tends to be organized by social categories. Information about the characteristics of, for example, women and men is organized and stored in different memory structures. Although there are advantages to storing social information in this way, separating "male" and "female" information in memory leads to an overemphasis of the differences between men and women. Several best-selling books about gender relationships suggest that the differences between men and women are vast and often inexplicable. Psychological theory and research helps us see, however, that gender diversity—the extent to which men and women are different—is more perceived than actual.

THE INDIVIDUAL IS A SOCIAL ACTOR   Not only are we social perceivers, but we also act within our social contexts in ways that have implications for diversity. We typically bring into our interactions with other people a set of beliefs and expectations about them. These expectations can function in two ways: they guide the way we act toward other people, and they influence the way others react to us. Here's an example. Psychological studies have demonstrated that most of us feel tension and uncertainty in interactions with physically disabled people. These feelings may stem from the belief that handicapped individuals have special "needs" with which we are uncomfortable or unfamiliar. Our beliefs about disabled people may lead us to avoid them or keep our interactions with them brief and superficial, thereby contributing to our perceptions of their "differentness" from us. Moreover, our suspicious and avoidant actions actually contribute to rather than ameliorate their marginalization and dependence on others. In other words, our behavior often sends signals to other people about their differentness and how they are expected to act, leading them to live up to (or, more commonly, down to) those expectations. In this way our behavior toward others actually alters the extent of difference in our social environment.

Finally, our actions toward socially different others are also driven by our feelings about ourselves. I have discussed the fact that we think of ourselves in terms of our social categories and affiliations. These social identities are value-laden; we are proud of being, for example, Jewish, Latino, or female. Because we are emotionally invested in our social categories and memberships, we want them to

Dimensions of social difference often become the basis for categorizing people into groups and thinking about them as group members rather than as individuals. What social category comes to mind here?

compare favorably with other social groups. The desire to make our social group "look good" compared with others invariably guides us to behave in ways that create or enhance differences between us. In short, the diversity we perceive in our schools or communities may result in part from our needs to feel good about our own social groups.

Diversity Is a Social Influence

To study the ways in which the individual and the social context are interdependent, we must recognize that our behavior is influenced by a variety of social forces, one of which is our "differentness" from others. Therefore, we not only perceive social difference in our environments, but many of us also experience diversity. We are aware that we are different from other people in many ways, such as in our skin color, family background, and religious beliefs. This experience is psychologically important because being different from others influences the way we think and feel about ourselves and the way we interact with other people.

INDIVIDUAL IDENTITY IS SOCIALLY CONSTRUCTED   Psychologists have learned that our identities—who we believe ourselves to be—incorporate the impressions and beliefs that others hold about us. The experience of diversity acknowledges that we live among people who themselves are constructors of their social world. In other words, other people categorize you based on dimensions of social difference (just as you tend to do to them). Other people may not know you personally, but as a member of some (often visibly apparent) social group about which they have prior knowledge, you are known to them to some degree. The "you" that is known to other people and based largely on your social group affiliation may differ sharply from how you view yourself. The discrepancy between our identities and the way other people identify us has profound implications for our psychological well-being and social adjustment. Imagine a disabled individual who views herself as intelligent, Italian American, athletic, Republican, and outgoing, but who is viewed by others in terms of her disability. How frustrating it must be to realize that other people think of you as "disabled" (with the negative qualities associated with being disabled) when you do not think of yourself in that way or when "disabled" is just one (and perhaps a relatively unimportant) part of who you are. One's social identities and the beliefs and assumptions that other people associate with those identities have important implications for one's psychological identity and well-being. In sum, a psychological appreciation of diversity must include an understanding of the experience of being different from others.

INDIVIDUAL BEHAVIOR IS SOCIALLY DETERMINED   The experience of diversity extends beyond how we identify ourselves to include how we behave. Any actions we take toward others that are guided by category-based expectations have implications for the perception of diversity. Similarly, others' behavior toward us follows their beliefs and expectations about us and influences how we experience a diverse world. Others' beliefs and expectations about the traits and behaviors of the members of a social group compose a role—a script for conducting oneself in the ongoing drama of life. However, social roles are a double-edged sword. On the one hand they are comfortable contexts in which to live because playing the "expected" role brings the approval of others. On the other hand, social roles are limiting; they constrain what a member of a social group should be or do. For example, there is still a strong collective belief in this society that women are best suited for roles that involve nurturant, supportive, and helpful behavior. Not surprisingly, women greatly outnumber men in such occupations as elementary school teacher, nurse, and secretary. Adopting this "female" role is associated with opportunities in those vocational areas—as well as with a cultural stamp of approval for playing the "woman" role appropriately—but it also places women at economic disadvantage. You can see, then, how our behavior is not ours alone but is shaped by cultural forces that stem directly from social differences.

SUMMARY

Although the raw material for social diversity exists in the actual ways people differ, we process that raw social information in a way that distorts, magnifies, or diminishes their actual social difference. We also act out expectations and feelings and directly or indirectly change the actual social differences we live with. Diversity, then, is partially a product of our information-processing tendencies and of our beliefs about other people. Who we are as individuals is also a product of our diverse social contexts. Our identities are shaped by others' beliefs and assumptions about the social categories that we occupy. Further, our behavior can be determined or shaped by the roles others establish for members of our social group. These interconnections between the individual and the diverse social world are the concern of a psychological study of diversity.

FOR THOUGHT AND DISCUSSION

1. If diversity refers to inclusion that redresses past injustice, why do we not make efforts to include members of *all* disadvantaged or discriminated-against social groups in our schools, companies, and organizations?

2. Multiculturalism endorses "melting-pot" ideals. Are there belief systems that endorse "boiling-pot" ideals? In other words, are there groups who believe that conflict, segregation, and judgment are inevitable or even desirable?

3. Who are you in social terms? How many social categories are you a member of? How important are these terms to your overall identity?

4. Using enrollment, admissions, or institutional research office data, generate a picture of the diversity of your college or university. Is the diversity in the student body reflected in the faculty, staff, and administration?

5. Does your personal identity differ from your social identity—the "you" others know? How does this discrepancy affect you?

6. What social roles do you occupy? In what ways are they beneficial or limiting?

REFERENCES

Beckham, E. (1997, January 5). Diversity opens doors to all: A multicultural focus helps stimulate more critical thinking. *New York Times Book Review,* 58.

Kleinpenning, G., & Hagendoorn, L. (1993). Forms of racism and the cumulative dimension of ethnic attitudes. *Social Psychology Quarterly, 56,* 21–36.

University of California Regents v. Bakke, 438 U.S. 265 (1978).

U.S. Bureau of the Census (1996). *Statistical abstract of the United States.* Washington, DC: Author.

Us and Them

Perceiving Social Difference Through Categories and Stereotypes

Our study of how we construct and maintain perceptions of diversity must begin with considering how we think about people who are different from ourselves. Two psychological concepts—the social category and the stereotype—frame our study of social thinking. Social categorization and stereotyping exert profound influence on the social world we perceive and live in and, as we shall see in later chapters, are themselves shaped by broader cultural forces such as religious belief systems and television programming. Thus they are pivotal concepts for understanding our role in constructing diversity. In this chapter I consider social categorization and stereotyping in turn, then discuss their implications for understanding people who are socially different from ourselves.

SOCIAL CATEGORIZATION

Every day we confront a dizzying mix of body shapes, physical characteristics, skin colors, clothing and hair styles, and maybe even languages. Perceiving and understanding the social diversity of our classrooms, workplaces, and communities involves a great deal of information processing. To ease this information-processing burden, we create categories in which we place people who have common social characteristics. **Social categorization** involves thinking about people as members of social groups rather than as individuals. Because social categories help us organize and simplify information associated with the individuals who inhabit our social lives, they increase the efficiency of our social information processing. However, the cost of greater efficiency is decreased accuracy.

Distilling our social environment through social categories changes the way we see that environment. As a result, the accuracy of our impressions and judgments of others is affected. In the following section we elaborate on how social categorization promotes efficient but impedes accurate thinking about other people.

What Do Social Categories Do?

SOCIAL CATEGORIES ARE EFFICIENT   What if you kept your class notes in a single pile on your desk, with notes from different classes and days haphazardly shuffled into the pile? Finding the notes for a specific class and day would involve sifting through the stack to check each individual page, a laborious task if they happen to be near the bottom! Obviously a categorization system, such as with notebooks and file folders, makes storing and locating any individual piece of class information much easier. The same principle operates in dealing with social information. Placing people in categories facilitates efficient social information processing, enabling us to combine individuals who have a similar quality or status into a group. Thinking about groups of people requires less cognitive effort than does thinking about individuals, leaving us with more available resources to handle the many other demands on our cognitive processes.

Researchers did a series of experiments designed to examine the cognitive efficiency of social categories (Macrae, Milne, & Bodenhausen, 1994). They asked participants to form an impression of a hypothetical person while they were simultaneously doing a cognitive task (listening to a lecture). The researchers reasoned that if using social categories helps to lessen the cognitive effort needed to form impressions, then people who are allowed or encouraged to use categories should have more cognitive resources available for the simultaneous but unrelated task and should thus perform better. In one study participants were shown a list of 10 traits (presented one by one on a computer) that described a hypothetical person named John. The traits included those typical of, for example, an artist (e.g., creative, temperamental) or a doctor (e.g., responsible, caring). Some of the participants saw an appropriate social category label ("artist" or "doctor") appear above the trait words; others did not see the category label. While they were doing the impression-formation task, participants were also listening to a tape-recorded factual lecture on Indonesian geography. After the tasks were complete, participants were given a 20-item multiple-choice test on the facts in the audiotaped lecture. The results confirmed the researchers' idea: Those who formed their impressions of "John" with the assistance of an explicit social category scored significantly better on the test of the lecture facts than those who did not have a category made available to them.

A follow-up study showed that this influence of social categories on the performance of a simultaneous cognitive task was not merely intentional—in other words, the participants did not deliberately behave in the expected way in order to produce the expected effect. In a similar study, Macrae and his colleagues

(Macrae et al., 1994) flashed the social category word for merely a fraction of a second on the computer—a technique called *priming*—and then presented the trait. Still, participants who formed impressions of "Jim" with the aid of a social category (albeit one that they did not recognize!) performed better on a simultaneous but unrelated cognitive task compared with those who did not receive a social category prime. Together, these studies demonstrate the ability of social categories to economize cognitive resources, such as attention and memory, and make them available for other needs.

SOCIAL CATEGORIES ARE INFLUENTIAL   It is well established that social categories and the beliefs that we associate with them influence our thinking and evaluation of people from other groups (Hamilton & Sherman, 1994). Social-category–based beliefs set up expectations for people from a particular group, and much research shows that these expectations influence our perceptions and judgments of people based on their group membership.

For example, researchers investigated the effects of class-based categorization on judgments of a child's academic performance (Baron, Albright, & Malloy, 1995). They had participants watch a videotape of a girl playing near her home and in a neighborhood playground. In one version, called the low-social-class condition, the home and playground were urban and run-down; in another version, the high-social-class condition, they were spacious, well kept, and obviously exclusive. The participants also watched a (bogus) tape of the child taking an intelligence test. The results showed that social class affected the participants' ratings of the child's academic ability but only when they had no information about her ability. Participants who had categorized the child as from a low socioeconomic background evaluated her test performance more negatively than those who believed she was an upper-middle-class student. However, this social categorization effect did not occur when the participants were given information about the child's academic abilities. This study shows how categorization affects the way we think about people but also suggests that the influence of social categories as a basis for judgments of others may be overridden by other, more relevant, information.

In another study, participants studied some information about a basketball player and then listened to a taped radio broadcast of an actual basketball game involving the player (Stone, Perry, & Darley, 1997). After the broadcast, participants rated the attributes and performance of the player. The information about the player, however, was manipulated in two ways. Participants were led to believe that the player was either African American or White (social information) and that he possessed either low or high athletic ability (individual information). The results revealed that participants' ratings of the player were influenced only by the social information. Those who believed the player was Black rated him as having higher physical and basketball ability than participants who believed he was White. However, they attributed more effort (court smarts and hustle) to the "White" player than to the "Black" player. This study also demonstrates the power of social categories to influence our perceptions of individuals and suggests that individualistic (and seemingly more accurate) information can be overridden by social categorical information.

To sum up, social categories simplify, and therefore alter, our picture of the social world. Social categories also actively influence the way we think about people in a particular group. Some of this influence, however, occurs through the operation of social stereotypes, a concept I will address later in this chapter. Before that, let us consider how we come to use a particular social category when people are members of many social groups and categories at the same time.

How Do We Select Social Categories?

Think of someone you know well, such as a roommate or friend. Make a mental list of the possible social categories to which this person could be assigned. Most people are part of many social groups; some are easily visible, others are not. We have considered why social categorization is fundamental to social information processing, but how do we select the social categories? Or do they select themselves? Psychological researchers have found that categorization is driven by attention. The more we attend to an aspect of a person—such as weight, race, or physical disability—the more likely it is that we will mentally "file" that individual with similar people we have noticed in the past (Smith & Zarate, 1992). Clearly, some aspects of other people draw our attention (such as a physical deformity), whereas others often go unnoticed (such as a hairstyle). Social categories tend to be based on qualities of other people that are perceptually salient, accessible, and important.

PERCEPTUAL SALIENCE   Our senses are naturally drawn to the noticeable, or salient, aspects of a stimulus. When we observe an object or scene we notice and remember its distinctive or unusual features much more than its mundane qualities. The same principle governs our social perception. One source of social categories, then, lies in the perceptual salience of individual characteristics.

Distinctive features activate categories for two reasons. First, people who share a distinctive characteristic tend to be associated in memory, even if they are different in many other ways. When we see, for example, an overweight person, we easily recall other overweight individuals we know. Because of their association in memory, we tend to think of them as a group. Second, information about salient categories is immediately available to the perceiver compared with other, less salient, categories. It is easier for us to notice and remember other information about physically disabled people than about, for example, gay men and lesbians because, unlike sexual orientation, physical disabilities themselves are salient and memorable. Some common, distinctive social categories include sex, race, and ethnicity (to the extent that it is perceptually salient, such as through language differences), as well as physical disability, obesity, economic status, and age.

The perceptual salience of a characteristic is partly due to the situation in which it is encountered. Shelley Taylor and her colleagues have found that "solo" status, such as being the only woman on a committee or the only Asian student in a class, commands others' attention (Taylor, Fiske, Etcoff, & Ruderman, 1978). In one study participants watched a group of six students discuss a topic; the groups consisted of each possible distribution of men and women (for example, six men, no women; five men, one woman, etc.). Participants then evaluated the contributions of a given group member. The results showed that the significance attributed to a group member's comments was inversely proportional to the size of his or her minority group. In other words, as people become more noticeable in a group, acquiring more solo status, their actions stand out and acquire greater importance in perceivers' eyes. This occurs even when the quantity of the member's contribution to the group remains the same across the various group types. Other research shows that evaluations of minority- or solo-status individuals are more exaggerated (Taylor & Fiske, 1978). In sum, distinctive attributes—whether that distinctiveness is inherent or situationally enhanced—is a basis for social categorization.

ACCESSIBILITY   Our social thinking is also governed by categories that are accessible. We are more likely to group people by frequently used categories or categories that have just recently been used than by categories we rarely use. If we are accustomed to thinking about people in terms of a certain dimension, we will tend to activate these categories to deal with new or unknown social situations, thus adding to their accessibility.

In a demonstration of the influence of accessible social categories on social perception, researchers primed the category "women" or "Chinese" (or no category) by presenting one of these words for very short durations to study participants via computer (Macrae, Bodenhausen, & Milne, 1995). After the priming task, participants viewed a videotape of a Chinese woman reading and were told they were to rate the editing of the tape. Thus participants' impressions of the person in the tape could be based on either social category: her sex or her ethnicity. In a final task, participants identified computer-presented trait words from a list that included some words that were typical of the social categories "women" (for example, "helpful") and "Chinese" (for example, "disciplined"). The results were striking. Those participants who were primed with the category "women" were faster in recognizing the women-typical, but slower in recognizing the Chinese-typical, traits than the participants who had no social category prime. Parallel findings occurred for those who were primed with the category "Chinese." They responded more quickly to Chinese-typical and more slowly to women-typical words than did people with no category prime.

This study makes two important points. First, when more than one social category can be used to think about someone, *accessible* social categories—ones that we have recently used—take precedence. Second, when an accessible social category is appropriated to process social information, other relevant categories are inhibited—that is, they become less helpful than if we had no social category to

We often think about people using social categories that are culturally valued. These Hasidic Jews likely categorize others based on their religious identity or gender—both prominent social dimensions in the Hasidic culture.

work with. Here we see another aspect of the efficiency of social categories: When one is activated for use, others are deactivated until the social information processing is complete.

CULTURAL IMPORTANCE Social categories are also established and maintained because of their cultural importance. As social information processors, we live and work within cultural contexts. Cultural traditions and beliefs influence our perceptions of others, including the social categories we use to organize those perceptions. Cultures develop specific ways of viewing the world, and these cultural convictions frequently feature social categories that are pertinent to that worldview. In Israel, for example, the distinction between Jew and Arab (or Muslim) is important to the cultural and religious beliefs of Israelis; the social categories "Catholic" and "Protestant" are just as vital for the people of Northern Ireland. In many conservative Christian religious groups, "saved" and "sinner" are prominent and culturally valued categories. These social categories are not only developed by cultural groups but are also enforced. For example, interracial marriage is frowned upon in many cultures (including our own) because it blurs culturally important social distinctions.

In short, our social categorizations are not random. Some categories select themselves by virtue of their visual distinctiveness; others because of their frequent use. Still other categories are derived from our cultural values and traditions. Armed with some basic knowledge about social categorization, let us further examine how social categories influence the diversity we perceive in our social world.

STEREOTYPING

In addition to economizing our cognitive resources, social categories are informative. When we categorize people based on a group membership, we risk discarding a great deal of individual information. We recover some of this information by developing a general description, called a **stereotype**, of the people in a social category and associating it in memory with that category. A stereotype is a set of beliefs about the members of a social group and usually consists of personality traits, behaviors, and motives. Stereotypes are also assumed to be inaccurate and overgeneralized beliefs about people from social groups (Allport, 1954). That is, when we stereotype people, we apply a set of beliefs that represent the summary qualities of a group to individuals from that social group. These group-based beliefs do not provide very accurate information for understanding individual group members.

To learn how social categories and stereotypes are linked in memory, try this: What traits and behaviors come to mind when I say "professor"? Intelligent? Absent-minded? Dork? You likely have little trouble accessing a general description of a typical professor because that stereotypical information is closely associated with the category "professor" in your mind. In addition to personal traits, that stereotype probably carries information about professors' education and income and perhaps their social and political attitudes. In terms of our file-folder metaphor, stereotypes are essentially file labels, brief summaries of the contents of a folder. They provide a general idea of what is in the folder and save us the work of sifting through every individual element for that information. As with social categorization, stereotyping conserves our cognitive resources but does so by changing the nature of our social surroundings.

Stereotypes Are Dispositional and Negative

The content of stereotypes is marked by two qualities. First, stereotypic beliefs tend to be dispositional; that is, they inform us about the inner qualities of individuals based merely on their group membership. Given that we cannot readily "see" an individual's personality traits or abilities, stereotyping is potentially valuable and advantageous in social interactions. The problem is that behavior is caused by *both* inner dispositional and outer situational factors. Thus stereotypes are overinformed by dispositional information and inherently inaccurate.

Second, the evaluative content of stereotypes tends to be negative. Research demonstrates that our stereotypes of many social groups—including African Americans, women, poor and unemployed people, gay men and lesbians, the physically and mentally disabled, and overweight people—are predominantly composed of negatively valued qualities (Allon, 1982; Brigham, 1974; Eagly & Mladinic, 1989; Farina, Sherman, & Allen, 1968; Furnham, 1982a; Gibbons, Sawin, & Gibbons, 1979; Herek, 1984). There are exceptions to this "stereotypes are negative" rule, but even people we positively stereotype (e.g., Asian Americans are intelligent technowizards) are limited by the narrowness and uniformity

Stereotypes are overinformed by atypical group members. Though they are not typical members of the category "gay men," the qualities seen in these men will be associated with the category and attributed to other gay men.

of those "positive" beliefs. In sum, the dispositional assumptions inherent in stereotyping are negative and inaccurate and are applied uniformly to each individual in that social category. Moreover, the negative traits and emotions associated with stereotyping form the basis for prejudice, a topic to be addressed in a later chapter.

Where Do Stereotypes Come From?

Operating together, social categorization and stereotyping influence our understanding of the social differences that surround us. We know that categorization stems from attention to others' distinctive or important social characteristics, but where do our stereotypes come from? Stereotypic beliefs derive from personal exposure to people from other social groups and from our attention to instances in which unusual events and people occur together, and they are learned from family and other cultural conduits.

PERSONAL EXPOSURE   When we know little about the members of another group, we rely on personal contact with or observations of them to inform our beliefs about the whole group (Rothbart, Dawes, & Park, 1984). Our observations of and experiences with socially different people contribute to stereotypes in two ways.

First, our stereotypic beliefs are informed by the social roles that we observe group members occupying. For example, we might observe that many more women than men are elementary school teachers and nurses. As a result we may assume that women as a group are nurturant and helpful, erroneously believing that women's association with these roles reflects a correspondent inner quality (Eagly & Steffen, 1984). In fact, social roles are more likely assigned by society than chosen by the individual, so the behaviors we observe of the members of a social group in a given role do not necessarily reflect their personalities or personal preferences.

Second, our stereotypes are likely to include beliefs that help us explain others' disadvantage or misfortune. Psychologists have demonstrated that belief in a just world—in which people generally get what they deserve—is a common way of thinking about others (Lerner, 1980). In light of **just-world theory**, when other people experience misfortune or tragedy, it is easier to hold them responsible for their plight than to admit that bad things can happen to undeserving people. Accordingly, when we observe a group of people who face disadvantage, we tend to suppose that they have an attribute or inner flaw that somehow caused their regrettable situation. For example, rather than being seen as victims of broader economic forces such as unemployment, poor people are stereotyped as lazy and unmotivated, dispositions that "cause" their disadvantage (Furnham & Gunter, 1984). (Just-world theory will be discussed in more detail in Chapter 9.)

DISTINCTIVE INDIVIDUALS AND BEHAVIORS   Our stereotypes would be more accurate if they represented the attributes of the most typical group members. The problem is that typical group members are neither noticeable nor memorable. In fact, it is the unusual individual that grabs our attention. Atypical group members stand out; their behavior and appearance are vivid and memorable. Hence, their attributes and actions exert disproportionate influence on our thinking about all the members of that social category (Rothbart, Fulero, Jensen, Howard, & Birrel, 1978). This influence is compounded when the social group itself is relatively small or unusual. Research on the **illusory correlation** demonstrates that the co-occurrence of an unusual behavior *and* a distinctive social category is particularly influential, leading us to erroneously believe that the two things are related (Hamilton & Gifford, 1976). Illusory correlations contribute to our stereotypes, causing them to reflect more unusual behavior or attributes than is warranted. As an example of illusory correlation, consider the drag queens who often march in gay rights parades and demonstrations. Cross-dressing is an unusual behavior that coincidentally occurs with the social category "gay." The rarity of that combination of occurrences sparks an assumption that they are related, contributing to the stereotypical (and erroneous) notion that gay men are transvestites or, more generally, sexual perverts.

In one study, participants read a series of sentences that described positive and negative behaviors exhibited by hypothetical members of a majority (Group A) or a minority (Group B) group (Johnson & Mullen, 1994). In a following task administered by a computer, participants read the sentences again, but this time the group information was omitted. They had to indicate, by pressing a key, whether the behavior was one that was described earlier as being committed by a majority- or minority-group member. The results revealed that participants overattributed negative actions to minority-group actors, and they were faster in making these decisions compared with the other pairs of information (positive act by a minority actor, any act by a majority actor). Thus stereotypes can arise when we erroneously connect unusual (and often negative) behaviors with unusual groups.

SOCIALIZATION   Finally, cultures and societies invest in collective views of social groups, called **cultural stereotypes.** For example, beliefs about overweight people are much different (and more negative) in the United States than in Mexico (Crandall & Martinez, 1996). Our stereotypic beliefs, in turn, are socialized by the steady influence of family members and television, two important conduits of cultural influence. Because children admire and imitate their parents, they accept parents' social attitudes rather uncritically. Parents' stereotypes are communicated to their children in many subtle ways, as in the kind of playmates that meet with their approval, warnings about neighborhoods to avoid, or casual use of racial or ethnic epithets in the home.

The characters and stories that we observe (or don't observe) on television also shape our beliefs about members of social groups, especially considering that the TV is on 7 hours per day in the average American home (Gerbner, Gross, Morgan, & Signorielli, 1986). Although TV characters and programs have become much more racially diverse in the past 20 years, the situation for other social groups is not nearly as positive. For example, women are still portrayed as victims much more often than men, and more violence is perpetrated against women than men on TV. When viewed repeatedly and uncritically, such portrayals feed our stereotypes of women as weak, subordinate, and exploitable.

Why Do Stereotypes Persist?

Psychologists have long regarded stereotyping to be part of a significant social problem (Allport, 1954). This is so not only because stereotypic beliefs tend to be negative, dispositional, and overgeneralized to individual group members but also because, once established, stereotypes are difficult to change. Therefore, the influence of stereotypes on our thinking about and behavior toward other people can subtly contribute to prejudice and discrimination toward people who are socially different from ourselves. Let us consider a few of the reasons for the persistence of stereotypes.

STEREOTYPES POSSESS A KERNEL OF TRUTH   Stereotypes persist because they seem to be accurate. Actually, most stereotypes *do* have an element of accuracy in them. For example, we tend to stereotype women as "emotional" relative to men. Research demonstrates that, compared with men, women *are* more attentive and sensitive to nonverbal expressions (Eagly, 1987). However, this actual and specific difference between the sexes is exaggerated and results in women being globally judged as more emotional.

Are stereotypes accurate? The accuracy of stereotypes can be assessed in two ways (Judd & Park, 1993). First, we can compare the extent to which we believe outgroup members have a given trait with the extent to which they actually possess the trait. For example, we tend to stereotype Asian Americans as math whizzes; but are they as intelligent in math as we believe they are? If so, then our stereotype of Asian Americans (at least regarding beliefs about math ability) is accurate. Second, we can compare our beliefs about how prevalent a trait is among outgroup members with the actual proportion of outgroup members who possess that trait. For example, given our stereotypes of Asian Americans' math ability, we may believe that 60% of Asian students are math or computer science majors. If that proportion is actually reflected among Asian American students, then our stereotype (again, regarding that trait) is accurate.

There is a surprising amount of evidence that demonstrates the accuracy of stereotypes (Judd, Ryan, & Park, 1991; Lee & Ottati, 1993). In one study, Black and White college students' perceptions of their own and the others' group were measured in the two ways described previously (Ryan, 1996). On the first measure of accuracy, the results showed that Blacks were more accurate in their beliefs about Whites than Whites were in their beliefs about Blacks. On the second measure, Blacks' judgments about the proportion of Whites who possessed a stereotypic trait were more accurate than Whites' judgments about the proportion of Blacks who possessed stereotypic traits. This study suggests that stereotype accuracy may be more prevalent among minority- than majority-group members, perhaps because people from minority groups have more to lose if they misjudge the actions of majority-group members.

STEREOTYPES CONFIRM THEMSELVES   A second explanation for the resistance of stereotypes to change is our tendency to confirm rather than disconfirm stereotypical expectations about other groups (Rothbart, Evans, & Fulero, 1979). Some stereotypes are important to us—we don't want them to be challenged. Further, stereotypic thinking is comfortable and easy and does not require vast cognitive resources. For these reasons we selectively attend to evidence that supports our stereotypes, lending the impression that they are more true than they are.

In a demonstration of the tendency for stereotypes to confirm themselves, researchers presented study participants with a photograph of a woman who was known (through pretesting) to be a typical-looking member of the category "older woman" (Brewer, Dull, & Lui, 1981). After viewing the photograph, participants were presented with statements about the woman that were either stereotype-consistent (e.g., "she likes to knit"), stereotype-inconsistent (e.g., "she is politically active"), or of mixed content (e.g., "she walks with a cane and runs her own business"). Using a computer to present the statements, the researchers measured how long it took participants to process each statement. After the computer portion of the study, participants' memory for the statements was also tested. The results showed that statements that were consistent with participants' stereotype of "older women" were processed in less time than stereotype-inconsistent statements and were easily recalled. Stereotype-inconsistent statements were processed slowly but were also remembered well by participants. Participants' ability to remember stereotype-inconsistent statements, however, may have been due to the extra time they spent studying the statements. Statements with mixed content (e.g., an "old" woman trait and a "young" woman trait) were processed slowly and not well remembered.

This research demonstrates that recognition and memory are better for information that is consistent with our stereotypes than for information that is contradictory or only partly relevant to our stereotypes. Could this occur because people are aware of, and therefore act out, what *should* happen when their stereotypes are activated? Not according to recent research on implicit stereotyping (Banaji, Hardin, & Rothman, 1993). That is, when our stereotypes are activated without our knowledge—such as through the use of a subliminal prime—we still tend to recognize and recall stereotype-consistent, rather than inconsistent, information.

STEREOTYPES DIVERSIFY THROUGH SUBTYPES   What happens, however, when we are confronted with one or more individuals who do not fit our stereotype for that group? When we encounter people who do not conform to our stereotype for members of that group, such as a female corporate executive, we can disregard them as "exceptions to the rule." This saves us the cognitive effort necessary to alter our stereotypic notions and protects us from threat should we be personally invested in that particular stereotype. However, as encounters with stereotype-inconsistent people increase, we realize that social categories may be too broad and inclusive and hence error-prone. In those situations, **subtyping** helps preserve the stereotype of the general category while incorporating new social information by grouping stereotype-inconsistent individuals together into a new subcategory of the original category. For example, as we become more aware of women in business management roles, we will think of them as a subgroup of the general group "women" and modify our general stereotype to accommodate the differentness of the subgroup.

Patricia Devine and Sara Baker had White students list abilities and characteristics they associated with the group "Blacks," as well as with several common subgroupings of Black individuals, including "streetwise," "ghetto," "welfare," "athlete," and "businessman" Blacks (Devine & Baker, 1991). Their interest was not only in the traits associated with each of these subtypes but also in how distinctive (or nonoverlapping) the subtypes were. Subtypes are likely to be most useful for accommodating atypical examples of a category if they are distinct from each other and from the larger category. Their results indicated that the "athlete" and "businessman" subtypes of Blacks were the most clear and distinctive. That is, the traits associated with the "athlete" (physical qualities and athleticism) and "businessman" (well-dressed, ambitious, intelligent) subtypes differed from each other and, further, were not reflected in the overall stereotype of Blacks.

These findings suggest that subtypes not only help organize social information that is too diverse for one category to handle but that they also do so in a way that doesn't require alteration of the stereotype associated with that category. Because Black "businessmen" are organized independently of Blacks in general, the positive traits associated with Black businessmen are not incorporated into the (largely negative) stereotype of Blacks. With respect to perceiving the social world, then, subtyping is a mixed blessing. Although subtyping does extend and diversify a social category, essentially allowing more difference to exist within a social group, it also protects our general (superordinate) stereotypic beliefs from change by creating new and separate cognitive groups for individuals who do not fit the stereotype.

CONSEQUENCES OF SOCIAL CATEGORIZATION AND STEREOTYPING FOR PERCEIVING DIVERSITY

Although they are valuable information-processing tools, social categories and stereotypes shape the diversity we perceive in our social surroundings. The very process of sorting people into categories limits the possible ways in which people can differ from group characteristics. Thus the diversity we perceive in our surroundings partially depends on how complex our categorization systems are. When we reduce people into simple categories, we see our world as less diverse than if we use categories that contain an array of general and subordinate social groupings. Simplistic categorizations require fewer cognitive resources but may also lead to difficulties in our interactions with members of other groups. The process of categorization, therefore, must balance the need to distill an overwhelming amount of social information with the need to have an accurate picture of our social world and the people in it.

Still, diversity also exists *within* social categories. Even if we believed the world was composed of two categories of people ("us" and "them"), we could still find diversity in the members of the other group. As is explained in the following discussion, we fail to recognize and appreciate this kind of social difference. Moreover, the true diversity within other social groups is dulled by stereotypical thinking. Together, social categorization and stereotyping have several specific implications for the social difference we perceive around us.

We Believe Groups Are More Different Than They Are

A natural consequence of categorizing objects into groups is to emphasize the distinctiveness of those groups. You will agree that a categorization system must maintain clear distinctions between categories to function efficiently. This cognitive tendency leads to a bias in our social thinking—we overestimate the difference between social groups. This bias has been documented in many studies that involve judgments of physical and social objects. In one study children viewed pictures of three boys and three girls and assigned trait words to describe each picture (Doise, Deschamps, & Meyer, 1978). Half of the children (determined randomly) were told in advance that they would be rating pictures of boys and girls, thereby increasing the salience of the social category of gender for those participants. The participants who were thinking in terms of gender described boys and girls as being more different than did those who did not make the "boy/girl" distinction. That is, fewer common traits were used to describe boys and girls by the children who were encouraged to categorize the photos by gender. This study shows that our perception of members of other social groups is influenced by the mere act of categorization. Applied to our own social contexts, this research suggests that some of the difference we perceive between ourselves and individuals from other social groups is spurious or manufactured, yet (as we will see in a later chapter) we behave as if those differences were genuine.

We Believe Individuals Within Groups Are More Similar Than They Are

A second consequence of thinking about people in terms of their group identification is that we tend to gloss over how different members of a social group actually are. Just as papers and notes placed into a file folder become more indistinguishable, social categorization causes us to overestimate the similarity of people in a social group. This bias is most evident when thinking about *out*groups, groups of which we are not a member. Termed the **outgroup homogeneity effect**, it means we tend to think that "they" (members of an outgroup) are all alike, but "we" (members of our own group, or *in*group) are a collective of relatively unique individuals.

There are good explanations for why we attribute more similarity to members of outgroups than is warranted. First, we categorize individuals based on a distinctive or salient characteristic. If people share a distinctive feature, we assume that they also share other qualities (Taylor, Fiske, Etcoff, & Ruderman, 1978). Second, we interact more with ingroup than with outgroup members, thus providing ourselves with more frequent reminders about the differences among individuals in our own group. As a result of the outgroup homogeneity effect combined with our stereotype of that group, we tend to view the members of an outgroup as "all alike" and in negative terms. These perceptions are fertile ground for prejudicial reactions such as resentment, fear, and avoidance.

In an examination of the outgroup homogeneity effect, Bernadette Park and her colleagues recruited business and engineering majors to list as many "types" or "kinds" of business and engineering majors as they could (Park, Ryan, & Judd, 1992). In other words, they looked at how diverse (or homogenous) people perceived their own group and a relevant outgroup to be by measuring the subtypes that they generated for each. As they expected, people generated more subgroups for their ingroup than for the outgroup. When this difference was accounted for, the outgroup homogeneity effect disappeared. In other words, the tendency to see outgroup individuals as more homogenous than one's own group members depends largely on having fewer subcategories in which to place them. In another study, Park, Ryan, and Judd (1992) manipulated the use of subgroups by having some participants sort outgroup members into subgroups before measuring their perceptions of outgroup individuals. The participants who were forced to sort outgroup members into a variety of subcategories rated them as more variable than did participants who did not do the sorting exercise.

The research discussed here shows that we have more complex cognitive structures (involving more subgroupings or types) for ingroups than we do for outgroups. One implication of this relative ignorance about who "they" are is that we might be highly influenced by evaluative information about outgroup individuals. Researchers tested this idea by having participants evaluate a bogus application to law school under the pretext that researchers were interested in which information was most diagnostic of law school performance (Linville & Jones, 1980). The application that they were given, however, was supposedly from either an African American or a White applicant and showed either weak or strong credentials. The participants (who were White) who reviewed the "strong" application rated the Black applicant as more intelligent, motivated, and likable than the White applicant. Those who reviewed the "weak" application had the opposite reaction: They rated the Black applicant as *less* intelligent, motivated, and likable than the White applicant. In other words, White participants' perceptions of a Black applicant were more influenced by a single piece of evaluative information than their views of a White applicant were, and this effect can be attributed to the less developed knowledge we possess about outgroup, compared with ingroup, individuals. Put another way, the complexity with which we think about our own groups relative to others' groups affects how we evaluate "them."

We Explain "Their" Behavior Differently Than We Do "Ours"

The categorization of others and ourselves into different social groups and the application of stereotypes to outgroup individuals causes us to offer very different explanations for each other's actions. The results of many studies show our tendency to commit the **ultimate attribution error** (Pettigrew, 1979). That is, when explaining the behavior of outgroup individuals, we tend to cite inner, dispositional causes; but when we explain our own actions or those of a fellow ingroup member we cite situational, circumstantial factors. In one such study, participants who were employed attributed others' unemployment to laziness, whereas the unemployed individuals themselves externalized their plight by citing the belief that immigrants were taking all of the jobs (Furnham, 1982b). This research indicates that we judge the behavior of outgroup individuals more harshly than we do our own group's actions. Interestingly, our judgment of outgroup members' behavior is moderated when we are socially similar in some way. For example, an employed person would be less likely to blame an unemployed individual for his own plight if he recognized that they attended the same church.

The ultimate attribution error has implications for our perceptions of diversity. Attributing the actions of socially different others to their personalities rather than to situational factors buttresses our stereotypic beliefs. Further, if "their" behavior is believed to be due to inner attributes, there is no reason to expect that they will change. This assumption affords our stereotypes predictability and additional resistance to disconfirmation.

SUMMARY

The social diversity around us is sharply distilled by our perceptions about groups and their members. Although social categorization and stereotyping simplify and lend order to one's social world, they exaggerate and maintain differences between groups of people. They also promote thinking about others in more negative than positive terms and attributing their behavior to unchanging inner qualities. Although few of us willingly adopt and use social categories and stereotypes, the extent to which they are acquired through socialization and cognitive necessity has real consequences for the social world we live in. Truly the social world we live in is, in part, a creation of our own thoughts, beliefs, and assumptions. Inevitably these beliefs are acted out in our behavior, causing us to actively construct diversity in ways that extend beyond the cognitive processes covered in this chapter. This idea will be examined in Chapter 3.

KEY TERMS

social categorization	cultural stereotypes
stereotype	subtyping
just-world theory	outgroup homogeneity effect
illusory correlation	ultimate attribution error

FOR THOUGHT AND DISCUSSION

1. What social categories are represented in your classroom? your dormitory or house? your neighborhood?

2. What social categories are most important or useful to you? Where did these category distinctions come from?

3. Think about your stereotype of some group; write down some of the beliefs, assumptions, and characteristics in the stereotype. Where did this stereotype come from? How is it maintained in your thinking?

4. In what ways are stereotypes cultural products?

5. Do social categorization and stereotyping lead to a more or less diverse world? Explain.

REFERENCES

Allon, N. (1982). The stigma of overweight in everyday life. In B. B. Wolman (Ed.), *Psychological aspects of obesity: A handbook* (pp. 130–174). New York: Van Nostrand Reinhold.

Allport, G. (1954). *The nature of prejudice*. Reading, MA: Addison-Wesley.

Banaji, M., Hardin, C., & Rothman, A. (1993). Implicit stereotyping in person judgment. *Journal of Personality and Social Psychology, 65,* 272–281.

Baron, R., Albright, L., & Malloy, T. (1995). Effects of behavioral and social class information on social judgment. *Personality and Social Psychology Bulletin, 21,* 308–315.

Brewer, M., Dull, V., & Lui, L. (1981). Perceptions of the elderly: Stereotypes as prototypes. *Journal of Personality and Social Psychology, 41,* 656–670.

Brigham, J. C. (1974). Views of black and white children concerning the distribution of personality characteristics. *Journal of Personality, 42,* 144–158.

Crandall, C., & Martinez, R. (1996). Culture, ideology, and antifat attitudes. *Personality and Social Psychology Bulletin, 22,* 1165–1176.

Devine, P., & Baker, S. (1991). Measurement of racial stereotype subtyping. *Personality and Social Psychology Bulletin, 17,* 44–50.

Doise, W., Deschamps, J.-C., & Meyer, G. (1978). The accentuation of intracategory similarities. In H. Tajfel (Ed.), *Differentiation between social groups: Studies in the social psychology of intergroup relations*. London: Academic Press.

Eagly, A. H. (1987). *Sex differences in social behavior: A social-role interpretation*. Hillsdale, NJ: Erlbaum.

Eagly, A. H., & Mladinic, A. (1989). Gender stereotypes and attitudes toward women and men. *Personality and Social Psychology Bulletin, 15,* 543–558.

Eagly, A. H., & Steffen, V. J. (1984). Gender stereotypes stem from the distribution of women and men into social roles. *Journal of Personality and Social Psychology, 46,* 735–754.

Farina, A., Sherman, M., & Allen, J. G. (1968). The role of physical abnormalities in interpersonal perception and behavior. *Journal of Abnormal Psychology, 73,* 590–593.

Furnham, A. (1982a). The Protestant work ethic and attitudes toward unemployment. *Journal of Occupational Psychology, 55,* 277–286.

Furnham, A. (1982b). Explanations for unemployment in Britain. *European Journal of Social Psychology, 12,* 335–352.

Furnham, A., & Gunter, B. (1984). Just world beliefs and attitudes towards the poor. *British Journal of Social Psychology, 23,* 265–269.

Gerbner, G., Gross, L., Morgan, M., & Signorielli, N. (1986). Living with television: The dynamics of the cultivation process. In J. Bryant & D. Zillman (Eds.), *Perspectives on media effects* (pp. 17–40). Hillsdale, NJ: Erlbaum.

Gibbons, F. X., Sawin, L. S., & Gibbons, B. N. (1979). Evaluations of mentally retarded persons: "Sympathy" or patronization? *American Journal of Mental Deficiency, 84,* 124–131.

Hamilton, D., & Sherman, J. (1994). Stereotypes. In R. S. Wyer & T. K. Srull (Eds.), *Handbook of social cognition* (pp. 1–68). Hillsdale, NJ: Erlbaum.

Hamilton, D. L., & Gifford, R. K. (1976). Illusory correlation in interpersonal perception: A cognitive basis of stereotypic judgments. *Journal of Experimental Social Psychology, 12,* 392–407.

Herek, G. M. (1984). Attitudes toward lesbians and gay men: A factor-analytic study. *Journal of Homosexuality, 10,* 39–51.

Johnson, C., & Mullen, B. (1994). Evidence for the accessibility of paired distinctiveness in distinctiveness-based illusory correlation in stereotyping. *Personality and Social Psychology Bulletin, 20,* 65–70.

Judd, C., & Park, B. (1993). Definition and assessment of accuracy in social stereotypes. *Psychological Review, 100,* 109–128.

Judd, C., Ryan, C., & Park, B. (1991). Accuracy in the judgments of in-group and out-group variability. *Journal of Personality and Social Psychology, 61,* 366–379.

Lee, Y., & Ottati, V. (1993). Determinants of in-group and out-group perceptions of heterogeneity: An investigation of Sino-American stereotypes. *Journal of Cross-Cultural Psychology, 24,* 298–318.

Lerner, M. J. (1980). *The belief in a just world: A fundamental delusion.* New York: Plenum.

Linville, P., & Jones, E. (1980). Polarized appraisals of outgroup members. *Journal of Personality and Social Psychology, 38,* 689–703.

Macrae, C., Bodenhausen, G., & Milne, A. (1995). The dissection of selection in person perception: Inhibitory processes in social stereotyping. *Journal of Personality and Social Psychology, 69,* 397–407.

Macrae, C., Milne, A., & Bodenhausen, G. (1994). Stereotypes as energy-saving devices: A peek inside the cognitive toolbox. *Journal of Personality and Social Psychology, 66,* 37–47.

Park, B., Ryan, C., & Judd, C. (1992). Role of meaningful subgroups in explaining differences in perceived variability for in-groups and out-groups. *Journal of Personality and Social Psychology, 63,* 553–567.

Pettigrew, T. F. (1979). The ultimate attribution error: extending Allport's cognitive analysis of prejudice. *Personality and Social Psychology Bulletin, 5,* 461–476.

Rothbart, M., Dawes, R., & Park, B. (1984). Stereotyping and sampling biases in intergroup perception. In J. R. Eiser (Ed.), *Attitudinal judgment* (pp. 109–134). New York: Springer-Verlag.

Rothbart, M., Evans, M., & Fulero, S. (1979). Recall for confirming events: Memory processes and the maintenance of social stereotyping. *Journal of Experimental Social Psychology, 15,* 343–355.

Rothbart, M., Fulero, S., Jensen, C., Howard, J., & Birrel, P. (1978). From individual to group impressions: Availability heuristics in stereotype formation. *Journal of Experimental Social Psychology, 14,* 237–255.

Ryan, C. (1996). Accuracy of Black and White college students' in-group and out-group stereotypes. *Personality and Social Psychology Bulletin, 22,* 1114–1127.

Smith, E., & Zarate, M. (1992). Exemplar-based model of social judgment. *Psychological Review, 99,* 3–21.

Stone, J., Perry, Z., & Darley, J. (1997). "White men can't jump": Evidence for the perceptual confirmation of racial stereotypes following a basketball game. *Basic and Applied Social Psychology, 19,* 291–306.

Taylor, S., & Fiske, S. (1978). Salience, attention, and attribution: Top of the head phenomena. In L. Berkowitz (Ed.), *Advances in experimental social psychology* (Vol. 11, pp. 249–288). New York: Academic Press.

Taylor, S. E., Fiske, S. T., Etcoff, N. L., & Ruderman, A. J. (1978). Categorical and contextual bases of person memory and stereotyping. *Journal of Personality and Social Psychology, 36,* 778–793.

3

Stereotypes in Action

CHAPTER OBJECTIVE

To show that our active role in altering and constructing social differences is not merely mental activity but can produce actual change in our social environments. Three concepts are discussed—the self-fulfilling prophecy, stereotype threat, and the influence of stereotypes on our communication about others—that show how our behavior toward the socially different alters true differences between us.

The Self-Fulfilling Prophecy, Stereotype Threat, and Stereotypic Communication

In Chapter 2 I discussed how the extent and nature of the difference we perceive in our social world is shaped by our use of social categories to divide it up and stereotypes to label it. Our reliance on group distinctions and labels not only informs our thinking about the people around us but also affects our behavior toward them. This chapter considers how stereotypes influence our behavior toward others and how that behavior can change the nature of our social context. Do our expectations of socially different others lead them to act in ways that confirm those expectations? Does talking about socially different others produce in them the very things we communicate? If so, then, as social psychologist William Swann (1985) has noted, we are architects of our own social realities. In this chapter I consider three areas of theory and research that document stereotypes in action: the self-fulfilling prophecy, the concept of stereotype threat, and the implications of stereotypes reflected in our language and communication.

THE SELF-FULFILLING PROPHECY

A **self-fulfilling prophecy** occurs when our expectations of an individual's personality or behavior cause that person to act in ways that confirm our expectations (Merton, 1948). Hence our "prophecy" (expectations, assumptions, or beliefs) for that person is self-fulfilling—through our own actions we bring out in her or him what we expected in the first place. Research evidence for the self-fulfilling prophecy is abundant; the effect has been documented in general social interactions, in interactions between researchers and research participants, and in rela-

Stereotypic beliefs about Black students' intelligence and motivation for school can undermine their school performance.

tionships between teachers and students (Brophy & Good, 1974; Jamieson, Lydon, Stewart, & Zanna, 1987; Jones, 1986; Rosenthal, 1974).

In the classic demonstration of the self-fulfilling prophecy, Robert Rosenthal and Lenore Jacobson (1968) led elementary school teachers to believe that some of their students had been identified through testing as "late bloomers," students whose academic promise was just now expected to develop. These students, however, were selected randomly and thus were no more (or less) promising than the other students. After 8 months, the students who had been labeled as "late bloomers" were viewed more positively by their teachers than the "average" students. Amazingly, the "late bloomers" improved in the classroom too; their IQ and standardized test scores improved significantly over the academic year. Many other studies have added support to this basic relationship: A teacher's expectations of a student's aptitude predict actual upward or downward change in the student's performance, in accordance with the expectations (Brophy & Good, 1974; Cooper & Tom, 1984).

This research gained national prominence and became a rallying point for people concerned that teachers' expectations—informed by stereotypes—undermined the educational opportunities of broad classes of students such as females, racial and ethnic minority students, and students from lower economic classes (Wineburg, 1987). However, two points help temper our interpretations of the early research on the self-fulfilling prophecy. First, although much research documents a relationship between teachers' expectations of students' ability and students' performance, in many studies the size of that relationship is small (Jussim, Eccles, & Madon, 1996). Second, the fact that teachers' expectations of students predict student classroom performance does not necessarily mean that the self-fulfilling prophecy is operating—there are other explanations for the link between what teachers expect and how students perform in school (Jussim et al., 1996). Let's consider them.

How Are Teachers' Expectations Related to Students' Achievement?

TEACHER EXPECTANCY EFFECTS   The tendency for teachers' positive expectations of students to be related to students' positive classroom performance (and negative expectations to negative performance) can be explained in three ways, as illustrated in Figure 3.1. First, the relationship could be due to the self-fulfilling prophecy. That is, teachers' positive expectations for a student (or a group of students) could lead them to pay more attention to those students in the classroom, offer more help on assignments, or be more encouraging in responding to their comments. Conversely, teachers who hold negative impressions and expectations of students might call on them less often in class, give them less time to answer a question, or point out more deficiencies than strengths in their work. These behaviors could, in turn, produce improvements or decrements in students' school achievement.

Do teachers really tip their hand about students they regard highly (or not so highly)? Much research says yes. In one study teachers were videotaped talking about real students of whom they held high or low expectations (Babad, Bernieri, & Rosenthal, 1991). Study participants then viewed short (10-second) clips of the teacher's face while he or she was talking, but with the sound turned down. Amazingly, participants were able to correctly identify whether the teacher was talking about a liked or disliked student. This study shows that our expectations of and liking for others leak through to our behavior in the form of identifiable facial expressions. Other studies show that women and minority students report more negative classroom experiences and interactions with professors and teachers than do male, majority-group students (Allen & Niss, 1990; Steele, 1997).

PERCEPTUAL BIAS   The relationship between teachers' expectations and students' achievement can also be due to a bias in evaluating students' classroom behavior or work. We know from Chapter 2 that stereotypic beliefs seek confirmation rather than disconfirmation. Similarly, our beliefs about an individual (without regard to his or her social group) can bias our perceptions of that person in a way that supports our initial beliefs. The perceptual-bias explanation differs from the self-fulfilling prophecy in an important way. In the self-fulfilling prophecy, students' behavior actually changes in accordance with the expectations of the teacher. In perceptual bias, teachers' expectations are not transmitted to students' behavior but operate when teachers evaluate students' work in expectation-

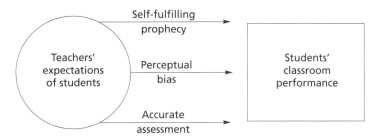

FIGURE 3.1

How are teachers' expectations of students related to students' achievement in the classroom?

consistent ways. Thus, although teachers' perceptual biases do not alter the extent or nature of social differences in a classroom (as the self-fulfilling prophecy does), they are no less unfair or discriminatory to students.

A great deal of research supports the existence of perceptual biases in attention to, memory for, and explanations of others' behavior. For example, when we are presented with information about an individual that is open to interpretation, we selectively attend to the information that is consistent with our preconceptions of that person (Hilton & von Hippel, 1990). Our memory for others' characteristics can be shaped by current beliefs about them. In one study researchers acquainted participants with the traits and behaviors of a hypothetical woman named Jane (Snyder & Cantor, 1979). Some of Jane's traits indicated she was extroverted; others, that she was introverted. Later, participants were asked to describe Jane's suitability to be either a saleswoman or a librarian. Participants who were considering her as a saleswoman recalled more of her "extroverted" qualities than did those considering her as a librarian; likewise, thinking of Jane as a librarian led participants to remember her "introverted" traits. Finally, the tendency for us to cite internal (personality) more than external (circumstances) factors when explaining others' behavior is itself an expression of an underlying perceptual bias (Gilbert & Malone, 1995). When we observe people, their actions and speech are much more salient than their situations. Thus, perceptually speaking, others' behavior seems to come from them, not their circumstances.

How could these perceptual biases in attention, memory, and explanation account for the relationship between teachers' expectations and students' behavior? A teacher with negative expectations of a student could attend more to the mistakes than to the strong points of that student's project. Low expectations of a student may prompt a teacher to recall less class participation than actually occurred. Similarly, a student who misses an exam may do so for a variety of reasons, both internal (she doesn't care about the course) and external (her mother is ill and requires care). However, the teacher is more likely to assume the former and refuse to grant a makeup exam. In each of these scenarios, the tendency for student "behavior" to reflect teacher expectations is due wholly to the teacher's (mis)interpretations of student actions—not to any actual change in the student's behavior or ability.

ACCURATE ASSESSMENT   Finally, the relationship between teacher expectations and student achievement could result from an accurate assessment of the student's abilities (Jussim, 1991). Teachers do not form arbitrary positive and negative impressions of students; rather, their expectations are likely rooted in the records, reports, or observations of the student's past achievement. For example, a student (or group of students) may be expected to do poorly in 11th-grade English because the teacher is aware that the student received a D in 10th-grade English. If the student does underachieve in the class, as expected, it need not be due to the teacher's influence or bias but to the fact that the teacher's expectations and the student's achievement were caused by the same factor: a poor record of past achievement. Researchers have found evidence that teachers' expectations for students sometimes correspond to students' classroom performance because their (teachers') expectations are accurate—they are based on a knowledge of pre-existing factors that affect students' achievement.

**Accurate Assessment or Self-Fulfilling Prophecy?
Research Evidence**

The relationship between teacher expectations and student achievement has long been assumed to be unfair and discriminatory (Wineburg, 1987). Two of the three explanations for this relationship discussed here—the self-fulfilling prophecy and perceptual bias—are unfair. But it is also possible that teachers' expectations predict student achievement fairly because those expectations are accurate. Therefore, it is important to determine how much of the effect of teacher expectations on student performance is accurate and fair and how much is unfair and discriminatory.

In two large-scale studies involving about 1,700 students in sixth-grade math classes, Lee Jussim and his colleagues measured teachers' perceptions of students early in the academic year, students' achievement in math across the school year, and students' motivation for achievement in math (Jussim, 1989; Jussim & Eccles, 1992). They reasoned that the self-fulfilling prophecy would occur if teachers' expectations for students in the fall term were related to students' math grades in the spring term after taking into account two factors: students' prior math achievement (the ability they brought with them from fifth grade) and students' motivation to do well in math.

The results indicated that teachers' expectations in the fall were strongly related to students' math grades in the spring. However, very little of this relationship was due to the self-fulfilling prophecy. Rather, about 70–80% of the effect of teachers' (positive or negative) expectations on students' math achievement was accurate. Students who were known to be good at math were expected to do well—and they did. Likewise, students who were known to struggle with math were expected to do poorly—and they did. The small remainder of the total effect of teacher expectations on students (20–30%) was due to the self-fulfilling prophecy (the researchers did not distinguish between the self-fulfilling prophecy and perceptual bias in these studies).

Who Is Susceptible to the Self-Fulfilling Prophecy?

These studies did find evidence of self-fulfilling prophecy (the remaining 20–30% of the effect of teachers' expectations), but the size of the effects on students was small. The small magnitude of the self-fulfilling prophecy found in these studies, however, does not indicate that the problem of the self-fulfilling prophecy in the classroom has been exaggerated. Rather, it is likely that teachers' expectations are self-fulfilling for some students or groups of students and not for others. Students from minority, disadvantaged, or stereotyped groups are particularly vulnerable to the self-fulfilling prophecy because stereotypes are often inaccurate. According to Jussim and his colleagues, inaccurate expectations possess greater potential to create self-fulfilling prophecies (Jussim et al., 1996). Minority or otherwise disadvantaged students are therefore more likely to be affected by teachers' expectations.

The studies of sixth-graders described previously were reanalyzed to test this question based on the students' sex, social class, and ethnicity (Jussim, 1989; Jussim & Eccles, 1992). In each of these social-group comparisons, students' fifth-grade math grades and motivation for math achievement were taken into account to rule out the possibility that the relationship between teachers' expectations and students' achievement was due to teachers' accurate assessment of students' math ability and motivation. Teachers' expectations were unrelated to student grades among boys, but they were related among girls. High teacher expectations for math achievement were associated with higher math grades and low expectations with low grades. What is this effect in practical terms? For the average female student in Jussim's studies, moving from the teacher with the most positive expectations to the teacher with the most negative expectations would result in a half-letter-grade drop in math class performance.

Similar results were observed when comparing students from low and high socioeconomic backgrounds. Students from lower socioeconomic status (SES) backgrounds were most vulnerable to self-fulfilling prophecies—low teacher expectations were associated with low math test scores and high expectations with high scores. The influence of self-fulfilling prophecies on economically disadvantaged students, however, was much larger than it was on females in general. If low-SES students moved from a teacher with the highest to one with the lowest expectations, their scores on a standardized test of math ability would drop by 21 to 45 percentile points (depending on their initial scores).

Finally, African American, compared with White, students were more influenced by teacher expectations in the same manner. As with economically disadvantaged students, the effect of the self-fulfilling prophecy was considerable. Moving from a teacher with the most positive to one with the most negative expectations would result in a drop of one and one half letter grades (e.g., B+ to C) in math class performance for the typical African American student in Jussim's studies.

In summary, these large-scale studies of elementary school students demonstrate that teachers' expectations of students are a strong predictor of students' school achievement. Most of this relationship stems from the fact that teachers' expectations are based on an accurate assessment of students' ability; naturally, students' achievement follows those expectations. For students from minority or stereotyped groups, however, teachers' expectations are more likely to be based on inaccurate, stereotypical ideas. For these students, teacher expectations often become a self-fulfilling prophecy. Thus students from minority groups—in particular, African American and economically disadvantaged students—are vulnerable to teachers' stereotypic beliefs. As we will see in the next section, students' vulnerability to stereotypes threatens not only their school achievement but also their psychological well-being.

STEREOTYPE THREAT

When children enter school, they enter a system that reflects a largely White, male, and middle-class culture. For example, African American culture and scholarship are devalued in American classrooms (Steele, 1992). Because Black culture is, for the most part, relegated to special times (for example, Black History Month), courses (The Black Novelist), or departments (African American Studies), it remains out of the mainstream of school curricula. Black students must be willing, therefore, to learn "White" history, art, and literature if they are to be educated. It is not surprising that when Black children are adopted and raised in White middle-class homes their intelligence test scores are equally as high as those of White adopted children raised in similar environs (Scarr & Weinberg, 1976). Similarly, scholarship that is relevant to women is often marginalized in Women's Studies programs or in courses such as Psychology of Women or Women in Art.

The American educational system also reflects White culture in defining "school achievement" (Oyserman, Gant, & Ager, 1995). Personal responsibility, hard work, and a healthy competitive attitude tend to predict success in school, and these reflect traditional White values. However, Blacks develop achievement strategies when they sense that schooling is a collective endeavor in which students work together and are dependent on one another for success. Similarly, the competitive nature of schooling is more consistent with cultural beliefs about males compared with females. Because boys and girls are socialized differently, boys are more prepared to "compete" for grades and honors in school than are girls.

These observations paint a picture of schools and schooling as culturally biased against Black and women students. Against this backdrop, Black and female students also face stereotypes about their group that contain beliefs about intelligence and academic ability. These stereotypes can be "heard" from teachers, fellow students, and family members, and from the broader culture in media images and representations. Regardless of their source, stereotypes about Black and female students' academic abilities threaten both their school achievement and their psychological well-being.

Stereotype Threat in African American Students

Beliefs about low intelligence and laziness have been part of the cultural stereotype of African Americans for decades (Devine & Elliot, 1995; Katz & Braly, 1933). Stereotypes about their "academic deficiencies" undercut the ambitions and accomplishments of African American students in school (Steele, 1992, 1997). In other words, Black students feel anxious and vulnerable in school settings because they sense that teachers' (and the surrounding culture's) assumptions about their ability set them up for failure. To defend against this threat, African American students tend to disidentify with school. That is, they relinquish the belief that education holds promise for them, that they can feel good about themselves as students, and that they can improve their life prospects through schooling. When students disidentify with school, their school performance drops and confirms stereotypic beliefs about African American students.

In a demonstration of **stereotype threat**, African American and White college students took a test composed of difficult questions from the verbal portion of the Graduate Record Examination (GRE). The students were told that the test either was or was not a measure of their intellectual ability. The African American students who believed their academic "deficiency" would not be detected by the test scored just as well as the White students. The African American participants who felt vulnerable to the test—that it was somehow able to "find them out"—scored much more poorly than the White participants (Steele & Aronson, 1995).

A follow-up study (Steele & Aronson, 1995) revealed some of the underlying components of stereotype threat. Under the procedure previously described, African American and White students believed they would be taking a test that either was or was not diagnostic of their intellectual ability. After completing some sample items to get an idea of the test difficulty, participants completed an exercise involving filling in the missing letters in a word. Some of the words chosen were related to the African American stereotype (for example, _ _ c e [race], _ _ z y [lazy]), whereas other words were related to feelings of self-doubt (for example, _ _ m b [dumb], _ _ _ m e [shame]). Finally, participants also rated their preference for a variety of music types, sports, and activities that were associated with the African American stereotype. The results showed that, more than any other group of participants, African American participants who anticipated taking a test that they believed could diagnose their intellectual ability completed the word fragments with more stereotypic and self-doubting words and reported less preference for Black-stereotypic activities.

This study shows that the African American participants who experienced stereotype threat were more aware of the stereotype about their group. Further, they wanted to avoid being stereotyped—their lowered endorsement of things African American reflects that. In keeping with this avoidance, only 1 in 4 African American participants who believed the test was diagnostic of their ability were willing to provide their race on a pretest demographic information sheet. All of the African Americans who anticipated taking a nondiagnostic test (and all of the White participants) provided their race. Finally, this research suggests that African American students respond to stereotype threat strategically. That is, they distance themselves from racial categorization and stereotypic associations only in threatening academic situations and only to avoid being viewed in stereotypic terms.

Steele and his colleagues' research shows that school performance among African Americans is related to stereotypes about their ability rather than to their actual ability, and when the threatening nature of those beliefs is removed, African American and White students perform equally well. Stereotype threat has also been observed in women and economically disadvantaged students who face stereotypes that include specific beliefs about intelligence and academic ability.

Stereotype Threat in Female Students

The notion that women are illogical and otherwise intellectually ill-suited for scientific pursuits is prominent in the stereotype of women, despite a lack of evidence (Hyde, Fennema, & Lamon, 1990). Female students who are aware of this stereotype, even if they disagree with it, carry an extra burden in math or engineering pursuits. In addition to mastering the material, they also run the risk of confirming what people already believe—that women are not good at math. Stereotypes about women's logical and mathematical deficiencies undercut the ambitions and accomplishments of women in math and science fields (Steele, 1997). In the short run, as was the case with African American students in academic domains, women's performance in math and science will suffer. In the long run, women may disidentify with achievement in math and science domains; in other words, they give up the belief that math and science fields hold promise for them and that their accomplishments in those areas will be appreciated. Both outcomes end up contributing to the stereotype that produced them.

Researchers tested this idea by giving men and women students a math test that was described as "able (or not able) to show gender differences." The women who believed their math "deficiency" would not be detected scored just as well as men, but the women who felt vulnerable to the stereotype of "math deficient" scored much worse than men (Spencer, Steele, & Quinn, 1999). This study demonstrates that women's poorer performance in math-related domains is due to their vulnerability to stereotypical beliefs about women's mathematical skills, not to their math ability. When that vulnerability is eliminated, women achieve equally to men.

Women are believed to possess poorer math and reasoning ability than men. These stereotypic expectations help undermine females' achievement in science.

Stereotype Threat in Economically Disadvantaged Students

Beliefs about the intellectual inferiority and laziness of poor people are widespread in our culture (Feagin, 1972; Hernnstein & Murray, 1994). As is the case with members of other stereotyped groups, these stereotypic beliefs burden economically disadvantaged students, lower their academic achievement, and push them to disidentify with school as a domain of promise and self-improvement. In a study similar to those reported earlier, French researchers gave participants who were from low or high socioeconomic backgrounds a test consisting of items taken from the verbal portion of the GRE (Croizet & Claire, 1998). The test was described either as "a test of verbal intelligence" or "an investigative tool for studying lexical processes." The low-SES participants who believed the test was diagnostic of their verbal intelligence attempted significantly fewer questions and scored worse than did low-SES participants in the nondiagnostic test condition and all high-SES participants. But when participants believed the test was not indicative of their intellectual ability, low- and high-SES participants scored equally well.

In summary, research on stereotype threat makes it clear that African Americans, women, and economically disadvantaged individuals are vulnerable to widely held stereotypic beliefs about their ability. Stereotype threat interferes with intellectual and academic performance and leads students to devalue school and achievement as a basis for self-esteem and self-improvement. It is important to remember that, from minority students' perspectives, disidentification with school achievement is a means of protecting psychological well-being from others' stereotypic expectations. Sadly, from teachers' (and other observers') perspectives, disidentification leads to the poor academic achievement that was initially expected of minority students, thus strengthening others' stereotypes of African American, female, and economically deprived students. In other words, this research also shows the power of stereotypic beliefs to generate their own fulfillment. Students who are believed to lack ability—due to stereotypes about their group—are not expected to do well by teachers and peers. These negative expectations contribute to a burdensome and unfriendly context for academic accomplishment, a context that brings about the expected behavior.

STEREOTYPIC COMMUNICATION

It is commonplace to talk to—and perhaps much more commonplace to talk about—people who are socially different from ourselves. For instance, students talk about fellow students who are members of a different Greek organization, sports team members talk about their rivals, and we all talk about people from different ethnic or cultural groups. When we talk about (or to) an individual from another social group, we tend to emphasize stereotypic characteristics of that group, refer to them as all alike, and subtly derogate the group (Ruscher, 1998). These communication tendencies exist despite communicators' insistence that they are not prejudiced toward the outgroup. Why? Stereotypes influence our choice of words and verbal expression when talking about people from other social groups, even when we don't recognize our negative feelings about that group.

Researchers in one study had pairs of participants talk about a hypothetical person who was described as "alcoholic" and about whom they were given a list of characteristics (Ruscher & Hammer, 1994). Half of the characteristics were consistent with the alcoholic stereotype (e.g., forgetful, disagreeable), and half were stereotype-inconsistent traits (e.g., motivated, successful). After forming impressions of the target person together, the two participants shared their impressions on videotape. The participants made more references to and spent more time talking about characteristics of the person that were consistent (compared with inconsistent) with the stereotype associated with his group. This conversational pattern was not due to forgetting the stereotype-inconsistent traits; a test of participants' memory after the discussion showed that they recalled both types of traits equally well. Other research finds this pattern when people talk about physically disabled and African American individuals (Ruscher, 1998).

Stereotypes are reflected in our communication patterns, not just in the terms we select to describe outgroup members but also in the linguistic structure of those terms. When we describe the expected or typical actions of outgroup members, we use abstract terms; but when we describe their unexpected or atypical actions, we use concrete terms. For example, imagine observing a male or female student giving an eloquent solution to a problem posed in your math class. Researchers find that people will use abstract terms such as "intelligent" to describe the expected action (males being good in math) and concrete terms such as "she answered the question" to describe the unexpected action (females being good at math; Maass, Milesi, Zabbini, & Stahlberg, 1995). This pattern is called the **linguistic intergroup bias** and is similar to the ultimate attribution error discussed in Chapter 2.

The linguistic intergroup bias reflects, in our communication, the dispositional nature of stereotypic thinking. Abstract descriptions tie the typical behaviors of outgroup members to underlying, unchanging qualities, and this lends stability to our stereotypes. Alternatively, when we observe a behavior that is atypical of an outgroup member, we can isolate that action through concrete descriptive terms and avoid having to confront the inaccuracy of our stereotypic beliefs.

Talking about outgroup individuals also makes the members of that group seem more similar. This occurs when we liken the person we are talking about to other members of that group we are familiar with, such as through past experience or media exposure. Ruscher and her colleagues found that when pairs of participants talked about a hypothetical outgroup individual ("Joe"), their conversation included more exemplars—examples of other members of that group who had similar qualities—when Joe's outgroup was emphasized than when it was not (Ruscher & Hammer, 1994).

Finally, our communications about outgroup members often reflect subtle prejudices. Do you talk differently to your elderly grandparent than to your friends? Probably, especially if the grandparent is hard of hearing. Communication with older adults is not only louder and slower, but also less understandable. Furthermore, louder and slower speech is perceived by older adults as patronizing (Ryan, Bourhis, & Knops, 1991). Presumably, this pattern of communication reflects stereotypic beliefs of the elderly as dim-witted. Other research measured the imperative verbs used by men and women "instructors" to teach the Heimlich maneuver to either a man or woman "student" (Duval & Ruscher, 1994). The researchers reasoned that the number of imperative verbs (e.g., "grab him around here," "pull up like this") used in a lesson was an indication of how simply the task was taught to the student. The results showed that men teaching women used significantly more imperative verb statements than they did when teaching other men (or than women did when teaching anyone). This suggests the operation of a stereotype: Men may see women as slightly less competent than males on tasks of physical skill or strength, thus requiring a more detailed, authoritative lesson.

In summary, research demonstrates that our communication with and about people from other social groups reflects the influence of stereotypes about those groups. We describe socially different others in stereotype-consistent terms, use references that liken them to other group members, and use derogative language with outgroup members in stereotype-consistent ways. Why do we communicate in stereotypical terms when we have no wish or intention to be prejudiced? Two answers are plausible. First, we define and evaluate ourselves and our own groups by pointing to others (Allport, 1954). Thus, even when we harbor no dislike of people from other social groups, talking about them in stereotypic terms helps us understand who *we* are and why *our* group is valuable. This explanation is strengthened by research that shows that when our group identity is threatened, we respond defensively with enhanced levels of the intergroup linguistic bias (Maass, Ceccarelli, & Rudin, 1996). Second, we hold stereotypic beliefs with varying certainty depending on the group, because we often have little actual contact with individuals from other social groups. Thus conversations with other, especially ingroup, individuals are ways to test the validity of our ideas and develop consensus for them (Ruscher, 1998).

MODERATORS OF STEREOTYPES IN ACTION

We have learned how stereotypes find their way into our behavior and how they affect people from social groups that we stereotype. However, our stereotypes don't exert a constant influence on our language and behavior for every social group. Rather, the influence of stereotypes on us — and subsequently on others — depends on how certain we are about our stereotypic beliefs and how much information we have about individual members of a social group.

Stereotype Certainty

We hold our stereotypic notions with varying degrees of certainty. Some are so ingrained we never question their "factuality"; others form on the shaky basis of hearsay and are held with some caution. As the certainty of our social beliefs increases, so does their tendency to generate their own fulfillment in others' behavior. Stereotypes about which we are certain issue a clear message to others about what we expect of them, as well as causing us to act out those beliefs more obviously. In sum, the more certainly we hold stereotypic expectations for members of an outgroup, the more we will "confirm" them in our interactions with those individuals.

Individuating Information

Stereotypes are particularly influential on our behavior when we have little other information about an individual beyond his or her social category, which, by the way, can often be known without interacting with the person. Information about an *individual* is more accurate and, hence, a better basis for making judgments and forming expectations than is stereotypic knowledge. Individuating information can be available from, obviously, personal experience. We are unlikely to think of our friends who are socially different from us in stereotypical terms because we know them. Our expectations for a friend's behavior, then, will likely be based on our first-hand knowledge of his or her attributes.

Second, we acquire individuating information through repeated interaction with a person. When a friend of mine learned that she was assigned an Asian

American roommate for her freshman year in college, she imagined that her future roommate was probably the "quiet, introverted, intelligent" type—stereotypical notions of Asian students. After living together for a few weeks, however, my friend realized that her roommate (and now friend) *was* intelligent, but was hardly quiet and introverted! Individuating information, gained through interaction, proved more useful than the "Asian student" stereotype for predicting what her roommate would be doing on a Friday night.

SUMMARY

In Chapter 2 we learned that stereotypes are beliefs about social groups and the people in them that consist of, at best, exaggerations of their actual attributes and, at worst, fabricated assumptions about them. If we could previously comfort ourselves with the thought that "stereotypes don't hurt anybody," we now know better. Stereotypes "act" to shape our social world in direct and indirect ways. Their direct influence operates through the self-fulfilling prophecy and stereotype threat, as others come to act out the roles that are scripted by our expectations of them. As people's behavior conforms to stereotypic expectations, actual differences between groups of people grow. As our social contexts become more defined by social categories, we remain separated from people who are socially different from us. Physical separation, in turn, heightens the need to rely on stereotypes in our thinking about socially different others, closing a circle of segregation and ignorance that enhances social differences around us.

A more subtle and indirect effect of stereotypes can be seen in the way talking about people from other social groups affects us, which in turn shapes the nature of our social contexts. Research suggests that when we talk to our friends and acquaintances about socially different people—hearing our friends' beliefs and experiences alongside our own—our stereotypic beliefs become more extreme (Myers & Bishop, 1970). So, although we may believe that talking about others leads to more validity or accuracy in our beliefs, the effect of discussing socially different others likely leads to less accuracy. Stereotypes, distorted and strengthened by discussion and communication, eventually find their way into our behavior and our expectations for people from other social groups, where they contribute to the social differences we experience around us. In sum, although social categories and stereotypes are useful information-processing tools, they act on our behavior in ways that make actual contributions to the social difference around us.

KEY TERMS

self-fulfilling prophecy
stereotype threat
linguistic intergroup bias

FOR THOUGHT AND DISCUSSION

1. Reflect on how teachers and professors, in your experience, have acted out different expectations for students. What types of students face differing expectations? What actions of the teacher demonstrated those expectations?

2. Have you experienced the negative effects of others' stereotyping of you? In what context did you experience it, what was the stereotypical belief, and what performance or ability did it interfere with?

3. If you have older relatives, such as grandparents or great-grandparents, living in your home or nearby, observe how family members talk to them. What changes in their communication style or vocabulary do you notice?

REFERENCES

Allen, B., & Niss, J. (1990, April). A chill in the college classroom? *Phi Delta Kappan, 607–609.*

Allport, G. (1954). *The nature of prejudice.* Reading, MA: Addison-Wesley.

Babad, E., Bernieri, F., & Rosenthal, R. (1991). Students as judges of teachers' verbal and nonverbal behavior. *American Educational Research Journal, 28,* 211–234.

Brophy, J., & Good, T. (1974). *Teacher–student relationships: Causes and consequences.* New York: Holt, Rinehart & Winston.

Cooper, H., & Tom, D. (1984). Teacher expectation research: A review with implications for classroom instruction. *Elementary School Journal, 85,* 77–89.

Croizet, J., & Claire, T. (1998). Extending the concept of stereotype threat to social class: The intellectual underperformance of students from low socioeconomic backgrounds. *Personality and Social Psychology Bulletin, 24,* 588–594.

Devine, P. G., & Elliot, A. J. (1995). Are racial stereotypes *really* fading? The Princeton trilogy revisited. *Personality and Social Psychology Bulletin, 21,* 1139–1150.

Duval, L., & Ruscher, J. (1994, August). *Men use more detail to explain a gender-neutral task to women.* Paper presented at the meeting of the American Psychological Society, Washington, DC.

Feagin, J. R. (1972, November). Poverty: We still believe that God will help those who help themselves. *Psychology Today,* 101–111.

Gilbert, D. T., & Malone, P. S. (1995). The correspondence bias. *Psychological Bulletin, 117,* 21–38.

Hernnstein, R., & Murray, C. (1994). *The bell curve: Intelligence and class structure in American life.* New York: Free Press.

Hilton, J. L., & von Hippel, W. (1990). The role of consistency in the judgment of stereotype-relevant behaviors. *Personality and Social Psychology Bulletin, 16,* 430–448.

Hyde, J., Fennema, E., & Lamon, S. (1990). Gender differences in mathematics performance: A meta-analysis. *Psychological Bulletin, 107,* 139–155.

Jamieson, D., Lydon, J., Stewart, G., & Zanna, M. (1987). Pygmalion revisited: New evidence for student expectancy effects in the classroom. *Journal of Educational Psychology, 79,* 461–466.

Jones, E. (1986). Interpreting interpersonal behavior: The effects of expectancies. *Science, 234,* 41–46.

Jussim, L. (1989). Teacher expectations: Self-fulfilling prophecies, perceptual biases, and accuracy. *Journal of Personality and Social Psychology, 57,* 469–480.

Jussim, L. (1991). Social perception and social reality: A reflection-construction model. *Psychological Review, 98,* 54–73.

Jussim, L., & Eccles, J. (1992). Teacher expectations: II. Construction and reflection of student achievement. *Journal of Personality and Social Psychology, 63,* 947–961.

Jussim, L., Eccles, J., & Madon, S. (1996). Social perception, social stereotypes, and teacher expectations: Accuracy and the quest for the powerful self-fulfilling prophecy. *Advances in Experimental Social Psychology, 28,* 281–388.

Katz, D., & Braly, K. (1933). Racial stereotypes in one hundred college students. *Journal of Abnormal and Social Psychology, 28,* 280–290.

Maass, A., Ceccarelli, R., & Rudin, S. (1996). Linguistic intergroup bias: Evidence for ingroup-protective motivation. *Journal of Personality and Social Psychology, 71,* 512–526.

Maass, A., Milesi, A., Zabbini, S., & Stahlberg, D. (1995). Linguistic intergroup bias: Differential expectancies or in-group protection? *Journal of Personality and Social Psychology, 68,* 116–126.

Merton, R. (1948). The self-fulfilling prophecy. *Antioch Review, 8,* 193–210.

Myers, D., & Bishop, G. (1970). Discussion effects on racial attitudes. *Science, 169,* 778–779.

Oyserman, D., Gant, L., & Ager, J. (1995). A socially contextualized model of African American identity: Possible selves and school persistence. *Journal of Personality and Social Psychology, 69,* 1216–1232.

Rosenthal, R. (1974). *On the social psychology of the self-fulfilling prophecy: Further evidence for Pygmalion effects and their mediating mechanisms.* New York: MSS Modular Publications.

Rosenthal, R., & Jacobson, L. (1968). *Pygmalion in the classroom: Teacher expectations and student intellectual development.* New York: Holt, Rinehart & Winston.

Ruscher, J. (1998). Prejudice and stereotyping in everyday communication. *Advances in Experimental Social Psychology, 30,* 241–307.

Ruscher, J., & Hammer, E. D. (1994). Revising disrupted impressions through conversation. *Journal of Personality and Social Psychology, 66,* 530–541.

Ryan, E., Bourhis, R., & Knops, U. (1991). Evaluative perceptions of patronizing speech addressed to elders. *Psychology and Aging, 6,* 442–450.

Scarr, S., & Weinberg, R. (1976). IQ test performance of Black children adopted by White families. *American Psychologist, 31,* 726–739.

Snyder, M., & Cantor, N. (1979). Testing hypotheses about other people: The use of historical knowledge. *Journal of Experimental Social Psychology, 15,* 330–343.

Spencer, S., Steele, C., & Quinn, D. (1999). Stereotype threat and women's math performance. *Journal of Experimental Social Psychology, 35,* 4–28.

Steele, C. (1992, April). Race and the schooling of Black Americans. *Atlantic Monthly,* 68–80.

Steele, C. (1997). A threat in the air: How stereotypes shape intellectual identity and performance. *American Psychologist, 52,* 613–629.

Steele, C., & Aronson, J. (1995). Stereotype threat and the intellectual test performance of African Americans. *Journal of Personality and Social Psychology, 69,* 797–811.

Swann, W. (1985). The self as an architect of social reality. In B. Schlenker (Ed.), *The self and social life* (pp. 100–125). New York: McGraw-Hill.

Wineburg, S. (1987). The self-fulfillment of the self-fulfilling prophecy. *Educational Researcher, 16,* 28–37.

Prejudice

CHAPTER OBJECTIVE

To demonstrate how social differences are evaluated; how they stem from needs to maximize self-esteem and minimize anxiety; and how prejudice is a natural by-product of social evaluations.

Evaluating Social Differences

We not only think about the social difference that surrounds us, as was discussed in the previous chapter, but we also *feel* about it. That is, we make sense of the social world not only by identifying and describing social differences but also by evaluating them. How good are "we"? Is my social group worthwhile? Are "we" better than "they" are? Like the perceptual tools of stereotypes and social categories, these evaluative questions also help us understand and order our social world.

Within this process of evaluating people who are socially different from ourselves, prejudice arises. **Prejudice** is unjustified negative judgment of an individual based on his or her social group identity (Allport, 1954). There are three components to this definition of prejudice—let's clarify each in turn. First, what does it mean that prejudice involves "unjustified" judgments or evaluations of others? Our feelings or evaluations of others based on their social group may be overgeneralized, such as believing that all Jewish people are scheming, business-savvy individuals. Also, they may be inaccurate or remain uncorrected by our experience with people from that group. In sum, prejudice is "thinking ill of others *without warrant*" (Allport, p. 6, italics added).

Second, prejudice involves negative rather than positive evaluations and judgments of others based on their group membership. Positive prejudice does exist, such as the feelings we have about physically attractive or wealthy people. But positive prejudice is comparatively infrequent and is not considered to be a source of discrimination and disadvantage for members of those particular groups. The range of negative feelings encompassed by prejudice is considerable and includes dislike, resentment, and fear, as well as prejudiced actions such as avoidance, use of ethnic slurs (or otherwise prejudiced epithets), discrimination, and physical confrontation.

Third, prejudice is a response to an individual that is based primarily on his or her group identity. Therefore, prejudice can be based on any group label, including such common ones as ethnicity, gender, social class, age, sexual orientation, religion, nationality or cultural identity, physical disability, or political affiliation. A proliferation of terms, such as racism, ageism, homophobia, or ethnocentrism, refer to prejudice against specific groups. Notice also that prejudice is not confined to people whose social group identity is visible; many important social categories, such as sexual orientation and religion, are invisible. Nevertheless, we develop biased and negative judgments about such people.

Summing up, prejudice involves evaluations—that tend to be negative—about others based on their social group affiliation or identity. We said earlier that evaluating socially different people lends meaning to our social world. To be sure, our evaluations of other groups do not pretend to be objective. Rather, judgments about others serve us and our needs. In this chapter we will consider how our evaluations of our own and others' social groups are connected to the need to enhance and preserve feelings of self-esteem, the need to reduce social and existential anxiety, and the need to be seen by others (and to see ourselves) as fair-minded, nonprejudiced people.

THE ROLE OF SELF-ESTEEM IN PREJUDICE

The need for self-esteem—defined as perceptions of personal worthiness and competence—is fundamental to human nature. The need to protect and enhance self-esteem, therefore, motivates many behaviors, including prejudice.

Maintaining a Positive Social Identity

Who are you? Try this exercise. List the terms, characteristics, or labels that are essentially descriptive of you on a piece of paper; list as many terms as you feel describe you. Recall from Chapter 1 that we can differ from others in many ways, both personal and social. Go through your list of self-descriptive words and indicate whether each is a personal or social quality. How much of your identity is based on personal characteristics? on social characteristics? According to **social identity theory**, we look to social categories and group memberships to help identify us, and we want these social affiliations to be as positive as possible. Our social identity can be derived from groups that are assigned to us (such as our race, gender, or perhaps religion) and acquired by us (such as our affiliations with clubs, teams, or organizations). Importantly, social identifications are a significant source of self-esteem (Luhtanen & Crocker, 1992).

PASSIVE SOCIAL IDENTITY MAINTENANCE   According to social identity theory, we desire a positive social identity; we want to be associated with social groups that are worthwhile and valued. This desire causes us to passively affiliate with groups that succeed. Robert Cialdini and his fellow researchers found that students wore more "team" clothing and colors—identifying themselves with the school football team—after the team had won than when it had lost (Cialdini et al., 1976). They also found that people distanced themselves from failing or disliked groups. Researchers called college students after their university team had either won or lost and asked them to describe the game. Students reflecting on a team loss used more "they" than "we" pronouns, compared with those who described a victory (Cialdini et al., 1976). In other words, we desire to share a group's glory but avoid their disgrace. We therefore enhance our social identity by affiliating with groups when they succeed. Likewise, our social identity is protected when we distance ourselves from unsuccessful groups.

ACTIVE SOCIAL IDENTITY MAINTENANCE We also actively pursue a positive social identity by forging comparisons between groups that boost rather than threaten our feelings of social worthiness. We create these favorable comparisons by selecting a lower-status, less successful, or disliked group as a comparison for our group. For example, if Carol feels uncertainty about the value and integrity of her sorority, she can compare her sorority to another in a way that restores her pride. She can pick a struggling or disliked sorority as a ready-made comparison or strategically select a dimension on which her sorority outshines a rival.

A great deal of research supports the claim of social identity theory that, when given a chance, we create favorable comparisons with socially different others. Amazingly, this occurs even when the groups have little real significance. Many studies have been conducted in which participants were divided into two groups randomly and given arbitrary labels such as "Red" and "Blue" (see Brewer, 1979, for a review). In these studies, participants were then asked to evaluate members of their own group and members of the outgroup. Even though the social distinctions in these studies were artificial and little interaction took place among group members, participants exhibited a consistent preference for ingroup, compared with outgroup, individuals.

This tendency to evaluate people in one's own group more favorably than people in a comparison outgroup is called **ingroup bias.** The ingroup bias is a well-established phenomenon and has been observed in a variety of real-world social groups (Furnham, 1982; Kelly, 1988). Do these comparisons bolster social identity? Yes, according to research. Participants who are allowed to make favorable comparisons with outgroups experience increased self-esteem compared with those who are not (Lemyre & Smith, 1985; Oakes & Turner, 1980). In other words, even small or temporary advantages in the status or competence of your group compared with another group reflect positively on you.

Who Exhibits the Most Ingroup Bias?

If ingroup bias enhances self-esteem, as the research shows, then we would expect people with low levels of self-esteem to engage in the most ingroup bias because

People from high-status, successful groups exhibit more ingroup bias than people from disadvantaged groups — why? They are likely more concerned about losing the privileged position and resources they enjoy than more disadvantaged people are, and they express this through prejudice and discrimination against the less fortunate.

they have the greatest self-esteem needs. Although this is intuitively sensible, it is actually people with *high* levels of self-esteem who exhibit the most ingroup bias (Crocker & Luhtanen, 1990; Crocker, Thompson, McGraw, & Ingerman, 1987). Similarly, individuals in high-status or successful groups exhibit more ingroup bias than people in lower-status, less successful groups (Crocker & Luhtanen, 1990; Mullen, Brown, & Smith, 1992; Sachdev & Bourhis, 1987). In sum, ingroup bias produces at least a temporary increase in one's self-esteem. But the people most in need of the emotional "lift" do not engage in it, whereas those who have little need for a more positive social identity do!

Why do people from competent, high-status groups demonstrate more ingroup bias than those from less privileged groups? The answer lies in realizing that emotional underpinnings of ingroup bias are not limited to enhancing self-esteem. Biased evaluations of an outgroup are also related to feelings of group deservingness and relative deprivation. That is, when your group is not receiving what you believe it should, what it has in the past, or what other groups are perceived to be receiving, a sense of relative deprivation ensues. Much research shows that the perception of relative deprivation is related to ingroup bias (Bobo, 1988). One study surveyed White Americans who described themselves as either collectively deprived (compared with Black Americans), individually deprived (compared with other people), or satisfied with their circumstances on their attitudes toward Blacks (Vanneman & Pettigrew, 1972). Only those White participants who perceived that their group was deprived expressed negative attitudes toward Blacks.

People from high-status, advantaged groups may perceive more deprivation and exhibit more ingroup bias for two reasons. First, compared with people from low-status groups, they have loftier expectations and ambitions for their group. As a result, their actual circumstances, even if satisfactory at some absolute level, feel relatively disadvantaged. Second, people from groups that possess status, power, or some other valued resource are more sensitive to losing resources they currently have than are those whose groups have never had such resources.

In summary, we actively evaluate social differences by placing value on our own and others' social groups. This evaluation process is not objective but tends to favor us and the groups we affiliate with at the expense of those groups we are not part of. Moreover, biased evaluation of social differences is grounded in needs for self-esteem and perceptions of deservingness. Our evaluation of social difference finds its natural extension in prejudice and discrimination. Preference and favoritism toward our own groups lead inevitably (although perhaps not directly) to indifference or dislike felt about others' groups, as well as to the negative behaviors usually associated with those feelings. The diversity of our social world, therefore, is partly a product of our own feelings of worthiness and deservingness and the social evaluations that derive from those feelings.

THE ROLE OF ANXIETY IN PREJUDICE

We have seen how our evaluation of social difference is driven by a need to protect and enhance a positive social identity and self-esteem and by personal feelings of deservingness. Social evaluations of our own and others' groups are also related to some negative emotions. Much research has established that our evaluation of our own and others' social groups is driven by anxiety, tension, and fear.

Managing Anxiety Through Social Identification

Many psychologists contend that all the fear and anxiety we experience in our day-to-day lives is, directly or indirectly, related to an underlying fear of death and the vulnerability associated with our mortality (Greenberg, Pyszczynski, & Solomon, 1986). Indeed, many typical life events—such as sickness, accidents, broken relationships, and lost jobs—remind us that we are feeble beings and that bad things can happen to us quite unexpectedly and unjustly. According to **terror management theory**, the realization that we are insignificant creatures living in an unjust, and often chaotic, world terrorizes us. This existential terror would cripple us if social and cultural groups didn't come to the rescue (Greenberg et al., 1986).

Social and cultural groups help us manage the terror associated with death and mortality by developing and maintaining systems of meaning or worldviews. These systems of meaning provide answers to questions of existence and lend order, meaning, and permanence to life. Worldviews also provide roles for individuals to adopt, contributing to our perceptions of purpose and value. Worldviews are composed of values, beliefs, rituals, and concepts that are woven into a coherent system and, over time, consensually validated by a group of individuals. Some common worldviews include religions, environmentalism, and capitalism.

Researchers have shown that people who are able to affirm their cultural worldview or defend it against threat are less anxious than people who cannot affirm or defend their worldviews (Arndt, Greenberg, Pyszczynski, Simon, & Solomon, in press). Thus worldviews shield us from existential anxiety and despair. Moreover, because worldviews are developed and maintained *socially*, identification with groups of similarly believing others is important for dealing with our own sense of vulnerability and mortality. When one's worldview is shaken by an event or experience, people should respond with increased identification with the worldview and the individuals who affirm it. Research supports this expectation. In a classic study psychologists (who were undetected) observed the behavior of a religious "doomsday" cult whose specific prediction for the end of the world proved to be incorrect (Festinger, Reicken, & Schachter, 1956). Instead of disbanding in embarrassment, the group's faith in their vision and cause was renewed.

In a more recent test of this notion, Christian participants completed a writing exercise in which they pondered their own death to temporarily heighten existential anxiety (Greenberg et al., 1990). Then they rated the likeability of a hypothetical Christian person. Compared with those who did not do the anxiety-enhancing writing exercise, the participants who did expressed more liking for the fellow Christian. This study shows that anxiety about death causes us to strengthen our social identifications. Similarly, Batson (1975) found that when Christian believers were confronted with evidence contradicting their beliefs, they responded not with a more moderate position but with greater faith in their beliefs. In sum, worldviews serve vital functions: They order life, impart meaning, and protect us from life's uncertainties. Threats to our worldviews are met with renewed identification with the supporting group and a defensive reaffirmation of the group's beliefs and values.

Meaning systems range from those that are limited and parochial, such as a fraternity or service organization, to the comprehensive, such as religious or scientific belief systems. Although each of us is a part of many social and cultural groups, we likely identify most strongly with those groups that sustain a comprehensive meaning system and in which we have a valuable contributing role. Religious belief systems are good examples of comprehensive worldviews because they answer many ultimate questions such as, Who am I? and Why am I here?

In summary, we are emotionally invested in social groups because the meaning systems they support stabilize our lives and protect us from threats posed by a meaningless existence and death. As a result, we are selfishly interested in the validity of those beliefs to which we're committed and in finding a special role in the group. Perhaps it is not surprising that we habitually engage in ingroup bias: Some of our social group identifications are deeply rooted in existential concerns.

Managing Anxiety Through Social Evaluation

In addition to coping with anxiety by reaffirming our faith in what we believe and our identification with those who share our beliefs, we also defend our world-views by derogating others who hold a different, challenging worldview. For example, the typical Christian may find the Jewish worldview foreign and potentially threatening because it does not recognize Jesus Christ as the Son of God. In the study described previously, Christians who were either temporarily death-anxious or not also evaluated a hypothetical Jewish individual (Greenberg et al., 1990). Christian participants who were acutely anxious about existential concerns evaluated the Jewish individual more negatively than did the participants who were not anxious.

In a similar study using different social groups, American students' death anxiety was made salient or not (using a writing exercise similar to the one previously described), after which they read an interview with a hypothetical person that expressed either pro-U.S. or anti-U.S. sentiment (Greenberg et al., 1990). Participants who were death-anxious expressed less liking for and less agreement with the anti-U.S. interviewee than participants who were not anxious. These studies demonstrate that anxiety about our own mortality and vulnerability cause us to dislike socially different others. By disliking "them" we validate and protect "our" worldview—its answers to questions and accompanying values.

We also evaluate socially different others negatively when we are in competition with them for some valued resource. This economic approach to ingroup and outgroup evaluation is called **realistic group conflict** because dislike of outgroups often has a tangible, material basis. In some classic field experiments with boys at summer camp, Muzafer Sherif (1966) showed that when boys were divided into teams for activities and camaraderie, the boys did show ingroup bias but did not exhibit negative attitudes or actions toward the other team. However, when Sherif introduced competition between the groups for recognition, awards, and tokens of accomplishment, the boys became openly hostile and antagonistic toward the outgroup members. Clearly, the boys felt threatened by the other team in the competitive situation.

According to Sherif, group conflict results when a group's aims and purposes, such as its desire for and intentions to gain a limited resource, conflict with those of another group. His research suggests that fear and anxiety contribute to negative evaluations of socially different people. Whether the boys were anxious about their ability to win the contests, about losing control of a resource, or about not getting what they felt they deserved, however, is difficult to determine from Sherif's research.

To sum up, we are emotionally invested in social groups because they maintain ways of believing that add much-needed order and meaning to our individual lives. Naturally, protecting "our" way of believing and doing things is important to us. This need for psychological security leads us to enhance our identification with the ingroup and those who support our values and to derogate outgroups and the validity of their beliefs. In other words, we perceive more social difference and engage in more prejudice when our values and resources are questioned or threatened. The diversity of our social contexts, then, is in part constructed on our fears and anxieties. We are more likely to prefer "us" and dislike "them" when we are aware of our vulnerabilities and limitations.

THE ROLE OF MAINTAINING APPEARANCES IN PREJUDICE

Prejudice is defined as holding negative attitudes and feelings toward other individuals based on their group membership. However, many studies that demonstrate ingroup bias find that participants rate both the ingroup and the outgroup positively (in absolute terms), with one's own group merely seen as *more* positive than the other group. Researchers have found, for example, that White students associate positive traits more quickly with the social category "Whites" than with "African Americans," but Whites are not seen as any less negative than African Americans (Gaertner & McLaughlin, 1983). Is this pattern of social evaluation — "both are good but we're better" — really prejudicial?

Social psychologists have learned that expressions of prejudice have changed over the years due to changes in the cultural and political landscape. Prejudice is expressed differently in our present-day climate of civil rights, political correctness, and tolerance than it was in times past (Gaertner & Dovidio, 1986). **Modern prejudice** is more subtle, easily justified, and, hence, difficult to detect than the "old-fashioned," overt prejudice of the pre–civil rights era.

Modern prejudice can take many forms, such as concealing one's true inner (and negative) feelings toward another by behaving in a careful, socially acceptable manner. In an early demonstration of modern prejudice, researchers asked White participants to evaluate their own group and African Americans (Sigall & Page, 1971). Half of the participants evaluated the groups via a questionnaire. Measured this way, participants' evaluations of Whites and African Americans were equally positive. The other half of the participants evaluated the groups while connected via electrodes to an imposing bank of equipment that they believed could detect their true inner attitudes and feelings. This measurement method, called the "bogus pipeline," caused participants to respond more truthfully. Compared with the questionnaire respondents, the "bogus pipeline" participants evaluated Whites more positively and African Americans more negatively. Thus this study shows that people may hide their true feelings about their own and other social groups.

Another form of modern prejudice involves open dislike and derogation of individuals for reasons that are related not to group membership but to the values attributed to those individuals (Sears, 1988). For example, Whites' dislike of African Americans has been shown to be partly due to Whites' belief that many African Americans have not embraced the central American values of hard work and self-determination (Kinder & Sears, 1981). Based on a set of values rather than on skin color or ethnic background, such prejudice appears less objectionable and is easier to justify and defend. In a series of studies, Crandall (1994) found that negative attitudes toward overweight people were related not to a general dislike of them but to the perception that overweight individuals repudiate the important American values of self-control and personal responsibility.

Finally, modern prejudice also arises when our stereotype about a group is inconsistent with our personal beliefs about that group (Devine, 1989). Stereotypes, as we have discussed, are socialized through family, media, and cultural influences and therefore are well learned and operate automatically. As a result, stereotypic thoughts, judgments, and actions are often difficult to inhibit and become the default response whenever we are exposed to an outgroup member. Our personal beliefs about a social group, however, may be more positive and informed than the stereotype that has been instilled in us. What's more, personal beliefs are more thoughtful and controllable. The automatic nature of stereotypes and the controllability of personal beliefs is an important distinction. It means that, even for individuals who espouse nonprejudiced ideals, one's immediate response to an outgroup member is negative and stereotype-driven. Thus, in terms of the automatic (stereotypes) and controlled (personal beliefs) components of prejudice, modern prejudice reflects the inability or unwillingness of people to "reprogram" their thinking about outgroup members in a way that replaces stereotypic beliefs with personal beliefs (Monteith, Zuwerink, & Devine, 1994).

In summary, research on modern prejudice has shown that we monitor our social evaluations and, insofar as we are able, present social attitudes and behaviors that are safe and justifiable. In light of this research, perhaps ingroup bias—in which people exalt their own group but stop short of derogating an outgroup—is an expression of modern prejudice. Compared to old-fashioned, overt prejudice, it *does* seem like progress to like "us" and not dislike "them." However, any evaluative distinctions between groups of people are inevitably linked to outcomes that are discriminatory. That is, even if our evaluations of socially different others are positive (but less so than our evaluations of our groups), we will divide resources in a preferential way. So, although others' groups may not be disliked, our preference for "us" will cause disadvantage for "them."

APPROACHES TO REDUCING PREJUDICE: PERSONAL CONTACT AND SELF-REGULATION

We now know that prejudice is anchored in cognitive structures such as categories and stereotypes and associated with personal needs for self-esteem, security, and social approval. Understanding what contributes to prejudice can also inform us about how to reduce prejudice. In this section, we consider two distinctive but effective approaches to reducing prejudice and promoting tolerance of socially different others.

Social categorization often goes hand in glove with physical categorization. That is, we perceive people as a group not only because they share a distinctive social quality but also because they are physically proximal—they tend to "hang out" together. For example, members of different racial groups often live in their own communities, attend different schools, shop at different stores, and attend different churches. It is not surprising, then, that we think of African Americans and Whites (or European Americans) as different groups! As we learned in Chapter 2, social categorization enhances the separateness of socially different groups of people. That separateness is not just a mental image; in many cases we are physically and geographically separated from outgroup individuals.

The stereotypes we hold about social groups and the influence stereotypes exert on our actions are due in part to the physical separation between members of different groups. Recall from our earlier discussion that stereotypic behavior occurs when we lack (or ignore) information about individuals. How can we acquire that information if we have no contact with those individuals? If our separation from people who are socially different from ourselves reinforces stereotypes and their associated negative feelings, then contact with those people should help break down stereotypes and prejudicial feelings of uncertainty, fear, or judgment that we often harbor about outgroup members. This idea is the essence of the contact hypothesis. Proposed by Gordon Allport (1954), the **contact hypothesis** says that physical contact with a member of a negatively stereotyped group (1) lessens the negative beliefs and feelings we hold about that individual and (2) improves our attitudes and feelings toward the group as a whole.

Is Any Contact OK?

Research on the contact hypothesis has established that several conditions must occur for contact with an outgroup individual to reduce stereotypes and negative feelings. First, this personal interaction should ideally be with an outgroup member of equal status—someone who has a similar set of life circumstances to your own (Brown, 1984). For example, negative beliefs and feelings about Jews would be reduced more effectively by interacting with a Jewish classmate than with a Jewish professor or administrator. Status differences are a convenient excuse for stereotypic beliefs, preventing personal contact from having its positive effects when they loom over an interaction.

Second, sustained personal interaction with an outgroup member reduces negative beliefs and feelings when that interaction is cooperative—when you and the other person are interested in and working toward a common goal (Dechamps & Brown, 1983). For example, neighborhoods with a mix of opposed racial or religious groups will reduce the suspicion and hostility between them by joining together to fight crime or beautify the streets. Additionally, research has shown that personal, cooperative contact must be sanctioned and supported by authority figures or institutions to effectively reduce prejudice (Cook, 1984).

Finally, although equal-status and cooperative contact are sufficient to reduce stereotypes about an *individual* from a disliked group, that goodwill does not generalize to the whole group unless the individual is seen as representative of the group (Desforges et al., 1997). Recall from Chapter 2 that stereotype-inconsistent

Personal contact between in-group and outgroup members is a vital condition for reducing prejudice between the groups' members. However, the contact must also occur between people of equal status and be cooperative in nature, and we must see the outgroup person as representative of his or her group.

information is often filed under "exceptions to the rule." However, when you have a positive interaction with an outgroup member you regard as typical of "them," it is more difficult to dismiss that person as an unusually friendly member of the outgroup and write the experience off as atypical.

Contact Lessens Our Reliance on Stereotypes

Our beliefs about members of other social groups are based on a single distinction—for example, we are White, they are Black—which, due to its distinctiveness or importance in the culture, masks many dimensions on which "we" and "they" are similar. These similarities tend to go unnoticed and unappreciated unless we have personal contact with an outgroup individual in the manner discussed previously. Imagine interacting with a physically disabled classmate about whom you believed stereotypical things. During the interaction, however, you might learn that you both have similar difficulties with your parents, or have both traveled to Europe, or like the same music groups. These dimensions are subtle groupings that include you both! Discovering your social similarities and shared group memberships causes the initial social distinction (physical disability) and its stereotype to fade in relevance and importance.

In addition to finding common ground, personal and friendly contact with an outgroup member provides you with lots of individual information. Individuating information becomes more salient than group-based information and is a more reliable basis for making inferences about outgroup individuals. Thus the distinctiveness of group labels and categories fades when we interact with people from outgroups. This was demonstrated in a study in which fourth-grade children were randomly assigned either to a classroom integrated with some students with learning disabilities or to a nonintegrated classroom (Maras & Brown, 1996). The nondisabled students' categorizations of the disabled students were observed over a 3-month term. At the beginning of the term, both groups used gender and disability to characterize the students in the class. In other words, you were either a disabled (or nondisabled) boy or a disabled (or nondisabled) girl. At the end of the term, students in the nonintegrated (control) class described their classmates in similar categorical terms. In the integrated class, however, students' descriptions were much more idiosyncratic; the ordering of the students in their classroom was not dominated by the "disabled/nondisabled" dimension. This study shows that personal, cooperative contact lessens the importance of social categories in our thinking about members of other groups.

Recall that stereotypes involve assumptions about the character and personality of outgroup members and that we tend to explain their behavior in dispositional terms, committing the ultimate attribution error. This tendency is partly due to lack of contact between ingroup and outgroup members. When we are separated from people who are different from ourselves we remain ignorant of the life circumstances and situational pressures they face, and of the fact that "their" behavior might be as much due to circumstances as our own is. Personal interaction gives us insight into others' situations and circumstances. As a result, we are more socially informed, less judgmental, and more willing to acknowledge that the negative traits we perceive in outgroup members (if they are true at all) may be caused by forces over which they have little control.

Application of the Contact Hypothesis

IN SCHOOL DESEGREGATION   In 1954 the U.S. Supreme Court declared racial segregation in schools unconstitutional. As a result schools opened their doors to students of all racial groups. This situation provided the opportunity for researchers to evaluate the contact hypothesis in an important, real-life setting. In a review of that research, Walter Stephan (1978) reported that only 13% of the studies examining the effect of desegregation on students' racial attitudes actually found support for the contact hypothesis. Worse, half of the studies found the opposite effect: Racial integration in the classroom heightened students' negative stereotypes and feelings about other-race students!

Although this seems disappointing, there are reasons to believe that school systems have not given the contact hypothesis a fair test. First, many school administrators in the 1950s were firmly against desegregation. Their racist attitudes did not foster a friendly or supportive environment for interracial student contacts. More important, although White and Black students did (and still do) have personal contact in schoolrooms, they have too few opportunities to interact in cooperative tasks. Research shows that it is common for students to compete against rather than cooperate with each other for grades and the teacher's attention (Aronson, Blaney, Stephan, Sikes, & Snapp, 1978). Moreover, the interaction of White and Black students is often overlaid with differences in socioeconomic status. Thus, even if a White and Black student worked cooperatively on a school project, status differences (such as family income or neighborhood affiliation) might preclude any softening of negative stereotypes between them.

IN CLASSROOM LEARNING Clearer evidence for the contact hypothesis comes from studies that examine how cooperative, equal-status learning groups affect students' stereotypes of socially different group members. In one study junior high school students learned English skills over a 10-week period in one of two ethnically mixed settings (determined randomly): a cooperative learning group or a traditional classroom (Slavin, 1979). At the end of the unit students listed their friends in the class. Compared with the classroom group, the cooperative learning group listed significantly more cross-ethnic friends. In a similar study, learning-disabled and normal students learned classroom material in either cooperative groups or in a conventional classroom setting (Armstrong, Johnson, & Balow, 1981). After the 4-week unit, learning-disabled students were viewed more positively by their nondisabled peers in the cooperative group than in the classroom condition. These experiments demonstrate that classroom interaction with socially different others that occurs under the proper conditions breaks down stereotypic beliefs and engenders positive feelings toward those individuals and their group.

In summary, physical contact provides opportunities for people of different and perhaps disliked social categories to relate and cooperate. Equal-status, cooperative interactions contribute to liking, they reveal shared interests, and they provide us with individuating information about others. However, contact and cooperation with socially different people is not our strong suit; it does not come naturally. If it is desired, then, contact between members of social groups should be fostered and rewarded by concerned agents such as churches, school boards, community service agencies, and local government.

Self-Regulation in Prejudice Reduction

As discussed earlier, modern forms of prejudice feature a strong element of personal ambivalence or conflict. Accordingly, modern expressions of prejudice require that people maintain a personal inconsistency, such as between public actions and private feelings, between behavior that appears group-based but is claimed to be value-based, or between endorsing negative stereotype content and positive personal beliefs about an outgroup. Another approach to reducing prejudice, then, consists of making people aware of the inconsistencies that support their prejudice and teaching them to regulate their own responses.

It has been shown that when people—particularly those for whom being nonprejudiced is important—become aware that they have responded in a prejudiced manner, they feel guilty and embarrassed (Devine, Monteith, Zuwerink, & Elliot, 1991). In that study, participants wrote about how they should and how they *would* interact with Black individuals and gay men in social situations. Researchers then measured participants' negative emotions, such as guilt, regret, and shame, following the writing exercise. The results demonstrated that, as the discrepancy between how one should and would act toward outgroup individuals increased, negative feelings also increased. However, this effect was greatest among people who thought of themselves as nonprejudiced.

Can the embarrassment and shame associated with recognizing our own prejudiced behavior motivate us to change? According to research by Margo Monteith (1993), yes, it can. In one study she had participants read and evaluate the credentials of a hypothetical gay law school applicant. Some of the participants were led to believe that they had evaluated the applicant negatively because of his sexual orientation, thus activating a discrepancy between their nonprejudiced intentions and the "results" of their action. Other participants received no such information. What happened? The discrepancy-activated participants—especially those who were nonprejudiced to begin with—had more negative feelings about themselves compared with the other participants. More important, the low-prejudice, discrepancy-activated participants had more thoughts about the discrepancy between their values and their actions, spent more time reading an article explaining why people are prejudiced against gays, and recalled more details from the article than all other participants.

This study is important because it shows that people with nonprejudiced values who act in prejudiced ways are not only disturbed by their own actions, they also actively try to determine what went wrong and how they can prevent future regrettable actions. Moreover, when their negative emotional reactions to such behavior were accounted for, participants' self-improvement efforts were weakened. In other words, personal regulation of prejudiced behavior is not likely to occur without first experiencing the embarrassment and shame of unintended, hurtful prejudice.

In a follow-up study, Monteith (1993) again made some participants aware of the discrepancy between their prejudiced responses and their preexisting attitudes. Participants then entered what they believed was an unrelated study in which they rated the funniness of a variety of jokes, some of which involved gay-bashing. The homophobic jokes were rated as less funny than the other jokes, but only among participants who possessed nonprejudiced values and were aware of the discrepancy between their values and actions. This study suggests that non-prejudiced people who experience the sting of being aware of their prejudice make an effort to become less prejudiced in subsequent situations.

Integrating the Contact and Self-Regulation Approaches to Prejudice Reduction

The research discussed here has important implications for understanding what intergroup contact—as a prejudice-reduction method—can and cannot do. Recall that Allport (1954) believed contact between members of antagonistic groups would reduce prejudice in part through revising our stereotypes about that group. However, stereotypes are firmly implanted by a socialization process that draws on family, media, and traditional beliefs about outgroups. Devine's (1989; Devine et al., 1991) research shows that stereotypes operate automatically, even among people who want to be nonprejudiced. In other words, our stereotypes are not as malleable as Allport had hoped. Therefore, the benefit of intergroup contact is to lessen our reliance on rather than to transform our stereotypes.

Personal, cooperative contact with people from other social groups and self-regulation of one's prejudiced responses are complementary approaches to reducing prejudice. That is, sustained contact is more likely to cause us to revise our personal *beliefs* rather than our stereotypes about outgroup members. The automatic influence of cultural stereotypes will cause discrepancies in people who hold personal beliefs that are more tolerant and egalitarian than are the stereotypes with which they are familiar. Therefore, learning to self-regulate one's prejudiced and stereotype-driven responses will be a second step in reducing prejudice in oneself.

SUMMARY

The social difference we see around us is not merely observed and recorded in memory but is, in part, a creation of our own emotional needs and evaluations. That is, we help construct the social diversity around us through our feelings about and evaluation of social groups and their members. Our basic emotional needs—to enhance and protect our self-esteem, to minimize anxiety and fear, and to appear fair-minded to others—lead us to draw clear evaluative distinctions between "us" and "them," especially when other groups pose a threat to our beliefs and resources. Prejudice, then, is much more a comment about who "we" are as individuals and group members than about who "they" are.

KEY TERMS

prejudice

social identity theory

ingroup bias

terror management theory

realistic group conflict

modern prejudice

contact hypothesis

FOR THOUGHT AND DISCUSSION

1. Think about sports fans. In terms of their social identity maintenance, what are "fair weather fans" like?

   Loyal fans stick with their team through losses and poor seasons. How might they cope with the disgrace of identifying with a loser?

2. Can you think of ways that you or other people express prejudice that are subtle and difficult to detect?

3. Is modern prejudice any *better* than old-fashioned prejudice? As a society, have we improved or regressed by becoming less overt and more subtle in our prejudices?

4. What is your dominant worldview? How do you draw personal value from the worldview?

5. When someone opposes or contradicts your beliefs or values, how do you react?

REFERENCES

Allport, G. (1954). *The nature of prejudice.* Reading, MA: Addison-Wesley.

Armstrong, B., Johnson, D., & Balow, B. (1981). Effects of cooperative vs. individualistic learning experiences on interpersonal attraction between learning-disabled and normal-progress elementary school students. *Contemporary Educational Psychology, 6,* 102–109.

Arndt, J., Greenberg, J., Pyszczynski, T., Simon, L., & Solomon, S. (in press). Suppression, accessibility of death-related thoughts, and worldview defense: Exploring the psychodynamics of terror management. *Journal of Personality and Social Psychology.*

Aronson, E., Blaney, N., Stephan, C., Sikes, J., & Snapp, M. (1978). *The jig-saw classroom.* London: Sage.

Batson, D. (1975). Rational processing or rationalization? The effect of disconfirming information on a stated religious belief. *Journal of Personality and Social Psychology, 32,* 176–184.

Bobo, L. (1988). Attitudes toward the black political movement: Trends, meaning, and effects on racial policy preferences. *Social Psychology Quarterly, 51,* 287–302.

Brewer, M. (1979). Ingroup bias in the minimal intergroup situation: A cognitive motivation analysis. *Psychological Bulletin, 86,* 307–324.

Brown, R. (1984). The effects of intergroup similarity and cooperative vs. competitive orientation on intergroup discrimination. *British Journal of Social Psychology, 23,* 21–33.

Cialdini, R., Borden, R., Thorne, A., Walker, M., Freeman, S., & Sloan, L. (1976). Basking in reflected glory: Three (football) field studies. *Journal of Personality and Social Psychology, 34,* 366–374.

Cook, S. (1984). Cooperative interaction in multi-ethnic contexts. In N. Miller & M. Brewer (Eds.), *Groups in contact: The psychology of desegregation.* New York: Academic Press.

Crandall, C. (1994). Prejudice against fat people: Ideology and self-interest. *Journal of Personality and Social Psychology, 66,* 882–894.

Crocker, J., & Luhtanen, R. (1990). Collective self-esteem and ingroup bias. *Journal of Personality and Social Psychology, 58,* 60–67.

Crocker, J., Thompson, L., McGraw, K., & Ingerman, C. (1987). Downward comparison, prejudice, and evaluations of others. *Journal of Personality and Social Psychology, 52,* 907–916.

Dechamps, J., & Brown, R. (1983). Superordinate goals and intergroup conflict. *British Journal of Social Psychology, 22,* 189–195.

Desforges, D., Lord, C., Pugh, M., Sia, T., Scarberry, N., & Ratcliff, C. (1997). Role of group representativeness in the generalization part of the contact hypothesis. *Basic and Applied Social Psychology, 19,* 183–204.

Devine, P. (1989). Stereotypes and prejudice: Their automatic and controlled components. *Journal of Personality and Social Psychology, 56,* 5–18.

Devine, P., Monteith, M., Zuwerink, J., & Elliot, A. (1991). Prejudice with and without compunction. *Journal of Personality and Social Psychology, 60,* 817–830.

Festinger, L., Reicken, H., & Schachter, S. (1956). *When prophecy fails.* Minneapolis: University of Minnesota Press.

Furnham, A. (1982). Explanations for unemployment in Britain. *European Journal of Social Psychology, 12,* 335–352.

Gaertner, S., & Dovidio, J. (1986). The aversive form of racism. In J. F. Dovidio & S. L. Gaertner (Eds.), *Prejudice, discrimination, and racism*. Orlando, FL: Academic Press.

Gaertner, S., & McLaughlin, J. (1983). Racial stereotypes: Associations and ascriptions of positive and negative characteristics. *Social Psychology Quarterly, 46*, 23–30.

Greenberg, J., Pyszczynski, T., & Solomon, S. (1986). The causes and consequences of the need for self-esteem: A terror management theory. In R. F. Baumeister (Ed.), *Public self and private self*. New York: Springer-Verlag.

Greenberg, J., Pyszczynski, T., Solomon, S., Rosenblatt, A., Veeder, M., Kirkland, S., & Lyon, D. (1990). Evidence for terror management theory: II. The effects of mortality salience on reactions to those who threaten or bolster the cultural worldview. *Journal of Personality and Social Psychology, 58*, 308–318.

Kelly, C. (1988). Intergroup differentiation in a political context. *British Journal of Social Psychology, 27*, 314–322.

Kinder, D., & Sears, D. (1981). Prejudice and politics: Symbolic racism versus racial threats to the good life. *Journal of Personality and Social Psychology, 40*, 414–431.

Lemyre, L., & Smith, P. (1985). Intergroup discrimination and self-esteem in the minimal group paradigm. *Journal of Personality and Social Psychology, 49*, 660–670.

Luhtanen, R., & Crocker, J. (1992). A collective self-esteem scale: Self-evaluation of one's social identity. *Personality and Social Psychology Bulletin, 18*, 302–318.

Maras, P., & Brown, R. (1996). Effects of contact on children's attitudes toward disability: A longitudinal study. *Journal of Applied Social Psychology, 26*, 2113–2134.

Monteith, M. (1993). Self-regulation of prejudiced responses: Implications for progress in prejudice-reduction efforts. *Journal of Personality and Social Psychology, 65*, 469–485.

Monteith, M., Zuwerink, J., & Devine, P. (1994). Prejudice and prejudice reduction: Classic challenges, contemporary approaches. In P. G. Devine, D. L. Hamilton, and T. M. Ostrom (Eds.) *Social cognition: Impact on social psychology* (pp. 323–346). New York: Academic Press.

Mullen, B., Brown, R., & Smith, C. (1992). Ingroup bias as a function of salience, relevance, and status: An integration. *European Journal of Social Psychology, 22*, 103–122.

Oakes, P., & Turner, J. (1980). Social categorization and intergroup behaviour: Does minimal intergroup discrimination make social identity more positive? *European Journal of Social Psychology, 10*, 295–301.

Sachdev, I., & Bourhis, R. (1987). Status differentials and intergroup behaviour. *European Journal of Social Psychology, 17*, 277–293.

Sears, D. (1988). Symbolic racism. In P. A. Katz & D. M. Taylor (Eds.), *Eliminating racism: Profiles in controversy* (pp. 53–84). New York: Plenum.

Sherif, M. (1966). *Group conflict and cooperation: Their social psychology*. London: Routledge and Kegan Paul.

Sigall, H., & Page, R. (1971). Current stereotypes: A little fading, a little faking. *Journal of Personality and Social Psychology, 18*, 247–255.

Slavin, R. (1979). Effects of biracial learning teams on cross-racial friendships. *Journal of Educational Psychology, 71*, 381–387.

Stephan, W. (1978). School desegregation: An evaluation of predictions made in *Brown vs. Board of Education*. *Psychological Bulletin, 85*, 217–238.

Vanneman, R., & Pettigrew, T. (1972). Race and relative deprivation in the urban United States. *Race, 13*, 461–486.

Women Relate, Men Act

Deconstructing Gender Diversity

CHAPTER OBJECTIVE

To discuss the content and consequences of gender stereotypes and to show that gender differences are socially and culturally constructed.

Of all the social categories and stereotypes we use to divide and organize the social world, none is more basic than the male–female distinction. The social categories of male and female and their associated stereotypes can effectively halve the complexity of our social world. Dividing the world into two distinctive, well-known social groups makes sense from an information-processing perspective. But how accurate are our social perceptions when filtered through the lens of gender difference?

Social categorization based on gender is widely used not only because of the simplicity of having two categories but also because these categories are so distinguishable. Men and women are very different people, or so it seems. In his best-selling book *Men Are From Mars, Women Are From Venus* (1994), John Gray gives practical advice on how to overcome the vast and significant differences between men and women to make better relationships. From the book title, Gray apparently regards men and women as akin to different species, virtually alien to one another and struggling to communicate with each other. But are men and women that different? If they are, in what ways, and how are those differences explained? If they are not, then why do gender differences remain such a strong part of our social world? These questions are addressed in this chapter on the psychology of gender diversity.

GENDER STEREOTYPES

Displayed in Table 5.1 are some of the attributes commonly associated with men and women; these qualities and beliefs make up our **gender stereotypes.** Your personal stereotypes may differ somewhat from the stereotypes in Table 5.1, and

TABLE 5.1 Stereotypic Traits and Abilities for Men and Women

Men	Women
independent	dependent
assertive	sensitive
not emotional	emotional
logical	religious
adventurous	attractive
competitive	cooperative
like math and science	like art and literature
have leadership ability	gullible

our gender stereotypes change when we are thinking about women and men of different racial status from our own. In general, however, these stereotypes are part of our culture. They are generally agreed-upon ways of thinking about men and women and define what is masculine and feminine.

The problem with gender stereotypes is not merely that women and men are presumed to be different; it is that men's qualities are more positively valued than women's qualities. Look again at the list of attributes in Table 5.1. In our culture, independence is valued over dependence, logic over intuition and emotionality, and assertiveness over interpersonal sensitivity. So gender stereotyping is a social problem because it is associated with **gender bias**—the tendency to value men and masculine traits over women and feminine traits. Let's examine some evidence for the claim that men are perceived as better, more competent, and more valuable people than women.

In the classic demonstration of gender bias, Philip Goldberg (1968) gathered published writings from a variety of professional fields and condensed them into a series of essays such as would be generated by a student on an exam. He then had participants read and evaluate the essays, which were labeled with a fictitious male (John McKay) or female (Joan McKay) student's name. The results showed that the same writing was evaluated more favorably when it bore a man's rather than a woman's name. Other demonstrations of gender bias have found that men's success is attributed to their ability, but women's success is attributed to the ease of the task (Feather & Simon, 1975).

Gender bias depends on what men and women are being evaluated for. For example, in one study equally qualified men and women "applicants" called about jobs that were traditionally masculine (e.g., security guard) or feminine (e.g., receptionist). The supervisors on the other end of the line tended to discourage or disqualify women who were interested in "men's" jobs and men who were interested in "women's" jobs (Levinson, 1975). In that study, the mere voices of men and women callers were sufficient to activate stereotypes, which then guided potential employers' behavior toward men and women in stereotype-consistent ways. A survey of male managers found that, compared with male employees, females were seen as less competent and motivated (Rosen & Jerdee, 1978). Thus gender stereotypes lead to more positive evaluations of men than of women. However, gender bias sometimes favors women, although this "advantage" is only gained in traditionally feminine tasks, abilities, or jobs. Because gender bias is driven by stereotypes of men and women, it is less likely to occur when people have other information (besides an individual's sex) with which to evaluate someone (Swim, Borgida, Maruyama, & Myers, 1989).

Gender bias is also evidenced by the fact that women's physical and psychological differences from men (notice that men are the standard) are often cast in terms of disease or disorder, and these "deficiencies" are then treated (Tavris, 1992). For example, premenstrual syndrome (PMS) describes the hormone-related mood changes that women allegedly experience each month. Research demonstrates, however, that only a small minority of women (about 5%) experience severe enough PMS symptoms to see a physician. Further, PMS seems to be, in part, a self-fulfilling prophecy. That is, women *report* experiencing PMS more regularly than is evidenced by physiological measures taken on them, suggesting that many women have lived up to society's stereotype for them—that they believe they have a disruptive monthly problem because everyone else expects it of them. PMS, then, is as much (perhaps more) a social belief about women as it is a physiological fact and provides a neat explanation for women's supposed moodiness and emotionality.

Women's perceived psychological differences from men are also framed as disorders. The clinical category "self-defeating personality disorder" and the similar pop-psychology concept of "codependency" feature symptoms that are thinly veiled extensions of the female stereotype: sacrificing one's own interests for others, overinvolvement in others' lives and problems, and taking too much responsibility for relationship problems. According to psychologist Carol Tavris (1992), these "disorders" are the latest attempts to define what is wrong with women. They provide a respected clinical justification for the "deficiencies" of women and also demonstrate that standards of mental health and adjustment are more masculine than feminine.

In summary, men and women are believed to be different types of people, possessing different attributes and abilities. Whereas men are generally regarded as independent, strong, and logical, women are regarded as dependent, sensitive, and emotional. Moreover, women's attributes are less positively valued than men's, resulting in a pattern of bias or discrimination against women that extends to many areas of life.

ARE THE DIFFERENCES BETWEEN WOMEN AND MEN ACTUAL OR PERCEIVED?

We have considered the ways in which men and women are believed to be different and some consequences of gender stereotyping. In Chapter 2 I showed that stereotypes seem to be accurate because they have some factual basis, even if that evidence is distorted or elaborated. Let's now examine whether some of the gender differences discussed here have any factual basis.

Intellectual Differences

Stereotypically, women are regarded as having better verbal ability than men. That is, they supposedly are better readers, have better language skills, and are more interested in art and literature than men. Is it true that women are more verbally skilled than men? In 1950, girls did outscore boys on tests of verbal skill, but by 1980 boys and girls were equal (Feingold, 1988). Other researchers reviewed over 160 studies that compared men and women on various verbal skills and tasks and found small differences, with women scoring higher than men (Hyde & Linn, 1988). A parallel but reverse gender difference is in the area of quantitative ability. Stereotypically, men are presumed to have a better "head for numbers," to be more logical, and to be more interested in math and science domains than women. Does this difference in ability really exist? Girls have closed the "math gap" that existed for decades and now score equal to boys on tests of math skills (Hyde, Fennema, & Lamon, 1990).

Psychological Differences

Gender stereotypes refer not only to differences in intellectual abilities and competence but also to psychological differences. Reviews of the research evidence suggest that women and men differ in four general domains of behavior: helpfulness, aggressiveness, gullibility, and sexual attitudes and behavior. The first three are discussed subsequently; the fourth is included in the discussion of evolutionary psychology at the end of the chapter.

HELPFULNESS AND EMPATHY   Most people (including women) perceive women as more empathic and helpful than men, more sensitive to the feelings and needs of others than men are. Much research data has established that men and women do behave differently in the areas of helpfulness (Eagly & Crowley, 1986). Studies that measure "heroic" helping—assisting someone in dire need or distress—show that men help more than women. However, studies that measure mundane expressions of help find the opposite: Women are more likely than men to do favors, express concern, or provide support to someone in need. Thus the direction of sex differences in helpfulness depends on the kind of helping observed.

Both large surveys and smaller experimental studies show that women respond with more empathy than men to a needy individual (Batson et al., 1996; Eisenberg & Lennon, 1983). Compared with men, when women talk they relate more personal experiences and show more support (Eagly, 1987). Another dimension of empathy involves sensitivity to nonverbal behavior; in this area researchers have found a reliable gender difference. Women are more attuned to subtle nonverbal cues in others' behavior and are better at interpreting nonverbal behavior than men are (Hall, 1978).

AGGRESSIVENESS   In general, research shows men to be more aggressive than women (Eagly & Steffen, 1986; Hyde, 1984). The magnitude of this gender difference in aggressiveness depends on how it is measured. Men are far more likely than women to commit violent crimes, such as murder, robbery, and assault. The research is not as clear, however, on gender differences in less physical forms of aggression, such as verbal taunts or insults. Some studies find that men and women do not differ, for example, in their willingness to use verbal insults (White & Kowalski, 1994). Aside from these gender differences in aggressiveness, females express more guilt about aggressive actions and are more concerned about being retaliated against than males are (Eagly & Steffen, 1986). Gender differences in aggression also disappear when a person is provoked and as people get older (Bettencourt & Miller, 1996). So aggressiveness is not solely determined by gender; there are many other factors that account for our aggressive actions.

Furthermore, gender differences in aggressiveness are often based on responses to surveys or questionnaires. Could these differences really be due to the way men, compared with women, present themselves to researchers and pollsters? Research does point to bias in questions designed to measure aggressive attitudes (Zur, 1989). When questions are posed in confrontational "us or them" terms, men affirm them more than women; but men and women are equally supportive of questions that frame aggression in humanitarian terms (e.g., "liberating oppressed people"). Thus perhaps some of the differences we observe between men and women in aggressiveness are not innate but are responses to society's different expectations for men and women.

GULLIBILITY   Popular stereotypes of women are that they are easily influenced, susceptible to persuasive appeals and claims. Some studies have shown women to be more easily influenced, whereas others provide no evidence of such a gender difference (Eagly, 1987; Eagly & Carli, 1981). When the results are summed up, women appear to be slightly more gullible and conforming than men. These gender differences also depend on factors such as the type of appeal made or whether the pressure is exerted by a group or an individual.

It has been suggested that comparing men and women on measures of gullibility and susceptibility to influence is a subtle expression of gender bias (Tavris, 1992). Indeed, posing the question, Are women more easily influenced than men? raises the specter of another "deficiency" in women that needs to be studied and explained. One might conduct the same studies to learn, Are men less trusting than women? Surely, lacking the ability to trust another person is just as deficient as being easily influenced. Thus gender bias might even have subtle effects on gender differences research.

To sum up, in view of the many ways that women and men could differ, reliably demonstrated gender differences are few in number and small in magnitude. As we can see from the studies reviewed herein, women and men are not different in intellectual domains, but they do differ in several psychosocial areas. Notice that several of the differences reviewed here are also reflected in our stereotypes of men and women (see Table 5.1). To what extent, then, are gender stereotypes

Gender stereotypes include beliefs about what men and women are good at. We expect elementary school teachers to be women because of our beliefs about their nurturance, helpfulness, and skills with children.

accurate summaries of the ways that men and women really differ? Janet Swim (1994) investigated the accuracy of gender stereotypes by comparing participants' perceptions of gender differences with more objective meta-analytic reviews of the research (reviews that quantitatively summarize many studies on the same topic). The results showed that participants (about 350 university students) accurately estimated gender differences on some behaviors and underestimated gender differences in other behaviors. Moreover, participants' responses were biased by favoritism toward women. In other words, all participants were more accurate in estimating positive female attributes than all other types of attributes. Also, participants' responses reflected ingroup bias. That is, women perceived greater gender differences in nonverbal behavior (a woman's "specialty") than men did, whereas men estimated greater gender differences on leadership ability (a man's "specialty") than women did. This study suggests that our gender stereotypes have some factual basis and may not be gross exaggerations of the truth. However, the findings are also limited because they describe gender stereotype accuracy in middle-class college students, a population in which gender differences may be small to begin with and in which gender equality may be a more salient and important value.

Are the psychological differences reviewed here reflective of a men's and women's "personality"? Or could gender differences be a natural response to differing social and environmental forces facing women and men? Next we discuss how gender differences are explained.

EXPLAINING GENDER DIFFERENCES

One of the most common questions posed by students in introductory psychology courses is, "Why are men and women different?" We now know that there are two sets of gender differences: those that are widely believed but not factual (such as that men are better at math than women) and those that are both believed and factual (such as that men are more aggressive than women). We consider explanations for each set of gender differences in this section, starting with why we regard men and women as different in domains in which they are clearly equal.

Stereotypes in Action

If men and women do not differ in any basic intellectual domains such as math or verbal ability, why do we continue to believe that they do and act as if the differences are actual? Two explanations derive from the influence of stereotypes on our perceptions and impressions of others. First, dimensions on which men and women differ are simply less common than dimensions on which they are similar. Therefore, news of gender differences is more unexpected, noticeable, and memorable. Moreover, many professional publications prefer to publish research that demonstrates differences between groups of people rather than research that does not. Because of this bias, we hear more about the few studies that find some evidence of a gender difference than about the preponderance of studies conducted that find no differences.

Second, even when faced with equal amounts of evidence—some studies that find gender differences and others that do not—we react differently to it. That is, because we prefer to have our stereotypes supported rather than threatened, we are more inclined to believe research that is consistent rather than inconsistent with our beliefs. For example, if presented with two identical research studies, one that found men had better math skills than women and one that found the opposite, we would tend to find reasons to affirm the former study and criticize the latter. These explanations, applications of concepts discussed in Chapter 2, show that stereotypic beliefs about men's and women's intellectual abilities persist because they seem to have more factual support than they actually do. It is our stereotypes that guide us to notice and remember supportive instances and research studies.

Socialization

The most prominent explanations for gender differences share the general notion that gender differences are acquired through exposure to the social environment. Both the immediate and broader social environments feature many socializing agents, including parents and other caregivers, teachers, peers, and television.

Although they differ in their particular predictions, the two socialization models discussed in this section agree that the differences between men and women are not inherent but learned.

GENDER DIFFERENCES ARISE OUT OF SOCIAL INTERACTION   One explanation for gender differences specifies that gender differences emerge when people interact with each other (Deaux & Major, 1987). The differences between men's and women's behavior that arise in interactions depend on two factors. First, we all have beliefs and expectations about the traits and abilities of men and women. The stronger our gender beliefs are, the more they will guide our interactions with members of the opposite sex in ways that confirm those very beliefs. Second, situations vary in the extent to which gender is relevant. The more "gendered" a situation is, the more active and influential our gender expectations will be in that situation. In short, this model characterizes gender beliefs as following the processes of a self-fulfilling prophecy while acknowledging that situations alone can activate our gender beliefs.

As an example, consider a male supervisor who must interview applicants for two positions: a manager and a secretary. Because the man subscribes to stereotypic beliefs about women's abilities and traits, he will bring these beliefs into all of his interviews. However, the situation—in this example, the position for which he is interviewing—will have an independent effect on his beliefs. Because of the gender-relevant nature of the secretary's role, those interviews will likely activate the supervisor's gender beliefs more than the gender-irrelevant interview situations. What does the social interaction model predict will happen in this scenario? The man will treat women differently (and more negatively) than men, especially in the gender-relevant situations. His treatment will also tend to alter how the female, but not the male, applicants respond. In effect, his beliefs combine with the situation to produce the expected gender difference.

Recognize that the gender difference described in this scene did not exist—or only potentially existed—*before* the supervisor and the applicants interacted. Thus, Kay Deaux and Brenda Major's (1987) "social interaction" model of gender differences makes an important point: Gender differences are, in part, context-dependent outcomes. Their model explains the process by which gender differences arise and what factors are important in that process; it does not, however, explain the origin of gender beliefs.

GENDER DIFFERENCES ARISE OUT OF SOCIAL ROLES   Another perspective on the socialized nature of gender differences looks to the social roles traditionally occupied by men and women. According to Alice Eagly (1987), gender differences arise when societies assign different responsibilities and roles to men and women and people make assumptions about the traits and abilities associated with those roles. As was discussed in Chapter 2, we often erroneously assume that men and women *choose* these different roles because they are inherently different types of people to begin with. Actually, the reverse is more accurate. Males and females start out very similar in their traits and abilities but become different partly as

Gender differences begin in the home, where boys and girls are sex typed—or directed into different activities and interests. Encouraging boys and girls alike to play sports and to contribute to domestic chores can counter the influence of sex typing.

a result of being assigned or "guided into" different roles, interests, and occupations that, in turn, draw out different skills and behaviors. Thus the gender diversity we observe around us is partially constructed by gender roles and role-appropriate behavior.

The roles traditionally occupied by men (such as livelihood provider) and women (such as child-care provider) in our society have given rise to general beliefs that women *relate*—they are nurturant, caring, relationship-oriented individuals—and men *act*—they are assertive, agentic individuals. Gender differences arise, then, when girls and boys learn the skills and behaviors that are required by their respective social roles. To competently discharge their roles, girls need to learn nurturance, cooperativeness, and dependence, and boys need to learn assertiveness, ambition, and independence. If gender differences are created by society's assignment of men and women to different roles, would those differences change if the role assignments could be changed? One researcher compared the child-rearing behaviors of single men who were raising children with similar women and found the fathers to be equally as nurturant as the mothers (Risman, 1987). So when men are placed in roles or situations in which they are expected to be nurturant, they respond with nurturant behavior—just as women do.

Likewise, women's superior skill at interpreting nonverbal behavior is an adjustment necessitated (for women) by being in subordinate positions to a greater extent than men are (Snodgrass, 1985). People who tend to be in "follower" rather than "leader" roles (as women are) will naturally develop better skills at decoding and interpreting the actions and intentions of their boss or supervisor. However, the influence of these roles on our actions is the same for men and women. If men were consigned to subordinate, low-status jobs in which female supervisors were questioning their ability and motivation or relationships in which they were financially dependent on their wives, surely men would likely become adept at "reading" other people, too.

This model of socialized gender differences differs in two ways from the previous one. First, it specifies where gender beliefs and expectations originate. Second, it says that gender differences are not restricted to social interactions but appear in a broader range of behavior and life contexts. Both models of socialized gender differences, however, have a similar promising message for addressing the gender differences that result in disadvantage for women. Gender differences can become less discriminatory to women if we rely less on gender stereotypes for information about women's and men's abilities. Also, we must recognize that it is more likely that men's and women's differing social role assignments cause them to adapt and behave differently than it is that men's and women's "true" differences cause them to choose their preferred roles. In the following paragraphs, I examine the influence of three prominent socialization agents on gender differences.

FAMILY INFLUENCES ON GENDER DIFFERENCES   Much of our behavior is learned by watching other people, a mode of learning that is especially important for children. Gender-appropriate behavior is modeled by parents, grandparents, and siblings in the typical home, and children are rewarded for reproducing the "appropriate" behavior. For example, boys learn very early that trucks, guns, and athletic gear are approved "boy" toys, and girls understand that dolls, clothes, and dishes are "girl" things. Moreover, gender-inappropriate behavior is often disapproved by authority figures, as when a little boy dresses up in Mom's clothes or when a little girl gets dirty playing with trucks outside. Most children also naturally strive to identify more with their same-sex than their opposite-sex parent, adding strength to gender-appropriate behavior patterns. So to the extent that girls learn that "their" activities are cooperative and nonaggressive and occur in the home and boys learn that "their" activities involve competition and dominance and occur on the playing field, the seeds of gender-based advantage and disadvantage, opportunity and limitation, are already firmly rooted in the home.

As previously mentioned, children also draw information about what women and men are like from observing their parents' and other adults' behavior in various social roles. In our society, at home men are providers and protectors, whereas women occupy homemaker and child-care roles. At work, men's roles involve power, decision making, and physical labor, whereas women's tend to entail helping, teaching, and supporting.

SCHOOL INFLUENCES ON GENDER DIFFERENCES   When children enter school, many already have clear notions about what boys and girls do and are like. These gender stereotypes are often supported and perpetuated in the schoolroom. According to the observational research of Barrie Thorne (1986), elementary school-rooms and playgrounds are markedly segregated by sex. Observing hundreds of students in several grade levels at several elementary schools, Thorne found that principals and teachers commonly referred to students as "boys and girls" and often compared boys' and girls' behavior (e.g., "The girls are ready, are the boys?"). Classroom seating arrangements tended to be divided along gender lines, as did other activities such as lunch and walking in hallways. Teachers frequently divided classes into girl and boy "teams" for learning competitions, a highly questionable practice that makes social categorization based on gender explicit and sets up a battle of the sexes for teacher approval and grades.

School recreation also tends to be divided along gender lines. Playgrounds become divided into boys' and girls' "territory," with girls' territory being closer to the school than boys' (Thorne, 1986). Further, boys tend to play with other boys in rougher, more competitive games than do girls (Maccoby, 1990). It is important to reiterate that, although these behavioral differences may not be caused by school influences, school is a place in which gender stereotypes are learned, rehearsed, and strengthened. Indeed, some of the gender segregation, such as the lunchroom seating patterns, reflected the students' preferences, showing that even children as young as 5 years old have already learned some lessons about how boys and girls differ and that these perceptions influence their behavior.

Gender stereotypes that persist in school are also evident in the fields of study chosen by women and men. Although females and males score equally well on standardized math tests in elementary and middle school, men achieve more than women in math and engineering fields (Hyde et al., 1990). Nine out of ten jobs in engineering, math, and the physical sciences are held by men, and the women employed in those fields earn about 75% of what men earn in comparable jobs (Hewitt & Seymour, 1991, as cited in Steele, 1997). In other words, through high school years, males and females have equal math ability and comparable academic achievement in math and science. But during college years and beyond, men's math and science achievement outstrips women's. Why is this?

Claude Steele (1997) suggests that stereotypes about women's logical and mathematical deficiencies undercut the ambitions and accomplishments of women in math and science fields. In other words, women feel vulnerable in those domains, and, as a result, they disidentify with math and science achievement. In other words, they stop believing that math and science fields hold promise for them and that their accomplishments in those areas will be appreciated.

Researchers tested this idea by giving men and women students a math test that was described as being either able or unable to show gender differences. The women who believed their math "deficiency" would not be detected scored just as well as men, but the women who felt vulnerable to the stereotype about being "bad at math" scored much worse than men (Spencer, Steele, & Quinn, 1999). This study demonstrates that women's poorer performance in math-related domains is due to their vulnerability to stereotypical beliefs about women; when that vulnerability is eliminated, women achieve equally to men. It also shows the power of stereotypic beliefs to generate their own fulfillment. Because women are believed to lack math ability, they are not expected to do well by teachers and peers. These negative expectations bias instructors and guidance counselors against women, lead to diminished opportunities for women to demonstrate their competence, and contribute to the general "unfriendliness" of math and science domains for women. Given those circumstances, it is not surprising that women's achievement goes down!

To sum up, school is a social context that is organized around gender categorizations (by teachers, administrators, and other students), and, naturally, gender stereotypes become part of that context. Our school experiences, from elementary school through college, reflect and perpetuate the gender stereotypes. Worse, stereotypes about males' and females' academic abilities, though untrue, can become true through the self-fulfilling prophecy.

MEDIA INFLUENCES ON GENDER DIFFERENCES   As will be shown in Chapter 7, children spend almost as much time watching television as they do at school. What does TV teach them about gender differences? Men outnumber women in the TV world, and, in general, men's characters have more power, independence, intelligence, and courage than female characters do; women, however, are younger and more romantically available. Men are portrayed as experts about products, whereas women are product "users." Men are bombarded by advertisements that appeal to their strength, competitiveness, and sense of adventure, whereas women typically view ads for cleaning, home care, and personal hygiene products. Stereotypic images and messages are worse in music lyrics and videos, in which men appear as sexually aggressive and rational, whereas women are sexually attractive, passive, and irrational (Freudinger & Almquist, 1978).

Clearly, the media construct images of and messages about women and men that perpetuate gender stereotypes. These vivid, repetitive portrayals influence our attitudes and perceptions, especially if we watch television uncritically. Viewing the social world on TV leads us to believe that men and women are much more different than they actually are and that these gender differences are inherent rather than natural responses to different social roles and circumstances.

Self-Construals

There is good evidence to indicate that the socializing effects of family, school, and media on men's and women's behavior may be mediated by the self-concept (Cross & Madsen, 1997). That is, socializing agents probably exert their influence on behavior indirectly by forming the way men and women mentally represent—or construe—themselves. Researchers have identified two general types of self-construals: independent and interdependent. Independent self-construals feature a mental representation of oneself that is separate from one's representation of others. People with independent self-construals strive to preserve their autonomy and individuality in behavior (Markus & Kitayama, 1991). Interdependent self-construals, on the other hand, feature representations of oneself that are intertwined with one's thinking about other people. People with interdependent self-construals strive for connectedness with others.

These types of self-construals map easily onto gender differences wrought by traditional social roles—women's roles promote nurturing and cooperative behavior, and men's roles promote assertiveness and independence. It is very likely, then, that women develop interdependent self-construals and men independent self-construals. These fundamental cognitive differences between men and women influence a variety of behaviors (Cross & Madsen, 1997). For example, research shows that women are more likely to attend to and remember information about other people in an interaction than men are (Josephs, Markus, & Tafarodi, 1992). Women's self-esteem, compared with men's, is more dependent on interpersonal outcomes, such as the reaction of a friend, than on achievement outcomes (Hodgins, Liebeskind, & Schwartz, 1996). These differences suggest that self-construals shape one's information processing in ways that reflect the prominence of interdependence (for women) or independence (for men) in the self-concept.

Evolution Theory

Many of the differences between men and women can also be explained in evolutionary terms. **Evolutionary psychology** explains behavior by noting how it perpetuates the genes of the individuals who display that behavior. In evolutionary terms, behavior patterns arise and persist because they help people successfully adapt to changing natural and social conditions, hence securing their genetic contribution to future generations.

Evolutionary explanations of gender differences are particularly compelling in the areas of sexual and courtship behavior (Archer, 1996). The basic prediction of an evolutionary model of gender differences in sexual attitudes and behavior is as follows. To maximize the perpetuation of their genes, males must aggressively pursue and mate with as many females as possible. Females, however, must carefully select and remain with a devoted and responsible mate to maximally perpetuate their genes. These cross-purposes are at the root of gender differences in sexual behavior, and much research evidence supports this general prediction (Buss, 1995). For example, men are more accepting of casual sex, take more initiative in sexual behavior, and engage in more casual sex than do women (Hendrick, Hendrick, Slapion-Foote, & Foote, 1985; Oliver & Hyde, 1993). Across very different cultures, men tend to be attracted to women for their youth and beauty, whereas women are attracted to men for their emotional stability, income, and ambition (Buss & Schmidt, 1993).

In addition to explaining gender differences in sexual attitudes and behavior, evolutionary psychology also addresses gender differences in domains that until recently have been thought to be due exclusively to socialization (Archer, 1996). For example, men's lower levels of nurturance, social connectedness, and emotional expressiveness have been traditionally attributed to their social roles and training. However, these differences can also be explained by noting the evolutionary advantage for males, who are in competition with other males for furthering their genes through liberal mating and procreation, to resist displaying signs of vulnerability, weakness, and excessive emotional attachments to others.

In summary, evolutionary psychology poses a strong challenge to the long-standing claims that gender differences are largely socialized. However, as John Archer (1996) explains, the present array of gender differences probably reflects both influences of the natural selection and evolution of adaptive behaviors among men and women and the presence of socializing agents. He speculates that perhaps our tribal ancestors, observing the different patterns of behavior among men and women, gradually created traditions, rites, and myths to infuse those stark evolved differences with meaning. If so, these social and cultural traditions would have begun to have their own effects on the behavior of men and women.

SUMMARY

Gender stereotypes exaggerate the actual differences between men and women and imply that such differences stem from internal, unchanging qualities. In other words, they contribute to—rather than break down—the notion that men and women are inherently different. Compared with males, females' stereotypical attributes and abilities are negatively evaluated, leading to a pervasive gender bias in our culture. Gender-stereotypic beliefs also generate their own fulfillment and result in lower educational and career opportunities for women in certain fields. Finally, the gender differences that have been reliably demonstrated can be explained by citing the different socialization of men and women and by understanding those differences as evolved and genetically adaptive behavior patterns.

KEY TERMS

gender stereotypes
gender bias
evolutionary psychology

FOR THOUGHT AND DISCUSSION

1. Consider how stereotypes of men and women depend on their racial or ethnic identity. What are the attributes of a "typical" Asian American male or female? African American? Hispanic?

   Explain how these stereotypic beliefs might generate their own fulfillment.

2. In what ways have you observed or experienced gender bias at school or work?

3. Consider the personal courtesies that men have traditionally been expected to extend to women: holding the door, giving up their seat on a bus or subway, and so forth. Are these acts chivalrous and kind or demeaning to women? Do they enhance gender differences or compensate for them? How have these social role expectations for men changed? Discuss.

4. Men and women are stereotypically regarded as good at math and science and art and literature, respectively. Recall some personal experience with this stereotype. How did it affect you?

REFERENCES

Archer, J. (1996). Sex differences in social behavior: Are the social role and evolutionary explanations compatible? *American Psychologist, 51,* 909–917.

Batson, D., Sympson, S., Hindman, J., Decruz, P., Todd, R., Jennings, G., & Burris, C. (1996). "I've been there too": Effect on empathy of prior experience with a need. *Personality and Social Psychology Bulletin, 22,* 474–482.

Bettencourt, B., & Miller, N. (1996). Sex differences in aggression as a function of provocation: A meta-analysis. *Psychological Bulletin, 119,* 422–447.

Buss, D. (1995). Psychological sex differences: Origins through sexual selection. *American Psychologist, 50,* 164–168.

Buss, D., & Schmidt, D. (1993). Sexual strategies theory: An evolutionary perspective on human mating. *Psychological Review, 100,* 204–232.

Cross, S., & Madsen, L. (1997). Models of the self: Self-construals and gender. *Psychological Bulletin, 122,* 5–37.

Deaux, K., & Major, B. (1987). Putting gender into context: An interactive model of gender-related behavior. *Psychological Review, 94,* 369–389.

Eagly, A. H. (1987). *Sex differences in social behavior: A social-role interpretation.* Hillsdale, NJ: Erlbaum.

Eagly, A., & Carli, L. (1981). Sex of researchers and sex-typed communications as determinants of sex differences in influenceability: A meta-analysis of social influence studies. *Psychological Bulletin, 90,* 1–20.

Eagly, A., & Crowley, M. (1986). Gender and helping behavior: A meta-analytic review of the social psychological literature. *Psychological Bulletin, 100,* 283–308.

Eagly, A., & Steffen, V. (1986). Gender and aggressive behavior: A meta-analytic review of the social psychological literature. *Psychological Bulletin, 100,* 309–330.

Eisenberg, N., & Lennon, R. (1983). Sex differences in empathy and related capacities. *Psychological Bulletin, 94,* 100–131.

Feather, N., & Simon, J. (1975). Reactions to male and female success and failure in sex-linked occupations: Impressions of personality, causal attributions, and perceived likelihood of different consequences. *Journal of Personality and Social Psychology, 31,* 20–31.

Feingold, A. (1988). Cognitive gender differences are disappearing. *American Psychologist, 43,* 95–103.

Freudinger, P., & Almquist, E. (1978). Male and female roles in the lyrics of three genres of contemporary music. *Sex Roles, 4,* 51–65.

Goldberg, P. (1968). Are women prejudiced against women? *Transaction, 5,* 28–30.

Gray, J. (1994). *Men are from Mars, women are from Venus.* New York: HarperCollins.

Hall, J. (1978). Gender effects in decoding nonverbal cues. *Psychological Bulletin, 85,* 845–875.

Hendrick, S., Hendrick, C., Slapion-Foote, J., & Foote, F. (1985). Gender differences in sexual attitudes. *Journal of Personality and Social Psychology, 48,* 1630–1642.

Hodgins, H., Liebeskind, E., & Schwartz, W. (1996). Getting out of hot water: Facework in social predicaments. *Journal of Personality and Social Psychology, 71,* 300–314.

Hyde, J. (1984). How large are gender differences in aggression? A developmental meta-analysis. *Developmental Psychology, 20,* 722–736.

Hyde, J., Fennema, E., & Lamon, S. (1990). Gender differences in mathematics performance: A meta-analysis. *Psychological Bulletin, 107,* 139–155.

Hyde, J., & Linn, M. (1988). Gender differences in verbal ability: A meta-analysis. *Psychological Bulletin, 104,* 53–69.

Josephs, R., Markus, H., & Tafarodi, R. (1992). Gender and self-esteem. *Journal of Personality and Social Psychology, 63,* 391–402.

Levinson, R. (1975). Sex discrimination and employment practices: An experiment with unconventional job inquiries. *Social Problems, 22,* 533–543.

Maccoby, E. (1990). Gender and relationships: A developmental account. *American Psychologist, 45,* 513–520.

Markus, H., & Kitayama, S. (1991). Culture and the self: Implications for cognition, emotion, and motivation. *Psychological Review, 98,* 224–253.

Oliver, M., & Hyde, J. (1993). Gender differences in sexuality: A meta-analysis. *Psychological Bulletin, 114,* 29–51.

Risman, B. (1987). Intimate relationships from a microstructural perspective: Men who mother. *Gender and Society, 1,* 6–32.

Rosen, B., & Jerdee, T. (1978). Perceived sex differences in managerially relevant characteristics. *Sex Roles, 4,* 837–843.

Snodgrass, S. (1985). Women's intuition: The effect of subordinate role on interpersonal sensitivity. *Journal of Personality and Social Psychology, 49,* 146–155.

Spencer, S., Steele, C., & Quinn, D. (1999). Stereotype threat and women's math performance. *Journal of Experimental Social Psychology, 35,* 4–28.

Steele, C. (1997). A threat in the air: How stereotypes shape intellectual identity and performance. *American Psychologist, 52,* 613–629.

Swim, J. (1994). Perceived versus meta-analytic effect sizes: An assessment of the accuracy of gender stereotypes. *Journal of Personality and Social Psychology, 66,* 21–36.

Swim, J., Borgida, E., Maruyama, G., & Myers, D. (1989). Joan McKay vs. John McKay: Do gender stereotypes bias evaluations? *Psychological Bulletin, 105,* 409–429.

Tavris, C. (1992). *The mismeasure of woman.* New York: Simon & Schuster.

Thorne, B. (1986). Girls and boys together . . . but mostly apart: Gender arrangements in elementary school. In W. Hartup & Z. Rubin (Eds.), *Relationships and development* (pp. 167–184). Hillsdale, NJ: Erlbaum.

White, J., & Kowalski, R. (1994). Deconstructing the myth of the nonaggressive woman. *Psychology of Women Quarterly, 18,* 487–508.

Zur, O. (1989). War myths: Exploration of the dominant collective beliefs about warfare. *Journal of Humanistic Psychology, 29,* 297–327.

Ethnic Diversity in Intelligence and Achievement

Not a Simple Matter of Color

CHAPTER OBJECTIVE
To illustrate the content and consequences of ethnic stereotypes that have at their core assumptions about intelligence, and to discuss the social and cultural context of ethnic group differences in intelligence and school achievement in particular.

Racial and ethnic categories are common ways of organizing the social world. Like gender, racial and most ethnic differences are perceptually salient social distinctions that are associated with different attributes and abilities. In their popular and controversial book *The Bell Curve* (1994), Richard Herrnstein and Charles Murray argued that class divisions in society are caused by differences in intelligence. That is, people with better jobs and incomes have them primarily because they are smarter than those who have poorer jobs and lower incomes. Herrnstein and Murray supported their assertion by pointing to research evidence that African Americans—who, as a group, have lower economic status than White Americans—are less intelligent than Whites.

The Bell Curve also proclaimed Asian Americans as superior to both Black and White Americans. Asian Americans' high-status jobs and greater income are, according to Herrnstein and Murray, due to their superior intelligence. This assertion was supported by the fact that, as a group, Asian Americans have greater economic status than do either White or African American ethnic groups. The ideas presented in *The Bell Curve* have been challenged and much of the research cited in the book discredited (Kincheloe, Steinberg, & Gresson, 1996). Regardless, *The Bell Curve* brought together current cultural stereotypes about African and Asian Americans as they relate to intelligence and achievement. The book also provided many White individuals with a tidy explanation for the economic disadvantages faced by Black Americans and the advantages enjoyed by Asian Americans at work and school.

Popular perceptions of African Americans and Asian Americans, in other words, center around beliefs about their intelligence and suitability for achievement in school and career domains. Because these beliefs are negative for African Americans and positive for Asian Americans, they support a kind of intellectual/achievement diversity that is color-coded: Blacks on the bottom, Whites in the

81

Stereotypic beliefs about the intellectual abilities of African Americans are negative, whereas beliefs about Asian American students' abilities are positive. However, both stereotypes can interfere with these individuals' respective school accomplishments.

middle, and Asians on top. This chapter confronts this particular kind of "color-coded" diversity by reviewing evidence for the prominence of beliefs about intelligence and achievement in our (generally White persons') stereotypes of Black and Asian individuals and by looking at whether these stereotypic beliefs have any factual basis. We also consider the questions of how racial and ethnic differences in intelligence and achievement are constructed and what consequences they have for African American and Asian American people.

Before we consider these questions, we must give some brief attention to the meanings of the terms *race* and *ethnicity*. For most of us, the term **race** brings to mind a category of people who share the same skin color and associated physical qualities. To refer to a racial minority group in the United States is usually to refer to some "non-White" group of people. Historically, our thinking about people in terms of racial categories has been imbued with associations of color: African Americans with the color black, Hispanic Americans with brown, and Asian Americans with yellow. In psychology, however, few people can agree on what race means or what constitutes a racial group (Jones, 1991). One problem with using race to group people is that there is more variability within so-called racial groups than there is between them (Zuckerman, 1990). For example, Brazilians, by virtue of their nationality, would probably be included in the racial group Hispanic or Latino. However, the lightest-skinned Brazilians are indistinguishable from many "Whites" and the darkest-skinned indistinguishable from "Blacks." If racial groupings are arbitrary and meaningless, why do they persist? According to Jean Phinney (1996), the concept of race endures because, in general, we observe that people of color tend to be treated differently than "White" people. Thus race is a handy pseudoexplanation for a variety of social outcomes and experiences.

Ethnicity concerns a cluster of (nonphysical) distinctives such as one's national or cultural origin, language, and perhaps religion (Phinney, 1996). In the United States, an ethnic minority group is typically a group of people whose culture of origin is not Western European. Ethnic group labels are more specific, and therefore more accurate, social constructs than old-style racial groupings. For example, although they would share the racial label "Black," African Americans and Caribbean Americans are ethnic groups with unique cultures, languages, religious traditions, and physical qualities. Although ethnic groupings are still somewhat arbitrary, ethnicity is preferable to race as a construct that structures our thinking about socially different people because it captures more of the dimensions on which we differ. With that introduction, let's turn to the focus of this chapter: understanding ethnic differences in intelligence and achievement.

STEREOTYPES OF AFRICAN AMERICAN INDIVIDUALS

What Do Whites Believe About Blacks?

Considerable research shows that White individuals negatively stereotype Blacks (Plous & Williams, 1995). In one study of racial stereotyping, White participants' racial stereotypes were primed by displaying "WHITE" or "BLACK" on a computer screen for about two tenths of a second—in other words, too fast to be consciously recognized. Nevertheless, the short exposure to the prime word affected how well participants recognized trait words that followed the prime. The Black prime facilitated participants' recognition of negative (for example, "lazy") compared with positive (e.g., "musical") Black stereotypical words, whereas the White prime facilitated recognition of positive (e.g., "ambitious") compared with negative (for example, "selfish") White stereotypical words (Wittenbrink, Judd, & Park, 1997). This research shows that Whites' negative stereotype of Blacks is well learned and operates beneath conscious awareness. The participants in the study did not realize they were making stereotypical racial judgments; nevertheless, the social category "Black" was more strongly associated with negative and "White" with positive attributes in participants' memories.

In another study, White university students were asked to identify the traits that make up the stereotype of Blacks. The most agreed-upon traits were: athletic, rhythmic, low in intelligence, lazy, poor, loud, criminal, and hostile (Devine & Elliot, 1995). Thus people also *consciously* associate negative traits with African Americans. But overt, public stereotyping of Blacks is less tolerated now than ever before. Psychologists who study **racism**—negative attitudes and behavior toward other-race individuals—agree that stereotyping of African Americans has become more subtle and justifiable compared with the pre-civil rights era (Dovidio & Gaertner, 1991). In keeping with the current social and political climate, people have developed ways to mask or rationalize their negative beliefs about Blacks, exhibiting what is called "modern" racism. One way is to deny personal belief in the negative cultural stereotype about Blacks. Participants in the study mentioned here did this: They were knowledgeable of the negative cultural stereotype but reported having positive personal beliefs about Blacks (Devine & Elliot, 1995).

How pervasive is the negative stereotype of African American individuals? Recall from Chapter 2 that when our social categories become too broad and inclusive, they are less accurate sources of social information. Our response is to divide the category into relatively more accurate subtypes. There is evidence that White people subtype Blacks and that the traits associated with these subtypes differ. White college students described African Americans overall in the following terms: hostile, poor, dirty, athletic, negative personality, musical, unintelligent, and lazy (Devine & Baker, 1991). However, the participants' stereotypes of Black Americans depended on which subtype they were associated with. Characteristics associated with the "streetwise," "ghetto," and "welfare" images of Black individuals were very negative and included having a negative personality and being unintelligent and lazy. However, Black "athlete" and "businessman" subgroups were thought of in much more positive terms, including having a positive personality, being ambitious, and, in the case of "Black businessman," being intelligent.

In summary, Whites' stereotypes of African American people are generally negative and, with the exception of subtypes such as athlete and businesspeople, are dominated by beliefs of laziness and low intelligence. Furthermore, stereotypical beliefs about Blacks' motivation and ability are seen by many individuals as an inherent, stable deficiency, echoing the basic message of *The Bell Curve*. This "deficiency" in ability and motivation serves as a handy explanation for the inequities experienced by Black persons in society and as a basis for discrimination toward Blacks in academic and employment settings. Is there any basis for these stereotypical beliefs?

Stereotypic Beliefs About African Americans' Intellectual Ability: Fact or Fiction?

Much evidence indicates that Black students receive lower grades in school and score lower on standardized tests of achievement than do White students. A national study of student achievement reported that African American students' standardized science test scores were 49 points poorer (on a 500-point scale) than White students' scores (National Assessment of Educational Progress, 1996). Math test scores showed a similar difference: Black students scored 27 points below White students (again, on a 500-point test scale). When reading proficiency was measured at the 4th, 8th, and 12th grades, Black and Hispanic students read below and White students above the expected grade reading level. Similar findings emerged on standardized tests of U.S. history: Significantly higher percentages of White students reached the grade-appropriate achievement levels compared with Black and Hispanic students.

Why do these achievement differences exist? Are they related simply to ethnic group differences in intelligence? Researchers reviewed the great number of studies comparing Black and White people on measures of intelligence (Loehlin, Lindzey, & Spuhler, 1975). They concluded that ethnic differences did exist in many studies, with White people on the average scoring higher than Black people, but the differences were small in magnitude and assuredly not due to one factor. Thus the popular debate on whether the differences between Whites' and Blacks' intelligence is due to genetics (inherited ability) or environment (home and school experiences) is oversimplistic. In fact, the debate itself seems to be fueled by people who have a preference for a simplistic solution (either the "environment" or "genetics" explanation), thus avoiding the complexities of the issue. More recent research reflects the same conclusions: Small average differences exist between White and Black Americans on measures of ability, but how much if any of that difference is due to inherited intelligence is undetermined (Demo & Parker, 1987; Simmons, Brown, Bush, & Blyth, 1978).

It is a common misjudgment, even among scientists, to interpret a statistically significant difference (that is, one that is not likely to be due to chance) between groups of people as meaningful or important or as if the difference applies to all the individuals in the groups equally. This misjudgment might lead us to believe that, because African American and White *groups* of people differ on measures of intelligence and achievement, all of the "White" group members are smarter than all of the "Black" group members. We must appreciate, however, that the differences observed *between* groups of Black and White individuals are dwarfed by the differences *within* those groups. The difference in intelligence between the lowest- and highest-scoring White students, for example, is much greater than the difference between the average White and Black American student. Obviously, there are other forces more potent than color or ethnic group that cause people to differ on tests of academic ability and achievement. What are they?

FAMILY, HOME, AND SCHOOL ENVIRONMENT   A 1973 national survey established that students' success in school was predicted by four factors: the levels of education of both mother and father, parents' occupational status, and having an intact (presumably, a two-parent) family. In the intervening 25 years, all of those predictors of school success have declined in the Black population, whereas only the prevalence of intact families has declined for White individuals (Kuo & Hauser, 1995). Thus African American students must overcome more obstacles to school achievement in the home than White students.

Additionally, Black students' lower achievement levels in school may be related to their in-home preparation for kindergarten. We will see in Chapter 7 that, compared with White children, ethnic minority (African American and Hispanic) children watch significantly more television. This tends to hinder, more than help, preschool language and thinking skills. Children who begin their education with some disadvantages will likely fall further behind throughout the schooling process. However, preschool "readiness" programs stimulate Black children's school achievement. Studies have demonstrated that preschool experiences that stress cognitive skills development and parental involvement among ethnic minority children are responsible for higher school achievement as many as 10 years later (Campbell & Ramey, 1995; Reynolds, Maurogenes, Bezruczko, & Hagemann, 1996).

These studies suggest that preschool interventions compensate for differences in the preschool home environment of Black and White children and give African American children a fairer start to their schooling. The fact that school achievement can be stimulated and improved suggests that preschool environmental factors are just as important as inherited intelligence in explaining the achievement differences between Black and White Americans.

When children go to school, we would like to think they are treated equally. Sadly, this is not true; research suggests that ethnic minority children meet another set of inequalities when they enter school. Data from the 1996 National Assessment of Educational Progress (NAEP) national surveys show that, compared with predominantly ethnic minority schools, schools with predominantly White students spend more per student on their education. This educational advantage remained when the economic differences between White and ethnic minority families were accounted for.

CULTURE BIAS AND STEREOTYPE VULNERABILITY IN SCHOOLING   As was pointed out in Chapter 3, Black children face a pervasive culture bias in schools in which African American history and culture are devalued and separated from the mainstream of school curricula. As a result, Black students must study and learn material (such as history and literature) that is disconnected from, and perhaps hostile toward, African American culture and values. Dealing with culture bias, then, may disadvantage Black students in school compared with White students. White cultural definitions of "school achievement" also prevail in the schools (Oyserman, Gant, & Ager, 1995). That is, school achievement is best predicted by individualistic values such as personal responsibility and a competitive attitude toward other students, and these reflect traditional White values. Blacks' school achievement, however, is best predicted by collective values such as the need for students to cooperate with each other in the learning process. Thus, compared with White students, African American students must frame academic achievement in unfamiliar ways, and, as a result, they are disadvantaged at school.

As was also discussed in Chapter 3, African American students are vulnerable to the stereotypic beliefs about their school ability and motivation held by teachers and students. As Claude Steele and his colleagues (1992, 1995, 1997) have demonstrated, Black students feel anxious in school settings because they sense that teachers do not expect them to apply themselves to and excel at their studies. This vulnerability leads to disidentification, a process of lowering the importance of school achievement to one's identity and self-esteem, and subsequently their school performance drops.

In summary, negative beliefs about intelligence and motivation dominate White Americans' stereotype of Blacks. Although there is evidence of actual differences between Black and White individuals on measures of intelligence and achievement, this difference is small and likely caused by the many differences in Blacks' and Whites' life experiences at home and in school. Perhaps chief among these life experiences is the fact that the American educational system reflects White culture, values, and beliefs and, therefore, is a more friendly environment for White than for Black students' achievement.

STEREOTYPES OF ASIAN AMERICAN INDIVIDUALS

What Do Whites Believe About Asian Americans?

In contrast to cultural stereotypes of African Americans, public perceptions of Asian Americans are quite positive. Asian Americans have been termed the "model minority" and are associated with such characteristics as intelligence and industriousness, being quiet and family-oriented, and having high ability in math and science (Osajima, 1988; Yee, 1992). This positive stereotype, however, is a recent development. Prior to the 1970s, White Americans' stereotype of Asian Americans incorporated such traits as "cunning," "sly," and "inscrutable" (Suzuki, 1989). However, even the positive "model minority" status may be a kind of award bestowed on Asian Americans because they embody the traditionally White values of hard work, responsibility, and family loyalty. In other words, Asian Americans are probably appreciated more for their expression of attributes valued by White Americans than for who they are as Asian Americans. As was the case with African Americans, beliefs about intelligence occupy a prominent place in the White stereotype of Asian Americans (Lee, 1996).

Stereotypic Beliefs About Asian Americans' Intellectual Ability: Fact or Fiction?

Much research has compared Asian American and White children and adults on measures of intelligence (Flynn, 1991; Yee, 1992). This research combines large national surveys and smaller studies and, overall, concludes that Asian Americans' average intelligence scores are no greater, and in some studies are lower, than the average intelligence scores of White individuals. However, this research also points out that Asian Americans' intelligence scores are more variable than those of White individuals. That is, the lowest and highest scores of Asian Americans on measures of intelligence are lower and higher, respectively, than the lowest and highest scores of White individuals. This may help us understand why Asian Americans outnumber members of other social groups in certain scientific fields such as computer science and physics; the most intelligent Asian Americans are brighter or more accomplished than the most intelligent White Americans. However, the typical members of each ethnic group do not differ in intelligence.

The Achievement Gap

Although Asian Americans possess no greater native intelligence than Whites, they achieve more in educational domains, and this is reflected in Asian Americans' higher achievement test scores. This achievement gap is observed in both verbal and quantitative areas but is greatest in quantitative. Asians also score higher on college entrance examinations and enter college with better grades than Whites (Chen & Stevenson, 1995; Flynn, 1991). Furthermore, national statistics indicate that about 40% of all Asian American adults have earned a college degree compared with 22% of White adults (U.S. Bureau of the Census, 1995). Two explanations have been offered for this tendency for Asian Americans to accomplish more in academic domains than White Americans do.

FAMILY SUPPORT FOR EDUCATION   One explanation for the achievement gap between Whites and Asian Americans is that Asian American families are more supportive than White families of their children's education and participate more in their schooling (Caplan, Choy, & Whitmore, 1992). This support can take many forms, from setting aside and monitoring study time to encouraging and assisting children in their learning. Indeed, high-achieving Asian American students tend to have parents who hold high standards for academic achievement. Perhaps it is no surprise that, compared with White students, Asian American students are more motivated toward school achievement and have more positive expectations for their education (Chen & Stevenson, 1995; Huang & Waxman, 1995).

OVERCOMING CULTURAL OBSTACLES TO ACHIEVEMENT   Asian Americans are not exempt from the cultural bias inherent in American schools and universities mentioned earlier. However, according to some scholars, their greater academic achievements may be due in part to the conviction that if they *do* overcome those obstacles, success and social mobility will result (Lee, 1996). In this view, Asian Americans' school accomplishments are the result of a persistent intention to succeed in spite of the fact that American schools exclude, marginalize, or devalue Asian culture and history.

Stereotype Vulnerability Among Asian Americans?

Whites stereotype Asian Americans as intelligent and high-achieving, particularly in scientific domains. Many Asian American students report, however, that this stereotype is more a burden than a benefit (Tan, 1994). Whereas African American students feel vulnerable about confirming others' stereotype of them, Asian American students deal with the fear that they will *disconfirm* others' beliefs about their ability. In other words, when people assume you are bright and full of potential, you don't want to burst their bubble. Moreover, like anyone subject to pervasive social expectations, Asian American students who are confronted with stereotypical beliefs about their "natural talent" in math and science will tend to internalize those assumptions. Thus a failing (or otherwise negative) grade at school becomes doubly threatening for Asian Americans compared with White students. First, a failing grade indicates a deficiency in one's effort or ability that most students, at one time or another, must face. In addition to the disappoint-

Asian American students are more successful in school in part because Asian American families participate more in and are more supportive of their children's education.

ment of not living up to the teacher's or professor's standards, school failures threaten Asian American students in another way. To underperform in school is to fail to live up to the expectations of one's peers, family, or community.

Researchers have found that parents of high-achieving Asian American students enforce disciplined study habits and allow fewer social distractions (in the form of activities with friends and jobs) to interfere with their schooling (Chen & Stevenson, 1995). However, in America "doing things with friends" is regarded as normal adolescent behavior and necessary for proper social development. Another study found that, compared with White students, Asian American ninth-graders achieved more in school but also described themselves as more isolated, depressed, and anxious. Asian American students were also less likely to enter into extracurricular activities and tended to blame themselves for their loneliness (Lorenzo, Pakiz, Reinherz, & Frost, 1995). These studies suggest that Asian Americans' superior school accomplishments come at the expense of personal well-being.

Other researchers took a sample of Asian American undergraduate students and matched them with non-Asian (mostly White) students with the same gender, SAT scores, level of parental education, and type of high school attended. In other words, the two groups of students were equated on important environmental variables and precollege achievement. They followed these two groups of students through college and found some striking results. First, compared with the White American students, Asian American students had lower GPAs, were more often on academic probation, and took longer to graduate despite taking the same number of courses as their non-Asian counterparts. Asian students were also more likely to withdraw from school for medical reasons than their White counterparts. And finally, although Asian American students were more likely to be science majors, their grades were no better than those of non-Asian science majors (Toupin & Son, 1991).

Taken together, these findings suggest that the expectations surrounding Asian American academic achievement, especially in the sciences, is a double-edged sword. High expectations for success generally breed success—a luxury not enjoyed by Black American students. However, such expectations have a downside. Asian American students may work harder at each course and assignment they face to assure success, thereby having less time for recreation, sleep, and a normal social life. They may choose a major or career (in the sciences) for which they are ill suited and struggle mightily to succeed in it. Finally, the high expectations confronting Asian American students can come both from parents and from the surrounding White culture. Stacey Lee (1996) found that Asian students who were struggling in their high school classes were reluctant to seek help for two reasons: They did not want to be "caught" failing to live up to the stereotype and they did not want to bring the shame of their inadequacy upon their families.

Positive beliefs about intelligence and academic ability dominate White Americans' stereotype of Asian Americans. Studies show that Asian Americans have no greater inherited intelligence than Whites but that they do accomplish more in school. Family support and participation in Asian American individuals' education explains much of this achievement gap. However, widespread cultural stereotypes about Asian American intelligence contribute to stress surrounding school endeavors and a vulnerability among Asian American students in the fear that they will fail to live up to those expectations.

RACIAL AND ETHNIC CATEGORIES AND STEREOTYPES AS CONSTRUCTORS OF DIVERSITY

"They" Are All Alike

Social categorization based on color, race, or even ethnicity lumps together individuals with diverse nationality, cultural heritage, and language. The category "African American" combines people of African heritage who are American-born and acculturated, African-born Americans, and individuals of Caribbean heritage. When called "African Americans" or "Blacks," people from these diverse groups are assumed to be much more similar than they are. Here we see the outgroup homogeneity effect (see Chapter 2) in action. Whites' stereotype of "Blacks" is applied uniformly to all members of that category, distilling vast amounts of difference among them. Furthermore, Whites' attitudes toward Black Americans that have been informed by events in U.S. history are improperly generalized to *all* Black individuals, regardless of their national and cultural background.

A similar distilling of diversity occurs through the use of the category "Asian Americans." This category combines many groups with distinct cultures and languages, such as Chinese, Japanese, Korean, and Vietnamese. By virtue of their sharing some distinctive physical characteristics, these diverse groups are assumed to be more alike than they are. We know that social categories that are too inclusive gain utility through subdivision. The subtyping process, however, does not reclaim the national and cultural diversity that is lost in the original categorization process. Rather, as discussed earlier, subtypes are derived from popular, and often stereotypical, portrayals and roles of group members. In summary, social categorizations based on race and ethnicity reduce the diversity of our social world.

"They" Are Different From "Us"

In addition to compressing within-race (or within-ethnic-group) differences, social categorizations based on race or ethnicity exaggerate between-ethnic-group differences. The physical qualities associated with ethnic groups—skin color, hair type, or the shape of facial features—are perceptually distinctive. People of different racial groups appear to be different, therefore we ascribe more difference to them than is truly there. Just to refer to a school or community as "racially diverse" reflects this bias. We would never refer to other dimensions of physical or genetic difference this way, as in "blood type diversity" or "eye color diversity." Why? Because unlike race, these dimensions are unknown or unnoticed. Further, because we tend to associate with people who are similar to us, White individuals typically have little contact with Asian and Black Americans. Lacking any personal experience with other-race people, we depend more heavily on stereotypic knowledge about them.

As was discussed earlier, stereotypes of Black and Asian Americans are inaccurate and misleading, especially where beliefs about intelligence and academic ability are concerned. Whites' stereotypes presume differences exist between them and Black and Asian American individuals, and these differences are attributed to unchanging dispositional qualities. In actuality, White and Asian Americans do not differ on measures of intelligence, and actual differences in achievement can be accounted for by the role of the Asian family and community in a child's education. White and Black Americans do differ on measures of intelligence and achievement, but, although some of that difference could be due to inherited intelligence, the size of the difference is small and is reduced by environmental interventions. In sum, stereotypes bolster the artificial difference imposed by racial categories.

The Political Context of Race Differences in Intelligence

It is important to acknowledge and understand the scientific evidence for ethnic group differences of any kind and the explanations for why those differences exist, despite the political sensitivity surrounding those issues. This sensitivity is greatest when confronting the explanations for ethnic group differences in intelligence and achievement. In our democratic society, in which all citizens are equal under the law and entitled to equal opportunity and protection, there is a strong bias in favor of "environmental" explanations. To conclude that intelligence is largely inherited and different for members of specific ethnic groups would make it difficult to maintain a democracy. It would mean that some people—identifiable by their ethnic-group status—were inherently less valuable or worthwhile than others, and, as a result, they would have much different life opportunities.

Stereotypes of Hispanic individuals may seem to have been overlooked in this chapter. However, few studies have examined Hispanic stereotypes exclusively, perhaps because many of the beliefs Whites hold about African Americans also apply to Hispanic people. Also, I have not mentioned stereotypes of White individuals in this chapter. This does not reflect the attitude that Whites are somehow exempt from being objects of research. Rather, researchers (who hail from many ethnic groups) tend to focus on stereotypes of minority groups because they believe that understanding will lead to social and political benefits for disadvantaged social groups.

KEY TERMS

race
ethnicity
racism

FOR THOUGHT AND DISCUSSION

1. How are racial stereotypes a self-fulfilling prophecy?

2. Explain how Black American and Asian American students experience racial stereotypes differently.

3. Research shows that the preschool home environment is vitally important to success in school. In your opinion, what are important components of that environment?

4. African American and Asian American students both face obstacles to school achievement. What are some of these obstacles? What can be done to make schools more reflective of and responsible for the melting-pot nature of our society?

5. Overcoming obstacles to achievement through *persistence* (common for Asian American students) is more valued than overcoming them through *disidentification* (common for African American students). Form an argument that disidentification is a more reasonable, adaptive response when one faces hindrances to school achievement.

REFERENCES

Campbell, F., & Ramey, C. (1995). Cognitive and school outcomes for high-risk African-American students at middle adolescence: Positive effects of early intervention. *American Educational Research Journal, 32,* 743–772.

Caplan, N., Choy, M., & Whitmore, J. (1992, February). Indochinese refugee families and academic achievement. *Scientific American,* pp. 36–42.

Chen, C., & Stevenson, H. (1995). Motivation and mathematics achievement: A comparative study of Asian-American, Caucasian-American, and East Asian high school students. *Child Development, 66,* 1215–1234.

Demo, D., & Parker, K. (1987). Academic achievement and self-esteem among Black and White college students. *Journal of Social Psychology, 4,* 345–355.

Devine, P., & Baker, S. (1991). Measurement of racial stereotype subtyping. *Personality and Social Psychology Bulletin, 17,* 44–50.

Devine, P. G., & Elliot, A. J. (1995). Are racial stereotypes *really* fading? The Princeton trilogy revisited. *Personality and Social Psychology Bulletin, 21,* 1139–1150.

Dovidio, J., & Gaertner, S. (1991). Changes in the expression of racial prejudice. In H. Knopke, J. Norrell, & R. Rogers (Eds.), *Opening doors: An appraisal of race relations in contemporary America* (pp. 119–148). Tuscaloosa: University of Alabama Press.

Flynn, J. (1991). *Asian Americans: Achievement beyond IQ.* Hillsdale, NJ: Erlbaum.

Herrnstein, R., & Murray, C. (1994). *The bell curve: Intelligence and class structure in American life.* New York: Free Press.

Huang, S., & Waxman, H. (1995). Motivation and learning-environment differences between Asian-American and White middle school students in mathematics. *Journal of Research and Development in Education, 28,* 208–219.

Jones, J. (1991). Psychological models of race: What have they been and what should they be? In J. Goodchilds (Ed.), *Psychological perspectives on human diversity in America* (pp. 3–46). Washington, DC: American Psychological Association.

Kincheloe, J., Steinberg, S., & Gresson, A. (Eds.). (1996). *Measured lies:* The Bell Curve *examined.* New York: St. Martin's Press.

Kuo, H., & Hauser, R. (1995). Trends in family effects on the education of Black and White brothers. *Sociology of Education, 68,* 136–160.

Lee, S. (1996). *Unraveling the "model minority" stereotype: Listening to Asian American youth.* New York: Teachers College Press.

Loehlin, J., Lindzey, G., & Spuhler, J. (1975). *Race differences in intelligence.* San Francisco: Freeman.

Lorenzo, M., Pakiz, B., Reinherz, H., & Frost, A. (1995). Emotional and behavioral problems of Asian American adolescents: A comparative study. *Child and Adolescent Social Work Journal, 12,* 197–212.

National Assessment of Educational Progress (1996). *The nation's report card* [On-line]. Available: www.nces.ed.gov/nationsreportcard/site/home.asp.

Osajima, K. (1988). Asian Americans as the model minority: An analysis of the popular press image of the 1960s and 1980s. In G. Okihiro, S. Hune, A. Hansen, & J. Liu (Eds.), *Reflections on shattered windows.* Pullman: Washington State University Press.

Oyserman, D., Gant, L., & Ager, J. (1995). A socially contextualized model of African American identity: Possible selves and school persistence. *Journal of Personality and Social Psychology, 69,* 1216–1232.

Phinney, J. (1996). When we talk about American ethnic groups, what do we mean? *American Psychologist, 51,* 918–927.

Plous, S., & Williams, T. (1995). Racial stereotypes from the days of American slavery: A continuing legacy. *Journal of Applied Social Psychology, 25,* 795–817.

Reynolds, A., Maurogenes, N., Bezruczko, N., & Hagemann, M. (1996). Cognitive and family-support mediators of preschool effectiveness: A confirmatory analysis. *Child Development, 67,* 1119–1140.

Simmons, R., Brown, L., Bush, D., & Blyth, D. (1978). Self-esteem and achievement of Black and White adolescents. *Social Problems, 26,* 86–96.

Steele, C. (1992, April). Race and the schooling of Black Americans. *Atlantic Monthly,* 68–80.

Steele, C. (1997). A threat in the air: How stereotypes shape intellectual identity and performance. *American Psychologist, 52,* 613–629.

Steele, C., & Aronson, J. (1995). Stereotype threat and the intellectual test performance of African Americans. *Journal of Personality and Social Psychology, 69,* 797–811.

Suzuki, B. (1989, November–December). Asian Americans as the "model minority": Outdoing Whites? or media hype? *Change,* 13–19.

Tan, D. (1994). Uniqueness of the Asian-American experience in higher education. *College Student Journal, 28*, 412–421.

Toupin, E., & Son, L. (1991). Preliminary findings on Asian Americans: "The model minority" in a small private East Coast college. *Journal of Cross-Cultural Psychology, 22*, 403–417.

U.S. Bureau of the Census. (1995). *Statistical abstract of the United States* (115th ed.). Washington, DC: Author.

Wittenbrink, B., Judd, C., & Park, B. (1997). Evidence for racial prejudice at the implicit level and its relationship with questionnaire measures. *Journal of Personality and Social Psychology, 72*, 262–274.

Yee, A. (1992). Asians as stereotypes and students: Misperceptions that persist. *Educational Psychology Review, 4*, 95–132.

Zuckerman, M. (1990). Some dubious premises in research and theory on racial differences. *American Psychologist, 45*, 1297–1303.

Diversity on TV

Reflecting or Constructing Our Social World?

CHAPTER OBJECTIVE

To confront the debate about whether television is a relatively passive reflector or an architect of the social difference around us.

We watch a lot of TV. In a typical household the television is on more than 7 hours per day (Nielsen, 1998). Children watch about 4 hours per day, but minority kids and children whose parents have no college education watch much more TV, as much as 6 hours each day (Tangney & Feshbach, 1988). This means that many children spend as much or more time watching television as they do in school or in activities with a parent. In short, TV is an imposing socializing agent, rivaling the school and family as an instiller of social attitudes and values. But what does TV teach us about our world and the people around us? Are the characters and programs on television a reflection of the real world, as many television producers argue? Or could it be that television constructs an image of the world that is different from what you and I experience?

To learn whether television programming reflects or constructs the diversity of our social world, we must consider two sets of questions concerning social representations and portrayals, respectively, on television. With regard to **social representations**, who are the people we see in the TV world? Is the social makeup of the TV world like the real world, and, if not, how does it differ? With regard to **social portrayals**, how are members of social groups portrayed on TV? Are they represented in stereotypical terms and shown in stereotypical roles? In short, what do we learn about the members of social groups from their television portrayals? In the following pages, research on the social representations and portrayals of people from several minority or underrepresented social groups is reviewed and discussed.

GENDER REPRESENTATIONS AND PORTRAYALS

TV Is a Man's World

In the real world, we know that there are about equal numbers of men and women. On TV, however, men outnumber women by a big margin. In a monumental survey of television programming over a 20-year period (1973–1993), George Gerbner (1997) found that for every woman who appears on the prime-time TV screen there are 2.5 men, and this disproportionate representation has remained stable for the past 20 years (Kubey, Shifflet, Weerakkody, & Ukeiley, 1995; Lemon, 1977). This stable finding is moderated by two factors: type of programming and the character's age. In Saturday morning programs, in which three male characters appear for every one female character, women are more underrepresented than in prime time. The male domination of the television world increases with the age of the characters. In the adult (ages 41–65) and older adult (age 65+) age groups, men outnumber women by four to one and six to one, respectively. Thus, although women have long been a minority group in terms of resources and power, their TV representation makes them a numerical minority, too. Moreover, women become much less visible (and men much more visible) as the TV population ages, a strange representation considering that in real life women live longer than men.

Women also suffer from underrepresentation in televised sports. Men's events are televised much more often than are women's events. There *are* many more men's than women's professional leagues and teams, suggesting that television just reflects the real (and obviously gender-disparate) state of American professional sports. However, when this disparity is controlled, women are still underrepresented on television. As a case study take professional golf. Throughout the summer months, both the men's and the women's professional golf tours (PGA and LPGA, respectively) hold weekly tournaments. By my count, the PGA has twice the television coverage of the LPGA, both in tournaments televised and in hours of coverage. Also, television commentary is not very friendly to women's sports endeavors, even when they are televised. Researchers have found that sports commentators subtly trivialize or explain away women's sports performances and use more sexually provocative camera angles for women than for men (Dyer, 1987; Messner, Duncan, & Jensen, 1993). Let us consider at length the ways television portrays women.

TV Portrayals of Women: Appealing, Romantic, and Dependent

Some of the huge discrepancy in representing men and women on TV is due to the greater cultural importance attached to youth and beauty for women than for men. As the saying goes: "Women get old, men become more distinguished." Hair color on TV reflects this gender bias. One study found that 14% of the prime-time male characters had gray hair compared with only 2% of the female characters,

Women's professional sports receive far less television coverage than men's. Here, golf pro Se Ri Pak holds up the U.S. Women's Open trophy she won in July 1998.

whereas 36% of the females were blonde compared with 7% of the men (Davis, 1990). Although older characters (age 45 and older) receive much less exposure in general, male characters still outnumber women by two to one. In other words, men are observed to age on TV to a much greater extent than women are. Such biased representation of women is not limited to television; it is also evident in motion pictures (Bazzini, McIntosh, Smith, & Cook, 1997).

The fact that women, relative to men, are not allowed to age on TV is closely related to the kinds of stories that can and cannot be told with older characters. According to Gerbner's research, women appear on the screen primarily to portray romantic, appealing figures, and there is apparently a short shelf life for them to be viably romantic (Gerbner, 1997). That is, for younger TV characters (under 40 years of age), 67% of women, compared with 33% of men, are involved in romance. For example, on *NYPD Blue*—one of the most-watched television dramas—there are four detectives (two men and two women) whose on-screen age appears to be less than 40 years. Story lines subtly but consistently portray the female detectives as objects of sexual attraction and develop romantic angles in the context of their professional police work. Moreover, the female detectives work together more than they work with male detectives and investigate less violent crimes, such as those involving child or spouse abuse. In the midlife years (roughly ages 40–60), however, this gender difference is reversed. About 20% of male midlife-aged characters but only 1% of female characters of that age are involved in romance (Gerbner, 1997).

Not surprisingly, women are depicted as more romantically "available" than men. Half of the women characters in prime-time television are single compared with less than 30% of the men. Indeed, most of the men shown in prime-time television are not identified as *either* single or married—as if that status were somehow irrelevant for men—whereas most women are clearly categorized by marital status. Additionally, provocative clothing is much more prevalent on female than on male characters (Davis, 1990). Thus, with respect to the demographic characteristics of men and women, TV makes distinctions that do not exist in real life. Worse, television portrayals objectify women, showing them as attractive, desirable, and available to men but not allowing them to age naturally on screen. Men, on the other hand, overpopulate the TV world, are allowed to get older in appearance, and have the dubious benefit of not being categorized based on their marital status.

In addition, women tend to be portrayed as emotional, dependent, less intelligent than, and subordinate to men. Women, far more often than men, are portrayed as victims of abuse or violence on television. In one survey of television programming, men gave advice or orders to women in 70% of their interactions (Busby, 1975; Lemon, 1977). This negative stereotype is reinforced by the low visibility of women characters on action-adventure programs (for example, *The Sentinel* or *The Pretender*), in which physical prowess, strategic planning, and derring-do are at a premium; 7 out of 10 actors on those shows are men (Davis, 1990). When women *do* play action-adventure heroines, such as in the shows *Wonder Woman* and *Xena: Warrior Princess,* they play overtly sexual figures who still often take their lead from a male superordinate.

The stereotypical differences between men and women on TV are also evidenced in the way they interact on the screen. One study of prime-time programs rated the "distancing" behavior in on-screen interactions. Distancing was defined as any action in which one actor maintained separation or moved away from his or her TV interaction partner and was thought to indicate one's control in social interactions. Male characters exhibited more distancing behavior than female characters, but only when interacting with a female (Lott, 1989). This study portrays men on TV as having more "say" in how interactions proceed, but this authority is only expressed when they interact with women.

Stereotypical portrayals of male–female interactions occur in films too. Mark Hedley analyzed scenes involving conflict between male and female characters (for example, an unwanted sexual advance) in 100 popular films (Hedley, 1994). He rated the powerlessness of the female characters as well as the outcome of the conflict. The results showed that female characters who had low amounts of power were more successful at deflecting the conflict (such as brushing off the advance) than were women rated high in power. This kind of portrayal of women is illustrated in the highly successful movie *Pretty Woman*. In that film, the economically disadvantaged, sometime-call-girl character played by Julia Roberts won love and riches from Richard Gere's character precisely because she was, or

In general, women on TV portray attractive, romantically available figures who are subordinate to men. Lucy Lawless's *Xena*—an action-adventure heroine with great physical prowess—helps counter stereotypic portrayals of women.

was perceived by him to be, weak, powerless, vulnerable, and naive. However, the story also required the woman to be uncommonly beautiful for this love to blossom. Many other films, such as the celebrated *As Good As It Gets* featuring Jack Nicholson and Helen Hunt, dramatize variations of the "high-status but empty man falls in love with low-status but compelling woman" theme. Collectively, the social message reflected in these scenes is one in which dependent and relatively powerless women are most "successful" in their interactions with men.

In summary, TV is a male-dominated world. Men are more visible and numerous on the small screen than are women. Women's TV "lives" are constrained by their ability to be youthful, attractive, romantic, and dependent figures. In other words, women on television portray stereotypical traits and roles to a much greater extent than do men. Television, therefore, presents a biased picture of the gender diversity that we observe around us.

AGE REPRESENTATIONS AND PORTRAYALS

The social difference in our world includes people of many ages and appropriate life stages. The world of television is not so diverse. Jake Harwood (1995) counted the older (defined as age 60+) main and supporting characters on 40 of the most-watched TV programs in 1995. Out of a total of 490 characters, only 29 were older adults. So, although 17% of the U.S. population is 60 years old or older, only 6% of the TV world is that age. His research also found that there are no lead and very few supporting characters who are older in the most popular shows watched by children and young adults. These figures show that older adults are underrepresented on TV, especially on programs aimed at younger viewers.

Who are those older characters and what attributes do they have? As examples, take *Frazier* and *The Simpsons,* two of the most popular current shows that have older adults in supporting roles. On *Frazier,* Marty, who is the on-screen father of the 40-something brothers Frazier and Niles, is a disabled, retired, grumpy figure who is portrayed as out of touch with and judgmental of his sons' lives. In story lines, Marty is often seen as a meddlesome, embarrassing character. On *The Simpsons,* Abe Simpson is the nursing-home-bound father of Homer. He is typically portrayed as a doddering, senile, and dependent individual who is a trivial and often disposable figure in his son's life. These are not kind portrayals, but they are typical for older TV characters.

Research has shown that older characters tend to be portrayed stereotypically—as dependent, lonely, disagreeable people who have various physical and mental limitations (Bishop & Krause, 1984; Gerbner, Gross, Signorielli, & Morgan, 1980). Moreover, older female characters are less visible on TV and are portrayed more negatively than older male characters (Dail, 1988). However, not all types of programming have such an age bias. Older adults are more visible and positively portrayed on daytime serials than in prime-time shows, although, even on soap operas, older women are still depicted in more negative terms than older men (Cassata, Anderson, & Skill, 1980). Older characters are more than twice as likely to be shown with some disability—such as an illness, injury, or significant maladjustment—than are younger characters. And, echoing the gender discrimination on TV that was previously mentioned, older women are much more likely to be portrayed as "disabled" than are older men (Gerbner, 1997).

Children are also underrepresented on TV, a surprising thought given the spate of Saturday morning "children's programming." These shows, however, typically feature animal (e.g., Barney), cartoon, or adult characters. Thus programming designed for children portrays an odd cast of characters that largely excludes real children. Although they constitute about 19% of the U.S. population, children (ages 0–10) make up only 6% of the TV cast of characters. Adolescents are similarly underrepresented on TV, making up 10% of the real world population but just 5% of the TV population (Gerbner, 1997).

In summary, the television world is vastly less age-diverse than the world we live in. Senior citizens and youth are underrepresented on TV and, when they appear, have less important roles. Older adults, particularly older women characters, are portrayed in negative and stereotypical terms. These representations send an implicit message, especially to heavy TV viewers, that the "important" people in our world are men and women in the prime of life.

Programs such as *For Your Love* present positive, stereotype-inconsistent images of African Americans, but, unfortunately, these programs are not very popular among White viewers.

REPRESENTATIONS AND PORTRAYALS OF PEOPLE OF COLOR

TV Is a Racially Segregated World

People of color, including African American, Latin American, Asian American, and other ethnic minority groups, make up one third of the U.S. population (U.S. Bureau of the Census, 1995). How are people of color represented on TV? An early review of the research on Black portrayals on television found that Black characters were severely underrepresented in the TV world of the 1960s and 1970s (Poindexter & Stroman, 1981). During those years minorities (a category that combined Blacks, Asians, and Native Americans) made up only 5% of all the characters on TV. Furthermore, Black characters had insignificant, low status, and low achievement roles. Blacks were also disproportionately cast as service workers (such as maid or busboy) and entertainers. In the past 20 years, however, the visibility of Black characters in prime-time programs has improved (Weigel, Kim, &

Frost, 1995). In 1978 White characters were on the screen 96% of the total show time, whereas Black characters appeared just 8% of the time. By 1990 Whites had similar visibility (93% of total show time), but Black characters were much more visible, appearing on the screen 17% of the time. In other words, Black characters now capture a proportion of TV screen time that is at least comparable to their proportion in the U.S. population. Moreover, the number of shows with a Black lead character and supporting cast or that address issues relevant to Black viewers has increased dramatically in the 1990s (e.g., *Cosby, Martin;* Weigel et al., 1995).

Interestingly, recent research reveals that Asian American individuals may be *over*represented on TV. Researchers surveyed over 1,000 prime-time television commercials and found that, although Asian Americans make up just 4% of the U.S. population, they constitute 8% of the "population" of people in TV advertisements (Taylor & Stern, 1997). This overrepresentation is thought to be related to the positive cultural stereotype about Asian Americans—that they are believed to be "industrious" and "polite." Indeed, Asian Americans' roles in the surveyed commercials were consistent with our stereotypes about them. That is, they appeared much more often in business or work than in family or home settings. Let us consider at length the television portrayals of people of color.

TV Portrayals of People of Color

Despite their advances in TV visibility, as mentioned earlier, portrayals of Black and Hispanic characters continue to be negative. Research shows that Black and White characters rarely interact on TV (Weigel et al., 1995). When they do share the screen, the interactions are more likely to be emotionally strained and noncooperative than same-race interactions. Further, TV scenes in which Black and White characters interact are more likely to feature male–male or female–female than mixed-sex interactions, perhaps reflecting our anxiety and negative attitudes toward interracial romance.

One area of programming in which racial stereotypes are blatantly played out is on reality-based police shows such as *Cops* and *America's Most Wanted*. On these shows, White "actors" (some scenes are dramatized, others are taped live) are more likely to be police officers than criminal suspects, and Black and Hispanic characters are more likely to be criminal suspects than police. Police are portrayed as needing to employ aggressive and violent behaviors to subdue criminal suspects. When police treatment of suspects is compared across races, Black and Hispanic suspects face more aggressive treatment than do White suspects (Oliver, 1994). These shows contribute to perceptions of Black and Hispanic persons (usually men) as lawless, violent, dangerous, and generally unproductive citizens.

The fact that violence on TV is associated with Black men influences the way we think about Black individuals in real life. In one study Thomas Ford (1997) had participants watch comedy skits from a popular television show that featured either stereotypical (e.g., poor, uneducated, and prone to violence) or neutral portrayals of Black characters. Then participants read about an incident in which a student reportedly assaulted his roommate. The assumed race of the student was subtly manipulated by his name; he was identified as either Todd or Tyrone (the assumed "White" and "Black" names, respectively). The guilt ratings of the alleged White offender were not affected by the type of programming viewed, but the ratings of the Black offender were. Participants were much more likely to judge "Tyrone" as guilty of the assault after watching stereotypical than neutral TV portrayals of Black characters. Identical results were found in a study in which participants were exposed to violent and nonviolent news stories and later made judgments about an alleged vandal who was either Black or White (Johnson, Adams, Hall, & Ashburn, 1997). In that study participants who read the violent rather than the nonviolent news story attributed a more violent personality and thus more responsibility for the vandalism to the Black actor than to the White actor. Finally, similar effects occur after participants watch music videos in which Black women are portrayed in stereotypical terms (Gan, Zillmann, & Mitrook, 1997). These studies show that portrayals of Black individuals (whether actors or real people) in stereotypical terms affects our real-life feelings and judgments about African American people. In sum, TV portrayals of Blacks can lead us to perceive the racial diversity of our real world in more TV-consistent terms.

Taken together, the findings reviewed here suggest that television has not had the positive influence on racial attitudes and perceptions that many (perhaps too idealistically) thought that it would. Although many Black television characters are visible and popular and portray positive traits and images, our racial stereotypes are as negative today as they were 30 years ago when Black individuals had no presence on TV. Why is this? Two explanations may be offered. First, although Blacks are more visible than ever on TV, with many Black characters having their own shows, evidence indicates that these shows are much more popular among Black than White viewers. For example, in 1991 the five most popular programs among Black viewers were *A Different World, The Fresh Prince of Bel Air, The Cosby Show, In Living Color,* and *Roc.* According to the Nielsen ratings, these shows ranked 13th, 22nd, 15th, 48th, and 73rd, respectively, among White viewers (Maines, 1992). In 1998 the top four shows among Black viewers (*The Steve Harvey Show, The Jamie Foxx Show, Monday Night Football,* and *For Your Love*) ranked 127th, 120th, 6th, and 120th, (tied) respectively, among White viewers. These figures suggest that positive depictions of minority characters are limited in their power to change perceptions and attitudes among Whites because White viewers do not watch them. Although White viewers also watch *Monday Night Football,* this show only contributes to cultural stereotypes of Blacks as athletic and aggressive. Second, many White viewers may see, for example, Bill Cosby's character in *Cosby* as atypical of Black people in general. Recall from Chapter 2 that stereotypes are protected from disconfirmation by dismissing inconsistent cases as "exceptions to the rule." Perhaps White viewers do this when they watch a Black character who does not fit into their stereotype of African Americans.

REPRESENTATIONS AND PORTRAYALS OF GAY, DISABLED, AND ECONOMICALLY DISADVANTAGED INDIVIDUALS

Historically, gay and disabled characters have been both infrequently and negatively portrayed on television. In the early TV decades, gay men and lesbian characters typically appeared as mentally unstable, morally corrupt individuals whose lives ended tragically before the end of the show—often by suicide (Russo, 1987). In recent years, however, gay and lesbian characters have appeared with greater regularity on TV. Currently, there are 23 lead or supporting gay characters on TV (Bruni, 1996). However, the portrayal of gay characters is mixed. Many male characters act out the effeminate, artsy, and ostentatious gay male stereotype, such as the characters Leon on *Roseanne* and Peter on *Ellen.* Also, gay characters tend to be portrayed one-dimensionally—their on-screen identity is dominated by their sexual orientation (or preference). On the other hand, characters such as Ellen on *Ellen* break down gay stereotypes by showing viewers that gay individuals live, work, and recreate just like everyone else and have lives that are not dominated by sex or sexual identity.

Among the most underrepresented people on TV are individuals with a physical or mental disability. Relative to their proportion in the population, disabled characters virtually do not exist on TV. When they do, they tend to be single, dependent, and self-pitying people who are portrayed as somehow responsible for their own plight (Donaldson, 1981). There are notable exceptions to this pattern. Chris Burke (an actor with Down's syndrome) played a character named Corky in the 1980s family drama *Life Goes On.* That show portrayed Burke's disabled character as possessing many positive attributes and competencies in a realistic manner. Additionally, two shows in the early 1970s, *Ironside* and *Longstreet,* featured detectives who were wheelchair-bound and blind, respectively. Too few of these programs and roles exist, however, to challenge our stereotypic beliefs about disabled individuals.

Finally, economically disadvantaged people are barely visible on television. Although "blue collar" programming has become popular in the 1990s, fueled by such shows as *Roseanne* and *Married . . . With Children,* poor people have very little representation on TV. George Gerbner's (1997) survey of 20 years of prime-time programming revealed that "lower socioeconomic class" characters made up just 1% of the population of people on TV. Nearly all of the characters (94%) on prime-time television hail from the middle class; just 1–2% are portrayed as economically disadvantaged. Thus television provides a distorted view of the socioeconomic diversity in our communities given that roughly 14% of the American population lives in poverty (U.S. Bureau of the Census, 1995). Because poor people are nearly invisible on TV, little research has studied how they are portrayed. However, in one study Martin Gilens (1996) analyzed television news magazine programs and found that stories about people from the economic underclass make subtle but consistent derogatory references to their ability, motivation, and values. The research reviewed in this section indicates that many social groups in our society are virtually invisible in the world of television. When they do appear, however, gay, disabled, and economically disadvantaged characters tend to be portrayed in derogatory, stereotypical terms.

THE INFLUENCE OF TELEVISION ON PERCEPTIONS OF DIVERSITY

The studies and findings discussed here lead us to conclude that television, through its programming and characters, distorts our perceptions of our social world. The more TV we watch, the more we live in the social world constructed and interpreted by television producers and writers. Television affects our perceptions of diversity in two ways. First, the cast of characters is primarily composed of men and women in the prime of life. These characters tend to act out stereotypical roles and stories in which men are empowered, dominant figures who make decisions and set agendas and women are subordinate, dependent figures who look desirable. Racial and ethnic minorities (other than African American), senior citizens, children, gay people, and mentally or physically disabled individuals as characters are at best marginalized through underrepresentation and at worst completely excluded from the television social landscape. So television restricts the visibility of some social groups, causing our world to seem less diverse than it is. This social segregation and exclusion on TV feeds the ignorance and fear we may already harbor about those who are different from us. Remember from our study in Chapter 3 that lack of exposure to or personal experience with members of other social groups means that we rely more heavily on stereotypes to guide our thinking about them.

Second, rather than breaking down the artificial differences imposed by social categories and stereotypes, television portrayals tend to reinforce them. If we watch enough TV, and watch it uncritically, we become more convinced of two things: (1) that men and women, White and Black individuals, and youthful and older adults are very different categories of people and (2) that the former are better than the latter. In other words, TV shows us a world in which social differences (what few of them we see) are large, important to maintain, and value-laden. As we know from earlier chapters, these perceptions feed stereotyping and separation between members of social groups. In short, television contributes more to a boiling-pot than to a melting-pot society by restricting our exposure to the socially different people who inhabit our world and by enhancing artificial differences between us and the people around us.

What can be done to address the contributing role of television programming in these social problems? How can television reverse the biased representations and stereotypical portrayals and more accurately portray the diversity of our social world? First, television writers, casting directors, and producers need to give greater visibility and voice to members of underrepresented social groups. Many popular shows have casts made up exclusively of able-bodied, White, young adults (see *Friends* or *Just Shoot Me,* for two of many examples). Programs such as these that have loyal viewing audiences could be encouraged to introduce a minority or disabled character. The common belief that "diverse" programming exists on cable TV is a myth. In fact, women, racial minorities, children, and older adults face the same underrepresentation on cable, public, and independent channels as they do on network TV shows (Kubey, Shifflet, Weerakkody, & Ukeiley, 1995).

Second, TV characters and stories need to challenge and disconfirm stereotypes of women. Some television shows have done this well. For example, the Public Broadcasting Service's *Mystery* series features Hetty Wainthropp, an older woman detective played by Patricia Routledge. Casting any woman as a detective, especially an older woman, helps break down stereotypical images of men as rational "actors" and women as emotional "appearers." Also, the characters who play these stereotype-inconsistent roles must be presented as normal people living fairly normal lives with whom the viewers can make some connection. The positive impact of such counterstereotypic depictions would be less effective if viewers perceived the women as unusual in some way (perhaps in their intelligence or education level).

Third, television needs to strive for more interracial contact. As discussed earlier, the casts and viewership of most TV shows tend to be divided along racial lines. Therefore, interracial interactions are infrequent and strained events on most TV shows. The principles of the contact hypothesis from Chapter 4 apply here. If television programs portray characters from different racial groups interacting personally working for some mutually valued goal or participating together in an activity of mutual interest, they will be effective models for teaching viewers the real-life value of such interaction.

KEY TERMS

social representations
social portrayals

FOR THOUGHT AND DISCUSSION

1. What current television shows and characters, in your opinion, challenge stereotypes? How do they do this?

2. Why is TV a male-dominated world? Consider some political and economic reasons.

3. Watch an episode or two of *All in the Family* (broadcast on many independent and cable channels). In that program the character Archie Bunker is often portrayed as ignorant and disliked by other characters for expressing his stereotypes and prejudices. Is this approach (ridiculing the bigot) appropriate or promising for reducing stereotypes in viewers? Explain your position.

4. Go to a website that displays television programs and ratings (on any browser follow the "TV" or "entertainment" link) and survey the current TV programs.

How many shows have male as opposed to female lead characters? What is their average rating?

How many shows have Black as opposed to White main characters? What is their average rating?

5. Aside from those covered in this chapter, what other social groups are under-represented or portrayed stereotypically on TV?

REFERENCES

Bazzini, D., McIntosh, W., Smith, S., & Cook, S. (1997). The aging woman in popular film: Underrepresented, unattractive, unfriendly, and unintelligent. *Sex Roles, 36,* 531–543.

Bishop, J., & Krause, D. (1984). Depictions of aging and old age on Saturday morning television. *The Gerontologist, 24,* 91–94.

Bruni, F. (1996, October 13). It may be a closet door, but it's already open. *New York Times.*

Busby, L. (1975). Sex-role research on the mass media. *Journal of Communication, 25,* 107–131.

Cassata, M., Anderson, P., & Skill, T. (1980). The older adult in daytime serial drama. *Journal of Communication, 30,* 48–49.

Dail, P. (1988). Prime-time television portrayals of older adults in the context of family life. *The Gerontologist, 28,* 700–706.

Davis, D. (1990). Portrayals of women in prime-time network television: Some demographic characteristics. *Sex Roles, 23,* 325–332.

Donaldson, J. (1981). The visibility and image of handicapped people on television. *Exceptional Children, 47,* 413–416.

Dyer, G. (1987). Women and television: An overview. In H. Baeher & G. Dyer (Eds.), *Boxed in: Women and television.* New York: Pandora Press.

Ford, T. (1997). Effects of stereotypical television portrayals of African-Americans on person perception. *Social Psychology Quarterly, 60,* 266–278.

Gan, S., Zillmann, D., & Mitrook, M. (1997). Stereotyping effect of Black women's sexual rap on White audiences. *Basic and Applied Social Psychology, 19,* 381–399.

Gerbner, G. (1997). Gender and age in prime-time television. In S. Kirschner & D. A. Kirschner (Eds.), *Per-spectives on psychology and the media* (pp. 69–94). Washington, DC: American Psychological Association.

Gerbner, G., Gross, L., Signorielli, N., & Morgan, M. (1980). Aging with television: Images on television drama and conceptions of social reality. *Journal of Communication, 30,* 37–48.

Gilens, M. (1996). Race and poverty in America: Public misperceptions and the American news media. *Public Opinion Quarterly, 60,* 515–541.

Harwood, J. (1995). *Viewing age: The age distribution of television characters across the viewer lifespan.* [On-line]. Available: http://falcon.cc.ukans.edu/~harwood/crr.htm#table4r.

Hedley, M. (1994). The presentation of gendered conflict in popular movies: Affective stereotypes, cultural sentiments, and men's motivation. *Sex Roles, 31,* 721–740.

Johnson, F., Adams, M., Hall, W., & Ashburn, L. (1997). Race, media, and violence: Differential racial effects of exposure to violent news stories. *Basic and Applied Social Psychology, 19,* 81–90.

Kubey, R., Shifflet, M., Weerakkody, N., & Ukeiley, S. (1995). Demographic diversity on cable: Have the new cable channels made a difference in the representation of gender, race, and age? *Journal of Broadcasting and Electronic Media, 39,* 459–471.

Lemon, J. (1977). Women and Blacks on prime time television. *Journal of Communication, 27,* 70–79.

Lott, B. (1989). Sexist discrimination as distancing behavior. *Psychology of Women Quarterly, 13,* 341–355.

Maines, J. (1992). Black and white in color. *American Demographics, 14,* 9–10.

Messner, M., Duncan, M., & Jensen, K. (1993). Separating the men from the girls: The gendered language of televised sports. *Gender and Society, 7,* 121–137.

Nielsen Television Index. (1998). [On-line]. Available: http://www.nielsenmedia.com.

Oliver, M. (1994). Portrayals of crime, race, and aggression in "reality-based" police shows: A content analysis. *Journal of Broadcasting and Electronic Media, 38,* 179–192.

Poindexter, P., & Stroman, C. (1981). Blacks and television: A review of the research literature. *Journal of Broadcasting, 25,* 103–122.

Russo, V. (1987). *The celluloid closet: Homosexuality in the movies* (2nd ed.). New York: Harper & Row.

Tangney, J., & Feshbach, S. (1988). Children's television-viewing frequency: Individual differences and demographic correlates. *Personality and Social Psychology Bulletin, 14,* 145–158.

Taylor, C., & Stern, B. (1997). Asian-Americans: Television advertising and the "model minority" stereotype. *Journal of Advertising, 26,* 47–61.

U.S. Bureau of the Census. (1995). *Statistical abstract of the United States* (115th ed.). Washington, DC: Author.

Weigel, R., Kim, E., & Frost, J. (1995). Race relations on prime-time television reconsidered: Patterns of continuity and change. *Journal of Applied Social Psychology, 25,* 223–236.

Social Stigma

Experiencing Social Difference

CHAPTER OBJECTIVE

To present a new perspective on diversity—the experience of being socially different. The chapter discusses the basic elements of social stigma and teaches that we are products of our diverse social surroundings.

We have seen in prior chapters that the diversity of our social world is, in part, a product of our own thought processes, needs, and actions. Through these processes we place ourselves in a "perceiver" mode, a mode in which we observe others and process social information. Thus the primary message in the preceding seven chapters has been: We influence diversity. A psychological consideration of diversity, however, is not limited to the processes by which we create, exaggerate, or overlook social differences. We are part of the diversity of our social contexts and thus *experiencers* of social difference. With this new perspective on our study of diversity, we are concerned with a new question: How does diversity influence us? In this chapter, we will confront some of the basic psychological elements involved in the experience of diversity.

UNDERSTANDING THE EXPERIENCE OF SOCIAL DIFFERENCE: BASIC COMPONENTS

Not long ago in my university library, on walking through a bank of book detectors near the exit, I set off the alarm. The shrill beeping of the alarm threw a hush over the reading room, and for a moment all eyes were on me. Not only was I acutely self-conscious, I was also instantly aware of being regarded by the surrounding library patrons as someone I was not—a book-stealing lowlife. I felt different, judged, and "typed" as a dishonest person. Living in a socially diverse world means that many of us will feel different. The experience of social "differentness" can take many forms, such as being excluded, mocked, misunderstood, or ignored. It is likely that you have experienced some of the consequences of being socially different, especially if you are a member of a racial or ethnic minority group, physically or learning-disabled, a gay man or lesbian, overweight, or economically disadvantaged.

Social scientists have long been interested in the experience of being socially different—or stigmatized—and its implications for one's identity, mental health, and social adjustment (Goffman, 1963; Jones, et. al., 1984; Katz, 1981). Stigma is a centuries-old term that refers to a physical mark symbolic of some negative status. The modern psychological usage of stigma conveys this meaning in social terms. To be stigmatized is to possess an attribute or status that has negative social implications. That is, one's attribute, or "mark," prompts in others stereotypic judgments, prejudice, or discrimination. **Social stigma**, then, refers to the experience of being socially discredited or flawed by a personal trait or characteristic. Let's consider the basic theoretical components of social stigma.

A Mismatch of Identities

The central concept for understanding stigma is identity—that summary of information that describes who you are. Take a few minutes and do this exercise in your notebook. On the left side of a page, describe yourself. List terms that answer the question, Who are you? On the right side of the page, list terms that answer the question, Who do people think you are? When you have finished, continue reading.

The descriptors in the left column form your **actual identity**, or the "you" you know yourself to be. The terms in the right column make up your **virtual identity**, or the "you" other people believe you to be. Look at the terms that compose your actual and virtual identities: They are probably not the same. Compared with how you know yourself, do others know you in terms that are inaccurate, negative, or unfair? If so, you feel stigmatized. Stigma—that feeling of social difference many of us experience—involves an inconsistency between one's actual and virtual identities (Goffman, 1963). In the great majority of cases, stigma is associated with a virtual identity that is more negative and/or more simplistic than one's actual identity. Occasionally, the opposite pattern of discrepancy occurs, when others have a more positive impression of you than you have of yourself; this will be discussed later in the chapter.

If stigma results when others' view of us is more negative than we know ourselves to be, could stigmatized individuals merely dismiss others' errant or prejudiced beliefs? This tends not to happen. A long history of thinking and research in psychology asserts that our identity is fundamentally social (Cooley, 1902; Mead, 1913). Understanding who we are is not just a simple matter of looking within ourselves. Rather, self-understanding depends vitally on who *other* people think we are. Part of our self-understanding, then, comes from internalizing others' views of us. Researchers have found that matching our self-views with others' views of us is an important need, both in short-term interactions and long-term relationships (Swann, Hixon, & De La Ronde, 1992). When friends and coworkers have a thorough and accurate impression of you, there is a level of comfort and predictability in your interactions with them. However, when other people have a more negative impression of you than you have of yourself, you sense vulnerability, tension, and unpredictability in interactions with them. The fact that others' beliefs about us are an important source of our own self-understanding poses a problem for stigmatized people. They face a chronic inconsistency between their own self-views and the negative views other people have of them.

Thus stigma involves a mismatch of identities—when the "you" reflected in others' behavior does not match the "you" you really are. Also, stigma cannot be experienced outside of a social context. The discrepancy between actual and virtual identities cannot be felt without some imagined or actual interaction with other people.

An Attribute–Stereotype Connection

Stigma can also be understood as a connection between an attribute and the stereotype associated with it. Recall from Chapter 2 that social categories and stereotypes are efficient social information-processing tools. By shifting our focus from the perception to the experience of diversity, we become aware that we can be categorized and stereotyped by other people. Most of us possess attributes that are associated with stereotypic knowledge. Dark skin coloring, physical disability, and extreme overweight are examples of attributes that prompt in others stereotypic thinking and prejudice. Some less common attributes that may spur stereotyping include a person's name or neighborhood, accent or dialect, or having one's body pierced or tattooed.

These attribute–stereotype connections are socially informative. They render us "known" and somewhat predictable to other people. However, as I discussed in Chapter 2, the "you" that other people know stereotypically is not likely to match the "you" that you know yourself to be. Others' stereotypic knowledge of us differs in three important ways from our self-knowledge: It is more negative, dispositional, and simplistic. Thus the experience of stigma involves recognizing that others see us in predominantly negative and characterological terms and that these terms are tied to just one (of our many) attributes.

In summary, these two conceptualizations of stigma are complementary. To possess an attribute that prompts negative stereotypic beliefs about you in other people is to have a virtual identity that is negative and inaccurate. Moreover, stigma is a potential by-product of a socially constructed identity. Because we look outward—to our interactions and social groups—for cues about who we are and what we are like, we must sometimes face the troubling prospect that we are not assumed (by others) to be the individual we know ourselves to be.

EXPERIENCING SOCIAL DIFFERENCE: CONTRIBUTING FACTORS

Stigma does not reside *in* an individual, as if one were branded with an unchanging mark. Rather, as explained previously, stigma arises out of social interaction. Although the experience of being socially different is essentially a matter of psychological identity, other factors contribute to stigma.

Differing Perspectives on Who You Are

Recall that the essence of stigma is the knowledge that others know a "you" that is different, more negative and assumptive, from the "you" you know yourself as. One explanation for two people reaching such divergent conclusions about an individual concerns their perspective and is summed up in the **actor–observer effect.** As behavioral "actors," our gaze and attention are naturally focused on external factors such as situations and circumstances rather than on our appearance or character. However, when others look at us they do not see situations or circumstances, they see us—our bodies and personalities. As a result, any distinctive attribute will have more impact on observers' perceptions of an individual than it will on the actor herself, especially if that attribute is associated with stereotypic knowledge.

To illustrate, my brother Warren has cerebral palsy. When others look at and think about him, they see his contorted stature and awkward movements. Their feelings and attitudes toward him are likely to be connected to that distinctive attribute. His many other attributes and abilities will be unobserved and unnoted. Essentially, he will be one-dimensionalized by many of the people with whom he interacts. When he thinks about himself, however, he doesn't see (in his mind's eye) his appearance or disability; thus his self-perceptions are not dominated by the attribute "disabled." Because of the divergent perspectives of actors and observers, the "you" you know yourself to be can differ from the "you" others see you as.

One of the implications of this perspective differential is that stigmatized individuals may be more motivated than nonstigmatized people to find out what other people see in them or think about them. If being stigmatized is recognizing that others see you more negatively than you see yourself, then stigmatized people should want to reduce or at least understand this discrepancy by taking others' perspective on themselves. Deborah Frable and her colleagues tested this idea in a fascinating study (Frable, Blackstone, & Scherbaum, 1990). They had stigmatized people of many types (e.g., obese, Black, physically unattractive, and facially scarred people) engage in a conversation with a nonstigmatized partner. These interactions were videotaped and subsequently viewed by each partner, who recorded his or her thoughts and feelings about the interaction. The participants were also asked to recall everything they could about their partner and the room.

The results showed that all stigmatized participants, regardless of their stigma type, displayed **mindfulness.** That is, they took their partner's perspective during

To be stigmatized is to realize that others see you in terms of one attribute—such as being a lesbian—and react to you based on the stereotype associated with that attribute, whereas you see yourself as having many different attributes.

the interaction and remembered more details about the interaction than their partner did. This research suggests that, in response to being misunderstood and judged by others, socially stigmatized persons are more vigilant in social situations and adopt the perspective of nonstigmatized interaction partners in viewing the situation and themselves. What, if any, benefit this perspective-taking posture has on the experience of social difference is still not well documented.

Situations Can Be Stigmatizing

Social difference can also be experienced situationally. That is, one's awareness of being stigmatized can be present (or high) in some contexts and not present (or low) in others. In this way, stigma can affect one's day-to-day self-perceptions and feelings of acceptance and competence. For example, athletic situations heighten the differentness of the physically disabled; academic situations have similar effects on learning-disabled people. When these situations are reversed, physically disabled and learning-disabled individuals are less aware of their differentness from others.

Thus a situation is stigmatizing if the situational demands or norms expose to others an attribute or part of yourself that is vulnerable to negative evaluation.

In that situation, it may be "found out" by others that you are different along some dimension, and they may make assumptions about you based on that difference. For example, I have a friend who enjoys playing games and with whom I have played many games. However, he has always avoided word games. This inconsistency only made sense when I learned that he was dyslexic and did not feel confident or competent in those game-playing situations. For him, the prospect of his reading disability being exposed to others was sufficiently threatening to make him avoid those situations. His stigma was only felt in situations that publicly spotlighted reading and spelling skills.

Social Differences Are Maintained by Culture

Finally, the relationship between an attribute and a stereotype is often embedded in cultural beliefs and norms. Stigma can exert chronic influence on an individual, particularly if the relationship between attribute and stereotype is embraced and maintained by one's surrounding culture. For example, overweight people are viewed in very negative terms, such as being lazy and undisciplined and lacking in self-control, and they face widespread discrimination (Allon, 1982). Research by Christian Crandall and his colleagues has shown that attitudes and feelings toward people who are overweight are grounded in traditional American values of personal responsibility, individualism, and self-discipline (Crandall, 1994; Crandall & Biernat, 1990).

In one study, a measure of antifat attitudes was positively related to other measures of social and political conservatism. Participants who expressed antifat sentiments tended to also endorse racist attitudes and support capital punishment, as well as traditional sexual values and practices (Crandall & Biernat, 1990). Interestingly, antifat sentiment was not confined to the thin participants, who may have been expected to attribute obesity to laziness. Even some overweight people held antifat attitudes, and these people tended to be the most politically conservative.

This research suggests that antifat sentiment stems from underlying cultural beliefs about individual responsibility and getting what we deserve in life. To further examine the cultural underpinnings of "fatism," Crandall (1994) conducted an experiment in which participants heard either a persuasive message about the uncontrollability of weight or a non-weight-related control message, followed by a measure of antifat attitudes. Relative to the control group, participants exposed to the "weight is uncontrollable" message liked overweight people more and viewed them as having more willpower. Therefore, when cultural beliefs about fatness were temporarily contradicted, people were less prejudiced toward overweight individuals.

To sum up, the experience of social difference is greatest when stigmatized individuals are marginalized in mainstream society and, hence, are understood by others only in the most stereotypic terms. Social stigma can be heightened situationally, as specific social contexts draw on attributes or abilities that may be negatively evaluated by others. Finally, social differences and the assumptions associated with them are often rooted in and maintained by cultural beliefs and values.

THE EXPERIENCE OF BEING SOCIALLY DIFFERENT

Having discussed social stigma—the experience of being socially different—in theoretical terms, let us sum up what this experience is like. Stigma is a complex social experience, involving cognitive, emotional, and behavioral components. Furthermore, stigma is often a mixture of negative and positive experiences. Others' negative stereotypes about stigmatized people often coexist with genuine feelings of sympathy for them (Katz, 1981).

Being Stereotyped

Cognitively, stigmatized individuals are aware that they are known differently to others than they are to themselves. This "spoiled identity" to which Goffman (1963) refers applies to the content and the structure of others' knowledge of stigmatized persons. Stigmatized people are categorized and stereotyped by others. As we know, stereotypic knowledge tends to be negative and inaccurate. Also, stereotypes tend to reflect characterological, and hence relatively unchangeable, terms.

The recognition that one is known stereotypically also means that stigmatized people are "one-dimensionalized" in others' eyes. It means that one aspect of their identity—perhaps not even one that the stigmatized person considers important—represents them to others. Furthermore, once established in people's minds, stereotypes are resistant to disconfirming information. So, although stigmatized individuals may not conform to the stereotype of their group, they face the frustrating problem of not being able to correct others' beliefs about them.

Being the Object of Ambivalent Feelings

Emotionally, to be stigmatized is to be the victim of prejudice. Stereotypic content and feelings are closely linked; it is difficult to think about someone in negative terms without harboring negative feelings for that person. These negative feelings can take many forms, including dislike, anger, or anxiety. However, negative reactions to stigmatized people are often accompanied by positive feelings. Sympathy, pity, or admiration are also common emotional responses to stigmatized people. Thus stigmatized individuals must deal with others' ambivalent feelings toward them (Katz, 1981).

Irwin Katz and his colleagues reasoned that **ambivalence** toward stigmatized people is rooted in two traditional and somewhat conflicting American values (Katz & Hass, 1988). The Protestant work ethic emphasizes self-reliance, hard work, and achievement, whereas humanitarianism stresses the equality and worthiness of all people. If people endorse these values equally, then it is possible to both dislike (for not working hard or taking personal responsibility for their lives) *and* support (for the disadvantages they face) the members of a stigmatized group. To test this idea, the researchers developed two questionnaires measuring pro-Black and anti-Black attitudes, respectively, and administered them to students at several northern colleges and universities (Katz & Hass, 1988). The results reflected students' ambivalence toward African American people. Anti-Black attitudes were correlated with the Protestant work ethic but not with humanitarianism; pro-Black attitudes were correlated with humanitarianism but not with the Protestant work ethic. And students' anti-Black and pro-Black attitudes were not related, meaning that it is possible to hold both kinds of attitudes at once.

In a follow-up study, Katz and Hass (1988) primed participants to think about either the Protestant work ethic or humanitarian values and then administered the two questionnaires previously described. Participants who were encouraged to think about the Protestant work ethic endorsed more anti-Black than pro-Black attitudes, but those who pondered humanitarianism displayed more pro-Black than anti-Black attitudes. Together, these studies suggest that social stigma involves experiencing both positive and negative attitudes from others.

Facing Discrimination

Finally, stigmatized people experience discrimination in many forms, the most common being avoidance or exclusion. Indeed, gaining acceptance is regarded as the chief problem for most stigmatized people (Goffman, 1963). Social interactions between stigmatized and nonstigmatized people are often marked by tension, awkwardness, and hostility. These strained interactions are associated with a wide range of discriminatory responses in such areas as employment, housing, and relationships (see Crocker & Major, 1989, for a review).

Behavior toward stigmatized individuals may also arise from the ambivalent feelings one may have about them. For example, you may want to help a blind person board a bus or subway but may be uncertain about what sort of assistance, if any, is needed; so you do nothing. Avoidance of stigmatized persons, then, should not be taken as evidence of simple dislike or resentment but rather as evidence of conflicting emotions and attitudes toward the stigmatized. Finally, discrimination against stigmatized individuals is often justified by holding them responsible for their own condition or lifestyle choice, such as occurs with overweight or gay people.

VARIATIONS IN THE EXPERIENCE OF SOCIAL DIFFERENCE

Positive Stigma

Thus far we have described stigma as a negative social experience. However, one can also feel socially different in positive terms. Positive stigma results when an individual possesses an attribute or status that prompts positive attitudes and feelings in others. The best example of positive stigma occurs in people who are phys-ically attractive. Physical attractiveness is a status that is culturally valued and is associated with a well-defined stereotype. According to the "beautiful is good" stereotype, physically attractive people are considered to be more friendly, intel-ligent, assertive, and emotionally stable than individuals with average or below-average looks (Eagly, Ashmore, Makhijani, & Longo, 1991; Jackson, Sullivan, & Hodge, 1995). Thus many attractive individuals will sense that others' over-whelmingly positive views of them do not fit with their self-views. Although it seems like an enviable "problem" to have, research indicates that positive stigma has negative consequences. Researchers in one study had attractive and unat-tractive women write an essay that was subsequently given a positive evaluation by a male evaluator seated in the next room (Major, Carrington, & Carnevale, 1984). Half of the women believed they could be seen by the evaluator (the blind on the two-way mirror was up); the other women believed that the man could not see them (the blind was down).

It follows that only the attractive women who were seen would believe that they were positively stigmatized in the eyes of the male evaluator, that they were known to him in unrealistically positive terms. The results showed that the at-tractive women who were seen by the evaluator were more likely to discount his positive evaluation than the women whose good looks went unnoticed. The at-tractive women who had been seen believed the praise was due more to their looks than to the quality of their essays. This effect did not occur in the unat-tractive women. Thus, despite some obvious advantages, physical attractiveness can be stigmatizing. It heightens one's psychological vulnerability, because praise and positive outcomes can never be fully separated from one's looks and attrib-uted solely to effort or ability.

Stigma by Association

Erving Goffman (1963) asserted that stigma could be experienced indirectly based on one's association with a stigmatized individual, a phenomenon referred to as **courtesy stigma.** Courtesy stigma is informed not by the specific stigmatizing attribute of your friend or family member but by what your association with that person seems to say about you. Courtesy stigma has been observed in, for ex-ample, the parents of developmentally disabled children. Obviously the parents are not themselves disabled, but their association with their disabled children imputes to them some social difference of their own (Birenbaum, 1992). Little is known about the actual and virtual identities underlying courtesy stigma and about whether the discrepancies are negative or positive or both. For example, are the parents of disabled children seen as saintly, devoted caregivers or as resigned to a thankless life circumstance? Regardless, courtesy stigma can have a range of negative consequences.

In one study of courtesy stigma, participants viewed a staged conversation between two men after being led to believe either that both of the men were

We can be stigmatized by our association with other stigmatized people, and this contributes to our avoidance of those individuals.

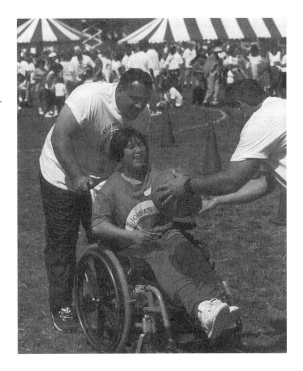

heterosexual or that one was gay and the other was heterosexual (Neuberg, Smith, Hoffman, & Russell, 1994). Participants' perceptions of the heterosexual man were more negative when he was interacting with a gay partner than with a heterosexual partner. In other words, the heterosexual man was stigmatized by his association with the gay interaction partner.

In another study, participants read scenarios about a fictitious male student who was described as either voluntarily rooming with a gay male or being assigned a gay male as a roommate. Compared with the student who did not choose, the student who chose a gay roommate was seen as having gay tendencies of his own and was described in gay stereotypic terms. However, these perceptions were observed only in people who had high levels of intolerance to begin with (Sigelman, Howell, Cornell, Cutright, & Dewey, 1991).

Finally, courtesy stigma may not be uniformly negative but may prompt both negative and positive reactions in others. In one study, participants read about an individual who either was or was not physically disabled and who was in a romantic relationship with a nondisabled partner (Goldstein & Johnson, 1997). Participants wrote their impressions of the partner and rated him or her on a variety of traits. The results indicated that partners of disabled individuals were viewed differently from those of nondisabled people. However, the difference combined both negative and positive impressions. That is, partners of disabled people were seen as more trustworthy and nurturant but less intelligent and sociable than partners of nondisabled people. This study shows that our attitudes toward people who are stigmatized by association reflect the ambivalent quality of our reactions to stigmatized individuals.

The research on stigma by association tends to be conducted from the perceiver's rather than the experiencer's perspective. That is, it measures others' attitudes toward people who are associated with stigmatized individuals rather than the attitudes and feelings of those who experience courtesy stigma. Thus it only suggests that the experience of social stigma is not limited to those who have a discrediting or discreditable mark but extends to people who affiliate with the marked individual. Even so, the research makes an important statement. If others perceive that associating with a stigmatized (such as a gay or disabled) individual will affect the way *they* are treated by others, it will lead to less interaction with stigmatized people. Stigma by association, then, has implications for both those who associate with stigmatized people and the stigmatized themselves, in the form of isolation and loss of social opportunity.

SUMMARY

We live in a socially diverse world. As a result, most of us are acquainted with the experience of being different from others. In this chapter we learned how social differences can be stigmatizing. We are stigmatized when our social difference prompts negative attitudes and feelings in others. Stigma arises out of social interaction and is experienced as a spoiled identity. When used, social categories and stereotypes are valuable information-processing tools; when experienced, they are often oppressive and demoralizing.

KEY TERMS

social stigma	mindfulness
actual identity	ambivalence
virtual identity	courtesy stigma
actor–observer effect	

FOR THOUGHT AND DISCUSSION

1. What social differences have caused you to feel stigmatized? Is this stigma situation-specific?

2. Stigmatized people suffer from the fact that stereotypes are resistant to disconfirming information. Given what you have learned about reducing stereotypes, develop a plan for improving the social prospects of the members of some stigmatized group of your choice.

3. The discrepancy between actual and virtual identities is the essence of stigma. If reducing the discrepancy is the goal, what are some of the implications of changing stigmatized individuals' actual identity? Virtual identity?

4. Identify a social group whose members prompt ambivalence in you. List and discuss your positive and negative responses and whether they are attitudes, feelings, or actions.

5. How is courtesy stigma related to the rejection and avoidance many stigmatized people feel?

REFERENCES

Allon, N. (1982). The stigma of overweight in everyday life. In B. B. Wolman (Ed.), *Psychological aspects of obesity: A handbook* (pp. 130–174). New York: Van Nostrand Reinhold.

Birenbaum, A. (1992). Courtesy stigma revisited. *Mental Retardation, 5,* 265–268.

Cooley, C. (1902). *Human nature and the social order.* New York: Scribners.

Crandall, C. (1994). Prejudice against fat people: Ideology and self-interest. *Journal of Personality and Social Psychology, 66,* 882–894.

Crandall, C., & Biernat, M. (1990). The ideology of anti-fat attitudes. *Journal of Applied Social Psychology, 20,* 227–243.

Crocker, J., & Major, B. (1989). Social stigma and self-esteem: The self-protective properties of stigma. *Psychological Review, 96,* 608–630.

Eagly, A., Ashmore, R., Makhijani, M., & Longo, L. (1991). What is beautiful is good, but . . . : A meta-analytic review of research on the physical attractiveness stereotype. *Psychological Bulletin, 110,* 107–128.

Frable, D., Blackstone, T., & Scherbaum, C. (1990). Marginal and mindful: Deviants in social interactions. *Journal of Personality and Social Psychology, 59,* 140–149.

Goffman, E. (1963). *Stigma: Notes on the management of spoiled identity.* New York: Simon & Schuster.

Goldstein, S., & Johnson, V. (1997). Stigma by association: Perceptions of the dating partners of college students with physical disabilities. *Basic and Applied Social Psychology, 19,* 495–504.

Jackson, L., Sullivan, L., & Hodge, C. (1995). Physical attractiveness and intellectual competence: A meta-analytic review. *Social Psychology Quarterly, 58,* 108–122.

Jones, E., Farina, A., Hastorf, A., Markus, H., Miller, D., & Scott, R. (1984). *Social stigma: The psychology of marked relationships.* New York: Freeman.

Katz, I. (1981). *Stigma: A social psychological analysis.* Hillsdale, NJ: Erlbaum.

Katz, I., & Hass, R. G. (1988). Racial ambivalence and American value conflict: Correlational and priming studies of dual cognitive structures. *Journal of Personality and Social Psychology, 55,* 893–905.

Major, B., Carrington, P., & Carnevale, P. (1984). Physical attractiveness and self-esteem: Attributions for praise from an other-sex evaluator. *Personality and Social Psychology Bulletin, 10,* 43–50.

Mead, G. (1913). The social self. *Journal of Philosophy, 10,* 374–380.

Neuberg, S., Smith, D., Hoffman, J., & Russell, F. (1994). When we observe stigmatized and "normal" individuals interacting: Stigma by association. *Personality and Social Psychology Bulletin, 20,* 196–209.

Sigelman, C., Howell, J., Cornell, D., Cutright, J., & Dewey, J. (1991). Courtesy stigma: The social implications of associating with a gay person. *Journal of Social Psychology, 131,* 45–56.

Swann, W., Hixon, J., & De La Ronde, C. (1992). Embracing the bitter "truth": Negative self-concepts and marital commitment. *Psychological Science, 3,* 118–121.

The Price of Being Socially Different

Consequences of Stigma

CHAPTER OBJECTIVE

To further study the experience of social difference by confronting the psychological and social costs of being stigmatized.

Our psychological study of the experience of social difference must consider how social stigma affects the individual. What consequences does being socially different have on the well-being and adjustment of stigmatized people? The cost of stigma exists on social and psychological levels; stigma affects social interactions and opportunities, as well as how stigmatized people view and evaluate themselves. Each of these domains of influence has important implications for mental health and adjustment. After discussing the general social and psychological consequences of stigma, I will consider the price of being socially different for one stigmatized group in our society—overweight people.

SOCIAL CONSEQUENCES OF STIGMA

Friendship and companionship play a vital role in preserving mental health and adjustment. Our friends listen when we are burdened and provide material and moral support when we are stressed (Cohen & Wills, 1985; Pennebaker, 1990). It is well documented, however, that stigmatized people face rejection and avoidance from others (Goffman, 1963). Stigmatized people also provoke negative emotional reactions in others, such as tension, uncertainty, or disliking. In general, stigma disrupts both the quality and the quantity of the social relationships of stigmatized people, and this should have aversive consequences for the well-being of stigmatized individuals (French, 1984).

In a fascinating classic experiment that demonstrates the negative effects of stigma on social interaction between stigmatized and nonstigmatized people, participants had a conversation with an individual—a confederate playing a role for the researchers—who was either physically disabled (a wheelchair-bound "amputee") or nondisabled (Kleck, Ono, & Hastorf, 1966). The participants were fitted with electrodes to measure their skin conductance, a physiological indicator of anxiety that lies beyond conscious control. The researchers also measured the duration of the interaction and the extent to which participants misrepresented their true (negative) attitudes about disabled people in the interaction.

Overall, participants exhibited more anxiety in interactions with disabled than with nondisabled partners. The interactions between participants and disabled partners were shorter than those between the able-bodied partners. Participants conversed with nondisabled partners for about 6½ minutes, whereas the interactions with disabled partners averaged about 5 minutes. Also, participants hid their true attitudes about disabled people from their disabled partner, displaying instead "disabled-friendly" sentiments. Interestingly, participants brought up topics in the conversation that were stereotypically positive, such as the belief that disabled individuals are more academically inclined than nondisabled people.

This study demonstrates some of the major social consequences of stigma. First, stigmatizing marks and conditions cause anxiety in others such that interactions with stigmatized people tend to be avoided or, if necessary, curtailed. Second, people carefully monitor their behavior toward stigmatized persons. This heightened vigilance about one's actions when interacting with stigmatized people may occur because we want to make them comfortable or because we do not want to reveal our own prejudice toward them or both. Regardless of the motive, stigmatized people experience interactions that are strained and superficial. Finally, stigmatized people are treated stereotypically. The connections between attributes and stereotypic traits and assumptions are often too well learned and automatic to inhibit. Even others' positive, well-intentioned actions toward stigmatized people are likely to reflect stereotypic ideas and to be perceived by stigmatized individuals as ingratiating or patronizing.

The Moderating Effects of Controllability on the Social Consequences of Stigma

The social consequences of stigma are not the same for every stigmatized person. Rather, they depend heavily on the underlying dimensions of stigmatizing conditions, one of which is controllability. **Stigma controllability** refers to who caused or is responsible for the stigmatizing attribute, status, or condition or to what extent it could have been prevented. Stigmatizing marks range in their controllability from those that are uncontrollable and assigned, such as race, ethnicity, or a genetically determined physical ailment, to those that are highly controllable, such as having a substance abuse problem, a criminal record, or a tattoo.

It is important to add that others' treatment of stigmatized individuals hinges on the *perceived* controllability of the stigmatizing condition, which may be independent of its *actual* controllability (as established by scientists or reflected in factual records). To illustrate, most people regard obesity as a controllable condition, caused by unrestrained eating, lack of exercise, or both. However, scientific evidence indicates that one's weight is fairly uncontrollable (Stunkard et al., 1986). Such evidence tends to have little impact on this widespread cultural belief that weight is controllable, and, as a result, overweight people tend to be blamed for their own plight.

A great deal of research has established that people with stigmas that are thought to be controllable are treated more negatively than those with uncontrollable conditions. Much research shows that controllable stigmas elicit more blame and anger and less inclination to help or provide support among perceivers than do uncontrollable stigmas. Perceptions of stigma controllability lead to more negative evaluations of people who are developmentally disabled, obese, unemployed or poverty-stricken, diseased, AIDS victims, speech-disabled, substance abusers, and amputees (Farina, Holland, & Ring, 1966; Furnham, 1982; Lewis & Range, 1992; Menec & Perry, 1995; Rodin, Price, Sanchez, & McElligot, 1989; Schwarzer & Weiner, 1991; Vann, 1976; Weiner, Perry, & Magnusson, 1988).

Other research shows that these negative attitudes and feelings translate into negative treatment of stigmatized individuals who possess a controllable stigma. In one study, participants were given the opportunity to administer electric shocks (under the pretext of sending a message) to an obese person whose obesity was described as either controllable or uncontrollable (Vann, 1976). Longer shocks were given to the obese person who was believed to be responsible for his or her weight.

In a more recent study, participants read a scenario about a man who had contracted AIDS due to one of four things: an AIDS-infected homosexual partner, an AIDS-infected heterosexual partner, a blood transfusion, or an AIDS-infected intravenous drug needle (Dooley, 1995). Participants' pity and anger toward and willingness to help the AIDS-infected individual were measured. The results indicated that pity was a crucial mediator of helpful intentions toward an individual with AIDS. That is, to offer help toward a person with AIDS, one is likely to first have to feel pity toward him or her. Compassionate feelings such as pity or sympathy, in turn, were produced by beliefs that AIDS was contracted in an uncontrollable manner (for example, through a blood transfusion). Participants' perceptions that an AIDS infection could have been prevented, such as in the homosexual and drug-use scenarios, produced anger toward the AIDS victim and an unwillingness to help him.

In summary, others' perceptions of the controllability of a stigma is a pivotal dimension for understanding the social consequences of stigma. But why is controllability information so important in understanding others' responses to stigma? Just-world theory argues that we have a general need to see the world—and the people and events in it—as reasonable, orderly, and just. In a just world, people get what they deserve. That people could be unemployed, disabled, or sick through no fault of their own, however, threatens beliefs in a just world in two ways. First, it suggests that *we* could suffer a similar tragedy. Second, it suggests that we are somehow obliged to help such individuals, perhaps giving some of our time and money to make their lives better. Researchers show that these threats are buffered by making the victim responsible for his or her own plight. Thus perceptions of stigma controllability are in part a defensive response to the threatening implications of stigma. Further, they justify negative attitudes and feelings toward stigmatized people.

The Moderating Effects of Visibility on the Social Consequences of Stigma

The social consequences of stigma also depend on the visibility of the status or condition (Frable, 1993a). **Stigma visibility** refers to how apparent it is to others and how difficult it is to conceal from others. Stigmatizing marks range in their visibility from the completely invisible, such as being gay or a paroled convict, to the completely visible, such as physical disability, obesity, or racial minority status.

Stigma visibility is a key moderator of stigma because those with invisible marks may avoid stigma altogether, provided such individuals can keep their stigmatizing conditions hidden from others. In other words, possessors of invisible but potentially stigmatizing attributes are not socially discredited—they are *discreditable*. As long as invisible or concealable failings go undetected by others, much of the negative experience of stigma is averted. This is perhaps best illustrated by the plight of lesbians and gay men, who are aware of widespread prejudice and discrimination they will experience if their sexual orientation becomes public knowledge (Berrill, 1990; Herek, 1991). The concealability of that attribute allows gay individuals to avoid some of those negative reactions by revealing their identity to potentially friendly, and concealing it from potentially hostile, people.

This does not mean that individuals with invisible stigmas experience no social difficulties. Deborah Frable (1993b) had university students from visible (such as ethnic minority or overweight) and invisible (such as being gay or hearing-disabled) stigmatized groups estimate what proportion of their peers shared their attitudes and preferences. The results revealed that students with invisible stigmas perceived more difference between themselves and their peers than did those with visible marks. In a second study participants viewed "uniqueness" adjectives (such as *different* or *outsider*) and "similarity" adjectives (such as *normal* or *commonplace*) presented by a computer and decided whether each adjective described them or not. Again, compared with people with visible stigmas, those with invisible stigmas described themselves with more "uniqueness" adjectives and were faster, and therefore more certain, in their responses. These studies show that people with hidden social flaws experience more marginality and differentness than do people whose stigma is obvious. Although Frable's studies did not establish this, feeling marginalized is likely to be associated with or to cause loneliness and social isolation.

People with invisible social flaws have another concern that affects their social well-being: whether to conceal or reveal their stigma. A concealed discreditable attribute can assume an important position in the stigmatizable person's daily life, determining (and often limiting) his or her social, employment, or recreational options and taxing his or her attentional and cognitive resources. Furthermore, individuals who choose to conceal their invisible stigmas develop friendships on somewhat false pretenses and must reconcile the benefits of those relationships with the social costs of revealing your discrediting attribute. That is, friends may be disillusioned or angry to learn that you are not who they believed you to be or that you did not trust them enough to confide in them.

Denying or hiding an important aspect of one's identity is associated with decrements to mental health (Pennebaker, 1990). Researchers have studied the well-being and social support of people who were diagnosed with AIDS and who either kept their condition private or revealed it to varying numbers of people (Crandall & Coleman, 1992). The results show that the highest levels of anxiety, depression, and stigma existed among AIDS victims who concealed their disease from everyone and among those for whom the diagnosis became public knowledge. In both of these situations the prospect of meaningful social support is dim. However, persons with AIDS who revealed their diagnosis to one other or to a few individuals reported higher social support and well-being. This study shows that invisible stigmas that are concealed prevent stigmatizable people from receiving others' support, understanding, and acceptance.

On the opposite end of the visibility spectrum are people with completely apparent stigmas. They cannot avoid being identified, labeled, and stereotyped; hence, their social plight is in being judged and rejected by others on sight. Visibly stigmatized people, then, are denied opportunities to interact with others. Aside from the implications for social support discussed previously, disrupted social interactions also affect one's social skills.

Carol Miller and her colleagues examined the effects of stigma visibility on social skill decrements by having obese and nonobese women engage in a phone conversation with a partner who was unaware of the woman's weight (Miller, Rothblum, Barbour, Brand, & Felicio, 1990). The conversation partners rated the obese women as less likable and friendly and thought they made poorer impressions than the nonobese women. Independent raters who listened to the taped phone conversations agreed: The obese women were seen as less likable, socially skilled, and attractive than the normal-weight women. One may speculate that these reactions were merely a fulfillment of the expectations of obese women for their interactions. However, obese and nonobese women did not differ on how likable and socially skilled they rated themselves in the conversation. This suggests that obese women's poorer social skills existed objectively prior to the conversation and were not just the realization of an expected social outcome.

Individuals with visible stigmas do not have the luxury of strategically concealing and revealing their stigma to maximize acceptance and social adjustment. Rather, they are caught in a vicious cycle of rejection and limited opportunity. Others' rejection disrupts the social prospects and skills of stigmatized people, which, in turn, contributes to even more avoidance and rejection.

The Moderating Effects of Stigma Peril on the Social Consequences of Stigma

A final dimension of the social consequences of stigma is the danger that other people associate with a stigmatizing condition (Jones et al., 1984), called **stigma peril.** The more peril is associated with a stigma, the more negative is its impact on the social prospects of stigmatized people. One aspect of stigma peril is contagiousness. People may be stigmatized by physical ailments that are perceived by others to be contagious, even when such contagion is irrational or highly improbable. The stigma felt by HIV/AIDS victims, for example, combines others' moral disgust with their irrational fear about contracting the disease, and it profoundly affects the social prospects of people with HIV/AIDS (Crawford, 1996; Herek & Glunt, 1988).

In a recent national telephone survey of American adults, Gregory Herek and John Capitanio (1998) measured whether respondents' attitudes toward people with AIDS were based on upholding cultural or personal values (for example, "I avoid people with AIDS because homosexuality is morally wrong") or on concerns about peril and personal risk (for example, "I avoid people with AIDS because I don't want to get AIDS"). The survey results showed that respondents' negative feelings toward AIDS sufferers and their support of policies such as mandatory AIDS testing were related to upholding personal values. However, behavioral intentions toward people with AIDS, such as not wanting to work alongside someone with AIDS, were related to fear of infection.

In sum, the peril associated with a stigmatizing condition contributes to our avoidance and exclusion of some stigmatized people. Another aspect of stigma peril draws on the concept of courtesy stigma that was discussed in Chapter 8. Stigmatized individuals are "perilous" if they are perceived to negatively affect nonstigmatized individuals' relations with peers and friends. Thus, our desire to avoid acquiring courtesy-stigmatized status likely adds to the rejection and isolation felt by stigmatized people.

PSYCHOLOGICAL CONSEQUENCES OF STIGMA

Self-Concept

The self-concept is the summary of one's self-knowledge and consists of traits, roles, and abilities. Identity and self-concept are similar terms, with identity referring to the most central or defining elements of the self-concept. Self-conceptions that are realistically positive, clear, and multifaceted promote psychological well-being (Campbell, 1990; Linville, 1985; Wylie, 1979). Many stigmatized people may struggle to maintain these mental-health-promoting qualities of the self-concept.

As was discussed in Chapter 8, the discrepancy between your actual self-views and the person you are believed to be by others is the essence of stigma. Accordingly, stigma could be reduced in two ways. First, stigmatized people could bring their virtual identity—who they are assumed to be—in line with their actual self-views. This would require a massive attitude-change campaign among the general public, a practical impossibility for most stigmatized individuals. However, it is this notion that is at the heart of public education campaigns on behalf of stigmatized groups, such as the developmentally disabled or welfare recipients. When stereotypes are broken down in society at large, stigmatized people become less socially discredited, and their self-concepts should reflect the more positive views held about them by others. And having a more positive self-concept contributes to well-being. A second route to reducing stigma is to align one's actual identity with one's virtual identity. In other words, stigmatized persons could internalize and fulfill others' beliefs about them, thereby reducing the mismatch between who they really are and who they are in others' eyes. Theoretically, this would reduce or eliminate stigma. Practically, however, it has two negative implications for the self-concept and psychological well-being.

First, we know from research on the self-fulfilling prophecy that stereotypic (and negative) expectations about others can elicit the expected negative behavior. Further, much research shows that one's self-views can be adjusted and rationalized to be consistent with one's actions (Cooper & Fazio, 1984). If, in order to reduce stigma, stigmatized individuals behave in the ways expected of them by others, their self-concepts will inevitably reorganize to reflect those negative qualities and detract from psychological well-being.

Second, in coming to view themselves as others view them, stigmatized people risk elevating their stigmatizing attribute to a master status in the self-concept. In other words, all of a stigmatized person's other abilities and qualities will become subordinate to and colored by the **master status attribute.** For example, imagine an overweight college student who, in an effort to fit in socially and reduce the stigma he experiences, begins to play the stereotypical (and expected) role of "the-jolly-clown-who-never-met-a-meal-he-didn't-like." Although this may improve his social prospects, he in effect becomes in others' eyes what he was assumed to be all along—a person with little self-control or dignity. In his efforts to reduce stigma, his weight has become the dominant aspect of his identity, not only to others but now also to him.

One of the consequences of having one's stigmatized status elevated in prominence is that stigmatized people think of themselves in more stereotypical terms. Researchers studied men's and women's self-descriptions when they were in same-sex or mixed-sex groups (Abrams, Thomas, & Hogg, 1990; Hogg & Turner, 1987). It was predicted that females would be aware of their stigmatized status in social situations in which they are in the minority. Indeed, after interacting in mixed-sex compared with same-sex groups, female participants' self-descriptions included more stereotypically female terms and greater acceptance of traditional sex roles. These studies show that stereotyping oneself may be a particular problem for stigmatized people because repeated interactions with nonstigmatized people and the focus those interactions bring to one's stigma may elevate their attribute toward master status.

What are the consequences of master status self-concepts for adjustment? People who have relatively few "facets" or sides to their identities or whose self-views are all closely intertwined are described as having simple self-concepts. That is, their self-views are not diversified but cluster around a small number of identities, such as viewing oneself exclusively as an "athlete." Research shows that simple self-concepts are psychologically vulnerable (Linville, 1985). The vulnerability arises when people experience criticism or a setback in an area that essentially defines them. If they have no other identities or abilities to turn to as a means to soften the sting, they are vulnerable to depression. In sum, stigmatized people who seek to lessen stigma by playing the expected role run the risk of reorganizing their self-concepts in a way that makes them vulnerable.

The negative consequences of social stigma for stigmatized individuals' self-concepts also extend to their possible self-concepts—the "you" (specifically, the set of some traits or abilities) that is possible or anticipated in some future situation (Brown, 1998). To demonstrate this, Lisa Brown had White, Latino, and African American students watch a videotape of a teaching assistant (TA) supervisor who would be evaluating them either in a future class (short-term interaction) or throughout the next semester (long-term interaction). The ethnicity of the teaching assistant in the videotape was manipulated so as to be either White or of the same group as the participant. The students' views of their possible selves in the future semester—what they would be like as TAs—were affected by both the ethnicity of the supervisor and whether they anticipated a short- or long-term interaction with him or her. Students of color who imagined a long-term rather than a short-term interaction with a White supervisor generated more negative possible self-views than the White students. The findings were reversed when students anticipated having a supervisor of their own ethnic background. Students of color generated more positive possible self-views when they imagined having a long-term rather than a short-term interaction with the minority supervisor than the White students did.

In sum, minority students who anticipated being evaluated by a White supervisor recognized that the supervisor's stereotypes would have a more negative impact as the length of the future interaction increased. Even before the interaction with the White supervisor occurred, then, minority students thought of themselves as less qualified and confident future teaching assistants than did White students. This study suggests that the negative implications of stigma for one's self-conceptions are not limited to the effect of present interactions on current self-views but extend to the effects of anticipated interactions on possible self-views.

Self-Esteem

Self-esteem refers to our feelings of personal value, worthiness, and competence. Self-esteem is associated with many mental health outcomes, such as lowered depression, anxiety, and pessimism and healthy reactions to criticism (Kernis, Brockner, & Frankel, 1989). Stigma stands to influence self-esteem in two ways. First, self-esteem is derived partly from the evaluations we receive from and observe in other people when we interact with them (Mead, 1934; Shrauger & Schoeneman, 1979). Over time, these evaluations become part of us. By definition, stigmatized people are aware of others' negative attitudes toward them. It follows that, through repeated interaction with others, stigmatized people will become aware of and internalize others' negative appraisals of them, thus lowering their self-esteem. Second, self-esteem is also developed by demonstrating competence and achieving positive outcomes (White, 1959). Competence is demonstrated to ourselves as we successfully manipulate and control aspects of our environment, and this competency contributes to feelings of worthiness and confidence. Stigmatized people, by virtue of being socially isolated, excluded, or discriminated against, are denied many opportunities to demonstrate personal competence, thus lowering their self-esteem.

This theoretical analysis says that because of others' negative attitudes and the discrimination experienced by stigmatized people, stigmatized individuals should have lower self-esteem than nonstigmatized persons. However, studies that compare the self-esteem levels of stigmatized and nonstigmatized people consistently find no difference between them, and in some cases stigmatized people have higher self-esteem (Crocker & Major, 1989). According to Jennifer Crocker and Brenda Major (1989), the self-esteem of stigmatized people appears to be equal to or higher than that of nonstigmatized individuals because of the chronic presence and effect of self-esteem defense strategies in stigmatized people (these strategies will be fully discussed in Chapter 10). They checked this hunch in several experiments by giving women and African American participants a negative evaluation and, for some participants, preventing them from thinking the kind of thoughts that typically protect against threats to self-esteem (Crocker, Voelkl, Testa, & Major, 1991). These studies showed that when stigmatized as opposed to nonstigmatized participants received a negative outcome and could not defend against it, their self-esteem goes down. When they were allowed to use a defensive strategy, however, stigmatized and nonstigmatized participants' self-esteem did not differ.

To summarize, the psychological effects of stigma are felt most immediately in threats to self-esteem. However, stigmatized people have adapted ways to defend their self-esteem from the negative attitudes and hurtful actions of others. The profound effects of stigma on the self-concept, however, are more subtle and pervasive; these, as a result, may be more difficult to defend against.

POSITIVE CONSEQUENCES OF STIGMA?

Not all of the consequences of stigma are overtly negative. Sympathy, pity, and offers of help are common positive responses to stigmatized individuals. However, research shows that these positive and perhaps well-intentioned reactions toward stigmatized people have negative effects. In one study African American and White participants solved anagrams cooperatively with a White partner in the adjacent room (Schneider, Major, Luhtanen, & Crocker, 1996). In half of the conditions, the partner sent a note to the participants containing some helpful tips on solving the next round of anagrams; the other participants received no help. The results showed that unsolicited help damaged the self-esteem of the African American participants but not of the Whites.

Other research had participants read scenarios about a physically disabled person being interviewed for and offered a job based on either merit (citing the applicant's qualifications) or sympathy (citing concern about the applicant's disability; Blaine, Crocker, & Major, 1995). The participants then responded as if they were the job applicant. Over several studies, the responses were consistent: Sympathy lowered self-esteem and motivation for work and increased the depression and hostility imputed to the job applicants.

In other words, the positive consequences of stigma may not be positive at all. Offers of help and expressions of sympathy can carry a demeaning message that you, as a stigmatized person, are assumed to need help. Often, such "positive" behaviors reveal the same stereotypic assumptions that underlie the negative consequences of stigma discussed previously. Also, positive reactions to stigmatized people may be motivated more by selfish concerns, such as a need to see oneself, or be seen by others as helpful than by genuine concern for stigmatized individuals. Finally, according to the competency-based model of self-esteem discussed earlier, stigmatized people who are constantly on the receiving end of sympathy and help may lose some control over their own environments and outcomes and, as a result, lose an important source of self-esteem.

A CASE STUDY IN STIGMA: BEING OVERWEIGHT

I have surveyed the general consequences of stigma for the social prospects and psychological well-being of stigmatized people. As a coda to this chapter, let's consider the social and psychological consequences associated with a specific social flaw in our society—being overweight.

The Nature of Overweight Stigma

As a socially discrediting mark, overweight combines elements of other physical disabilities (for example, mobility problems and beliefs about dependence and inactivity) with the character flaws associated with other perceived behavioral deviations (for example, alcoholism or homosexual orientation). Overweight people experience discrimination in virtually all areas of life, including employment, insurance coverage, social interactions, legal implications, college admissions, and self-concept (Allon, 1982). Overweight individuals even experience discrimination from their own parents. In several studies, Christian Crandall (1991) found that, compared with normal-weight students, overweight college students received less financial support for college from their parents; this dis-

The stigma associated with obesity is particularly negative because of widespread cultural beliefs about the controllability of weight and the associated assumptions of laziness and gluttony. These demonstrators are challenging the cultural assumptions about overweight.

crepancy was greater among females than males. This pattern of discrimination existed even after controlling for the parents' education level, income, and the number of children in the family who were attending college.

Much research has established that overweight individuals face very negative stereotypes about their abilities and character, including the general beliefs that they are unattractive, unhappy, weak-willed, and asexual. For example, Hiller (1981) had students write stories about characters who were either overweight or thin. The results showed that students were more likely to write sad or negative stories about the overweight characters and to make them more unpleasant characters than was the case with the thinner characters. In another study examining the stereotypes of overweight people, participants rated overweight individuals as less active, attractive, intelligent, hardworking, popular, successful, and outgoing than normal-weight persons (Harris, Harris, & Bochner, 1982). Other researchers placed personal ads in two metropolitan newspapers: One indicated that the woman who advertised was 50 pounds overweight; the other indicated that she had a history of substance addiction (Sitton & Blanchard, 1995). Fewer men responded to the ad for the overweight woman, suggesting that overweight is perceived more negatively than substance abuse.

Overweight stigma is embedded in broader cultural beliefs about personal responsibility and thus varies widely across cultures. Researchers surveyed students in the United States and Mexico and found that antifat attitudes were significantly lower among the Mexican participants than in the United States (Crandall & Martinez, 1996). Mexican students were less likely than Americans to believe in the controllability of weight, whereas American students attributed lower willpower and more blame for their own condition to overweight people. These findings indicate that antifat attitudes are directly influenced by Western ideology, namely, belief in a just world and a tendency to make internal, controllable attributions for others' fates.

Another study examined ethnic differences in overweight stigma within the American population. African American and White female participants rated photographs of Black and White women who were thin, of average weight, or overweight (Hebl & Heatherton, 1998). White participants viewed the overweight models as less attractive, intelligent, popular, and successful than the moderate or thin models. Black participants, however, rated the models much more even-handedly; on one measure (popularity) the overweight model was rated higher than either of the other models. In other words, there is more stigma attached to overweight for White than for African American women.

Psychological and Social Consequences of Being Overweight

Stigma due to overweight is associated with low self-esteem, loneliness, and personal dissatisfaction (Allon, 1982; Maddox, Back, & Liederman, 1968). In a study demonstrating the implications of stigma for self-esteem, overweight and normal-weight women made attributions for a positive or negative interpersonal evaluation (being accepted or turned down for a date) by a male peer (Crocker, Cornwell, & Major, 1993). After receiving the evaluation, participants' self-esteem and negative feelings were measured. Compared with getting a positive evaluation, negative interpersonal feedback from a male judge was more detrimental to the overweight women than to the normal-weight women. The overweight women attributed the negative evaluation to their weight, not to the judge's prejudice toward overweight people, and this resulted in their lowered self-esteem and increased negative mood.

Overweight is also associated with negative social outcomes such as hostility and avoidance in others. Recall from earlier in this chapter the study (Vann, 1976) that found that participants delivered more intense electric shocks to overweight people who were believed to be in control of their weight than to those who were overweight through no fault of their own. In other words, the assumption of controllability underlies people's estimation that the overweight are deserving of punishment.

Natalie Allon (1982) studied adolescents regarding their experiences with overweight peers. Many peers of overweight teens reported making an effort to disguise their preoccupation with their peer's weight in order to engage in a socially appropriate interaction. Further, they reported that their overweight peers evoked in them feelings of fear, pity, and repugnance that interfered with normal social relations with them. The youth often assumed their overweight peers to be too awkward, physically limited, or unattractive to participate fully in many social activities.

These findings suggest that overweight people have fewer social opportunities than normal-weight people, a situation that might account for the poorer social skills that were demonstrated in research reviewed earlier (Miller et al., 1990). Recall that, relying on information gleaned through a short phone conversation with an overweight or normal-weight woman, evaluators (though unaware of the woman's weight) rated the overweight conversation partner as less likable and attractive and as having poorer social skills than the normal-weight partner. In other words, there are actual differences between obese and nonobese individuals' social behavior, and these social deficits are noticed by others.

Research on the stigma of overweight provides a snapshot of the experience of social difference and gives us a clearer sense of the difficulties and issues that face stigmatized individuals in their daily lives. To be sure, stigmatizing conditions differ in their underlying dimensions, and these in turn change the nature of stigma. Other stigmatized people encounter different stereotypes, and their stigma has much different implications for coping and well-being. Nevertheless, this survey of the consequences of stigma adds support to the general notion that "social difference constructs us."

SUMMARY

The social and psychological costs of being socially different are high. Stigma disrupts the social relationships of stigmatized people, undermining the important stress-buffering and supportive effects of having friends and acquaintances. Spoiled social relationships can also undermine one's social skills, which further contributes to psychological maladjustment. Stigma also has adverse implications for the self-concepts and self-esteem of stigmatized people. These general consequences are reflected in the experience of overweight individuals in our society. Although stigma often elicits positive behavior from others in the form of help or sympathy, the net effect of such experiences is negative for stigmatized people.

KEY TERMS

stigma controllability	stigma peril
stigma visibility	master status attribute

FOR THOUGHT AND DISCUSSION

1. Is there a difference in the perceptions of a stigmatizing condition whose cause was uncontrollable and is untreatable (such as a birth defect) and an uncontrollable stigma that *is* treatable (such as a facial birthmark)? Explain.

2. Stigmatized people who are denied general social acceptance often find it in groups of similarly stigmatized individuals, such as an overweight person might do in a Fat Acceptance Group. What is a benefit and a drawback of this for adjustment?

3. Discuss why positive behaviors toward stigmatized people (sympathy, assistance) are often experienced negatively.

4. Practically, what can be done on your campus to improve the social opportunities of physically disabled students?

REFERENCES

Abrams, D., Thomas, J., & Hogg, M. (1990). Numerical distinctiveness, social identity, and gender salience. *British Journal of Social Psychology, 29,* 87–92.

Allon, N. (1982). The stigma of overweight in everyday life. In B. B. Wolman (Ed.), *Psychological aspects of obesity: A handbook* (pp. 130–174). New York: Van Nostrand Reinhold.

Berrill, K. (1990). Anti-gay violence and victimization in the United States. *Journal of Interpersonal Violence, 5,* 274–294.

Blaine, B., Crocker, J., & Major, B. (1995). The unintended negative consequences of sympathy for the stigmatized. *Journal of Applied Social Psychology, 25,* 889–905.

Brown, L. (1998). Ethnic stigma as a contextual experience: A possible selves perspective. *Personality and Social Psychology Bulletin, 24,* 163–172.

Campbell, J. (1990). Self-esteem and the clarity of the self-concept. *Journal of Personality and Social Psychology, 59,* 538–549.

Cohen, S., & Wills, T. (1985). Stress, social support, and the buffering hypothesis. *Psychological Bulletin, 98,* 310–357.

Cooper, J., & Fazio, R. (1984). A new look at dissonance theory. In L. Berkowitz (Ed.), *Advances in experimental social psychology* (Vol. 17, pp. 229–266). New York: Academic Press.

Crandall, C. (1991). Do heavy-weight students have more difficulty paying for college? *Personality and Social Psychology Bulletin, 17,* 606–611.

Crandall, C., & Coleman, R. (1992). AIDS-related stigmatization and the disruption of social relationships. *Journal of Social and Personal Relationships, 9,* 163–177.

Crandall, C., & Martinez, R. (1996). Culture, ideology, and antifat attitudes. *Personality and Social Psychology Bulletin, 22,* 1165–1176.

Crawford, A. (1996). Stigma associated with AIDS: A meta-analysis. *Journal of Applied Social Psychology, 26,* 398–416.

Crocker, J., Cornwell, B., & Major, B. (1993). The affective consequences of attributional ambiguity: The case of overweight women. *Journal of Personality and Social Psychology, 64,* 60–70.

Crocker, J., & Major, B. (1989). Social stigma and self-esteem: The self-protective properties of stigma. *Psychological Review, 96,* 608–630.

Crocker, J., Voelkl, K., Testa, M., & Major, B. (1991). Social stigma: The affective consequences of attributional ambiguity. *Journal of Personality and Social Psychology, 60,* 218–228.

Dooley, P. (1995). Perceptions of the onset controllability of AIDS and helping judgments: An attributional analysis. *Journal of Applied Social Psychology, 25,* 858–869.

Farina, A., Holland, C., & Ring, K. (1966). The role of stigma and set in interpersonal interaction. *Journal of Abnormal Psychology, 71,* 421–428.

Frable, D. (1993a). Dimensions of marginality: Distinctions among those who are different. *Personality and Social Psychology Bulletin, 19,* 370–380.

Frable, D. (1993b). Being and feeling unique: Statistical deviance and psychological marginality. *Journal of Personality, 61,* 85–109.

French, R. (1984). The long-term relationships of marked people. In E. Jones, A. Farina, A. Hastorf, H. Markus, D. Miller, & R. Scott (Eds.), *Social stigma: The psychology of marked relationships* (pp. 254–294). New York: Freeman.

Furnham, A. (1982). Explanations for unemployment in Britain. *European Journal of Social Psychology, 12,* 335–352.

Goffman, E. (1963). *Stigma: Notes on the management of spoiled identity.* New York: Simon & Schuster.

Harris, M., Harris, R., & Bochner, S. (1982). Fat, four-eyed and female: Stereotypes of obesity, glasses and gender. *Journal of Applied Social Psychology, 6,* 503–516.

Hebl, M., & Heatherton, T. (1998). The stigma of obesity in women: The difference is Black and White. *Personality and Social Psychology Bulletin, 24,* 417–426.

Herek, G. (1991). Stigma, prejudice, and violence against lesbians and gay men. In J. C. Gonsiorek and J. D. Weinrich (Eds.), *Homosexuality: Research implications for public policy* (pp. 60–80). Newbury Park, CA: Sage.

Herek, G., & Capitanio, J. (1998). Symbolic prejudice or fear of infection? A functional analysis of AIDS-related stigma among heterosexual adults. *Basic and Applied Social Psychology, 20,* 230–241.

Herek, G., & Glunt, E. (1988). An epidemic of stigma: Public reaction to AIDS. *American Psychologist, 43,* 886–891.

Hiller, D. (1981). The salience of overweight in personality characterization. *Journal of Psychology, 108,* 233–240.

Hogg, M., & Turner, J. (1987). Intergroup behavior, self-stereotyping and the salience of social categories. *British Journal of Social Psychology, 26,* 325–340.

Jones, E., Farina, A., Hastorf, A., Markus, H., Miller, D., & Scott, R. (1984). *Social stigma: The psychology of marked relationships.* New York: Freeman.

Kernis, M., Brockner, J., & Frankel, B. (1989). Self-esteem and reactions to failure: The mediating role of overgeneralization. *Journal of Personality and Social Psychology, 57,* 707–714.

Kleck, R., Ono, H., & Hastorf, A. (1966). The effects of physical deviance on face-to-face interaction. *Human Relations, 19,* 425–436.

Lewis, S., & Range, L. (1992). Do means of transmission, risk knowledge, and gender affect AIDS stigma and social interactions? *Journal of Social Behavior and Personality, 7,* 211–216.

Linville, P. (1985). Self-complexity and affective extremity: Don't put all your eggs in one cognitive basket. *Social Cognition, 3,* 94–120.

Maddox, G., Back, K., & Liederman, V. (1968). Overweight as social deviance and disability. *Journal of Health and Social Behavior, 9,* 287–298.

Mead, G. (1934). *Mind, self, and society.* Chicago: University of Chicago Press.

Menec, V., & Perry, R. (1995). Reactions to stigmas: The effect of targets' age and controllability of stigmas. *Journal of Aging and Health, 7,* 365–383.

Miller, C., Rothblum, E., Barbour, L., Brand, P., & Felicio, D. (1990). Social interactions of obese and non-obese women. *Journal of Personality, 58,* 365–380.

Pennebaker, J. (1990). *Opening up: The healing power of confiding in others.* New York: William Morrow.

Rodin, M., Price, J., Sanchez, F., & McElligot, S. (1989). Derogation, exclusion, and unfair treatment of persons with social flaws: Controllability of stigma and the attribution of prejudice. *Personality and Social Psychology Bulletin, 15,* 439–451.

Schneider, M., Major, B., Luhtanen, R., & Crocker, J. (1996). Social stigma and the potential costs of assumptive help. *Personality and Social Psychology Bulletin, 22,* 201–209.

Schwarzer, R., & Weiner, B. (1991). Stigma controllability and coping as predictors of emotions and social support. *Journal of Social and Personal Relationships, 8,* 133–140.

Shrauger, S., & Schoeneman, T. (1979). Symbolic interactionist views of self-concept: Through the looking glass darkly. *Psychological Bulletin, 86,* 549–573.

Sitton, S., & Blanchard, S. (1995). Men's preferences in romantic partners: Obesity versus addiction. *Psychological Reports, 77,* 1185–1186.

Stunkard, A., Sorenson, T., Hanis, C., Teasdale, T., Chakraborty, R., Schull, W., & Shulsinger, F. (1986). An adoption study of human obesity. *New England Journal of Medicine, 314,* 193–198.

Vann, D. (1976). *Personal responsibility, authoritarianism, and treatment of the obese.* Unpublished doctoral dissertation, New York University.

Weiner, B., Perry, R., & Magnusson, J. (1988). An attributional analysis of reactions to stigmas. *Journal of Personality and Social Psychology, 55,* 738–748.

White, R. (1959). Motivation reconsidered: The concept of competence. *Psychological Review, 36,* 953–962.

Wylie, R. (1979). *The self-concept* (Vol. 2). Lincoln: University of Nebraska Press.

10

To further examine the experience of diversity by learning about some strategies by which stigmatized people manage the consequences of stigma that were reviewed in Chapter 9 and by considering the implications of using those strategies.

Coping With Being Socially Different

Stigma Management

I have discussed how being socially different is often associated with rejection, limited social opportunities, and chronically threatened psychological well-being. What response can be made to this social problem? In this chapter we explore individual strategies for coping with social stigma—termed **stigma management** (Goffman, 1963). In devoting this chapter to learning about ways in which stigmatized people manage the rejection and disadvantage they face, I do not assume that redressing the social problem of stigma is best left to stigmatized individuals themselves. Interventions for managing stigma can also come from governing agencies, as in the form of educational campaigns to promote tolerance and reduce stereotypes, or programs to promote equal opportunities in school, housing, and work.

In reality, we all have developed strategies for improving the quality of our lives. Socially stigmatized people only differ in that they have more to cope with than do those of us who possess "majority" status or are members of relatively advantaged groups. In the following pages I describe several stigma management strategies and discuss their implications for social adjustment and psychological well-being. The strategies are organized into those that are primarily aimed at improving interpersonal outcomes, such as acceptance, and those that generally focus on improving psychological outcomes, such as self-esteem. Finally, to complete the case study of stigma begun in Chapter 9, we consider the stigma management concerns of overweight people.

Stigmatized people may realize greater acceptance in society through social action. Such social change can be led and stimulated by visible role models such as gay actor Ian McKellen.

STRATEGIES FOR GAINING ACCEPTANCE AND SOCIAL OPPORTUNITY

Withdrawal

One strategy by which stigmatized individuals may cope with the negative social implications of stigma—namely, rejection, strained interactions, and loss of opportunity—is to simply avoid people who treat them stereotypically. How can **withdrawal** from the nonstigmatized world increase one's acceptance and social opportunity? There are two possible ways, each requiring that withdrawal from circles populated by nonstigmatized people be associated with increased connection to a circle of similarly stigmatized people.

First, associating with similarly stigmatized people should afford stigmatized individuals greater acceptance and more normal social interaction within those ingroups. Indeed, there is no rule that states that acceptance in nonstigmatized majority groups is a better quality of acceptance than is offered by one's own kind. Associating with ingroups provides friendships, support, and a social context in which one's stigma is a nonissue. Disadvantaged social groups—especially if they have many members—also develop organizations and services that meet the social, educational, and occupational needs of their members, further enhancing the opportunities of stigmatized people.

Second, stigmatized people may realize greater acceptance and social opportunity in the nonstigmatized world through social and political activism. Minority and disadvantaged groups that press for change in society *do* have influence, and stigmatized people can benefit from the social and political power of their ingroup. Perhaps more important, participation in the social activism of their group can help redefine their stigmatizing attribute into a positive label. For example, the National Association to Advance Fat Acceptance (NAAFA) is a support and advocacy group for overweight individuals. This organization helps its members deal with prejudice, educates others about the stigma of overweight, and addresses the difficulties of buying clothes, getting and keeping jobs, and buying health insurance among overweight people. Through this group many overweight people have refused to accept the negative cultural stereotype of obesity and, working together, have encouraged the public to confront and reconsider their beliefs about fatness.

As a stigma management strategy to increase social acceptance, withdrawal has two distinct disadvantages. First, withdrawal is physically and socially isolating from the broader, nonstigmatized culture. Friendships with nonstigmatized people, as well as the opportunities and resources associated with them, become less available. Second, people who are marginalized from the nonstigmatized majority and more socially identified with their stigmatizing attribute risk experiencing *greater* stereotyping and prejudice. Recall that stereotypes guide our social perception when we have little experience or contact with socially different others. Therefore, withdrawal into a group of similarly stigmatized people may heighten the prominence of one's attribute or status to others and prompt ever more stereotyping and discrimination.

Passing

Passing concerns methods and strategies for minimizing one's stigmatizing attribute or condition or concealing it from others. To "pass" is to be known by others as normal, as if you possessed no discrediting or discreditable attribute. All of us have attempted to pass at one time or another, behaving so as not to draw others' attention to something we wanted to conceal. For example, students who are not prepared to discuss a reading in class are vulnerable to being exposed to their classmates as a "slacker" or a "poser" (my students' terms). From students' perspectives, to pass or go unrecognized in this situation is desirable and can be accomplished by subtly avoiding eye contact with the professor.

Stigmatized people have considerably more at stake when considering passing; let's consider some of the advantages and drawbacks. The chief advantage of passing is that you, as a stigmatizable (rather than stigmatized) person, are accepted, known to others as normal, and afforded a full range of social opportunities. This is particularly beneficial in short-term interactions when passing does not require great effort or monitoring. Passing, then, depends on the concealability of one's stigmatizing or stigmatizable attribute or status. For example, a deaf individual who could read lips might well pass as a hearing person in many contexts, but a blind individual would not be able to easily conceal his or her cane or guide dog.

There are considerable drawbacks for those who attempt to pass as normal (Goffman, 1963). First, stigmatizable people must invest great energy in concealing their failing, particularly when passing becomes a way of life. The effort consists of two parts: filtering one's own behavior and speech for inadvertent cues or references that might raise suspicion in others and being alive to the "safety" of social situations. For example, consider a lesbian who opts to pass as heterosexual at her workplace. To pass successfully, she must monitor her own speech for references (such as admired gay writers or gay organizations or events) that might disclose or raise suspicion about her identity to her coworkers. Because she has come out to a small group of friends, she must also try to keep her "gay" social circle separated from her work-related "hetero" social world. That is, if stigmatized people have revealed their attribute to selected people, those people become potential, if unwitting, cover-blowers. In short, to pass effectively, nearly all of one's daily activities must be scrutinized from the perspective of others; this is a daunting information-processing burden. As was mentioned in Chapter 8, Deborah Frable and her colleagues showed that stigmatized people are mindful in social situations, attending to overt and subtle behaviors of people with whom they interact and noting details of the situation (Frable, Blackstone, & Scherbaum, 1990). Such mindfulness is likely to be fatiguing and stressful.

A second drawback associated with passing is that stigmatizable individuals will feel divided loyalties to both the group composed of similarly stigmatized people and the group to which passing gains one admittance. For example, a lesbian or gay man passing as heterosexual may be privy to the jokes and barbs of heterosexuals about gay people. At once that person may sense the warmth of inclusion, the guilt of being a party to homophobia, and defensiveness at being the (undiscovered) butt of the joke. Additionally, the undetected gay person must still monitor passing issues and thus may feel obliged to laugh along in order to avoid being suspected as a sort of "gay sympathizer." And, as if it weren't bad enough, the gay person also faces the possibility of criticism from his or her gay friends for being hypocritical or for not supporting them in their gay identity.

According to Erving Goffman (1963), to pass is to confront the tension between managing information that could lead to one's discovery and managing the restraints that being known and stigmatized impose on one's social interactions. The overall effect of passing versus openness on one's psychological and social well-being is therefore difficult to judge. The benefits of being treated and known as a nonstigmatized person must be weighed against the cognitive investments needed to pass, as well as the social costs if one is "discovered." Furthermore, many scholars argue that disclosure of one's true identity is an important aspect of healthy adjustment (Cass, 1979; Miranda & Storms, 1989). A review of research on passing among gay individuals concluded, however, that disclosing to *oneself*—coming to terms with being gay—was more predictive of self-esteem than revealing one's gay identity to others (Savin-Williams, 1990).

Exploiting Stigma

The stigma management strategies discussed previously seek to improve the social reception of stigmatized people by minimizing the focus or impact of their stigmatizing attribute on interactions. Other strategies accomplish the same end by other means. We now consider behaviors in which stigmatized people may strategically exploit their attribute or status to improve their social prospects.

SELF-PROMOTION   In regard to managing the negative implications of stigma, **self-promotion** refers to demonstrating to other people that you, as a stigmatized person, are multidimensional and competent in several domains. For example, wheelchair athletes who play basketball or race in a marathon show the nonstigmatized world that they are comparable or even superior to nonstigmatized people in abilities or roles that are unrelated to their stigmatizing attribute.

Self-promotion has two primary advantages. First, it proactively changes one's virtual identity. Recall that stigma is the experience of being known by others in a more negative or simplistic way than you know yourself. If stigmatized people show others their "hidden" talents and assets, they help reform the image that other people have of them into something more positive, multifaceted, or both. And, if stigma decreases, acceptance and social opportunity should increase.

Second, self-promotion is a compelling strategy because it allows others to see and evaluate one's competencies in spite of (what others assume are) the hindrances and disadvantages of being stigmatized. That is, others may well augment their positive reactions to a stigmatized individuals' display of talent or skill because they are perceived to have overcome special disadvantages or adversity.

COMPENSATION   As another form of stigma management, **compensation** involves stigmatized people deliberately presenting to others behavior that contradicts the assumptions held about their abilities or character. This strategy seeks to compensate for an inadequacy assumed (by others) to characterize a stigmatized person by presenting evidence to the contrary. As with self-promotion, compensating for a presumed failing strives to reshape the virtual identity of stigmatized people and reduce stigma. Research suggests not only that compensation is used by stigmatized people but also that it improves their social image.

Amerigo Farina and his colleagues examined compensation in a study that was described as "how personal characteristics affect perceivers' perceptions and attitudes" (Farina, Allen, & Saul, 1968). Participants were told that they (as the "target" individual) would be presented to the "real" participants (the perceivers) as a student who was either mentally disabled or normal, followed by an interaction between the "target" and the "perceiver." The "target" participants believed, however, that the researchers were interested in the *perceiver's* behavior, thus re-

Stigma is lessened when one is viewed by others in multi-dimensional terms, as in the case of award-winning actress Camryn Manheim.

ducing their concern about being temporarily stigmatized (in another student's eyes) as mentally disabled. This was done to allow their responses to be as genuine and unselfconscious as possible.

The perceivers studied information about the target person; either the target was described as "mentally disabled" or that label was not mentioned. The students then played a game that involved moving a marble through a maze using two knobs to control the pitch of the maze. This game was chosen because it called on abilities and skills that would be regarded as lacking in mentally disabled people—namely, mental and motor skill. The results were revealing: The targets who believed they were known to their partner as mentally disabled performed better on the maze game than those who believed they weren't labeled. In other words, those participants who were temporarily stigmatized in a peer's eyes compensated for their failing by demonstrating greater proficiency on a test of mental skill than those who were not stigmatized.

The social benefits of compensation were observed in a study in which students reviewed application folders of a bogus female college applicant who was stigmatized by being overweight (a picture of an overweight student from another college was included in the folder; Blaine & Grahe, 1994). The applicant's personal statement included a reference about being "interested in extracurricular activities" or "interested in participating in the Fitness Center." The latter was seen as a strategic effort to address public perceptions of the controllability of overweight. Participants then evaluated the applicant on a range of dimensions.

The results showed that the overweight applicant who "atoned" or compensated for her overweight by indicating her interest in fitness programs generated more positive perceptions in others compared with the applicants who did not attempt to compensate. Participants liked her better, predicted greater success in college, and were more willing to be her friend. Moreover, participants reacting to the "compensating" applicant saw overweight as less controllable than those reacting to the control applicant.

Together, these studies suggest two things. First, stigmatized people can and do present themselves in ways that compensate for the negative assumptions of others that contribute to their stigma and rejection. Second, when employed, compensatory self-presentation has social benefits; it improves one's virtual identity and prompts greater acceptance in others.

STRATEGIES FOR PROTECTING SELF-ESTEEM AND WELL-BEING

High self-esteem and a self-concept consisting of positive terms held with certainty are cornerstones of psychological well-being. As was discussed in Chapter 9, stigma has negative implications for self-esteem and self-concept. To counter the general threat to well-being posed by stigma and stigma-related outcomes, stigmatized people may draw on several **self-protective strategies.** Self-protective strategies are cognitive in nature and involve thinking about one's stigma and the experiences associated with it in ways that are beneficial to self-esteem and well-being (Crocker & Major, 1989). These stigma management strategies and their consequences are explained in this section.

Attributing Negative Outcomes to Prejudice

As objects of prejudice and discrimination, stigmatized individuals chronically experience negative events and receive negative feedback from others. Such outcomes could be due to some inadequacy or incompetency in the stigmatized person or to prejudice in others. The former attribution would threaten and the latter protect the self-esteem and self-concepts of stigmatized people. Because it is often difficult to determine exactly why something occurred, attributing negative outcomes to prejudice is a plausible and adaptive strategy for stigmatized people.

In a test of this strategy, Jennifer Crocker and her colleagues had Black college students receive a negative evaluation from a bogus White evaluator who could either see them or not (Crocker, Voelkl, Testa, & Major, 1991). The researchers reasoned that it would be impossible for participants to attribute negative feedback to prejudice when the evaluator could not see and therefore identify them as Black. The results of the study showed that receiving a negative evaluation from a White evaluator lowered Black participants' self-esteem, but only when they could not be seen. In other words, participants who were afforded the opportunity to blame the negative evaluation on prejudice did not have lowered self-esteem. Similar results were obtained when women received negative feedback from a male evaluator (Crocker, Cornwell, & Major, 1993).

These studies illustrate the benefit to well-being of attributing negative outcomes to prejudice. However, they may have oversimplified the conditions under which stigmatized individuals receive negative feedback from others by having just two conditions: one in which prejudice can and one in which it cannot be blamed for the outcome. Other research has further studied this stigma management strategy by varying the likelihood that a negative experience is due to someone else's prejudice (Ruggiero & Taylor, 1995, 1997). Karen Ruggiero and Donald Taylor (1995) had women university students do a test that was evaluated by a male judge randomly selected from a panel of male judges. The women were told that 100%, 75%, 50%, 25%, or 0% of the judges held sexist attitudes and discriminated against women. Thus women received negative feedback about their ability along with some probability that it was due to discrimination. They were then asked to rate how much their failure was due to the quality of their answers and how much to discrimination. The only women who faulted the prejudice of the male judge for their poor test scores were the women in the 100% condition—those who were certain that their evaluator was discriminatory. In the other conditions women took responsibility for their negative experience by blaming the quality of their work—even in the 75% condition, in which discrimination was very likely! Similar results were observed when the participants were Black and Asian (Ruggiero & Taylor, 1997). Taken together, this research suggests that, although attributing negative outcomes to prejudice protects the self-esteem of stigmatized individuals, the strategy may only be used when it is likely to be a fair and accurate attribution.

Attributing negative experiences to others' prejudice is not, then, a talisman for magically turning negative experiences into positive ones. There are negative implications for overusing this stigma management strategy. If stigmatized people abuse the strategy by overattributing their negative experiences to others' prejudice, they may dismiss constructive, as well as prejudicial, criticism. Further, chronic attributions of negative experiences to prejudice may be perceived by others as defensive and paranoid. Given the burden stigma places on one's social interactions, stigmatized individuals may have learned to moderate their responses to negative and possibly discriminatory outcomes in the interests of better social relations. If so, stigmatized people may be balancing their needs for self-esteem with their needs for acceptance and social opportunity.

Devaluing Negative Outcome Dimensions

A second stigma management strategy for protecting psychological well-being involves devaluing the areas in which stigmatized individuals or members of their group receive negative outcomes. The principle behind this strategy is intuitive: When you receive criticism in an area that is not important to you, it doesn't hurt as much. This is applicable to stigmatized people in two ways. First, they experience more criticism and negative experiences than nonstigmatized people, and, second, they are less likely to be able to change the outcome than nonstigmatized people.

For example, overweight individuals would likely receive chronically negative feedback on dimensions related to appearance or physical competence, such as dating or athletics, respectively. Altering the outcomes by losing weight may not be an option if the individual is comfortable with his or her weight or is unable to lose weight. So, rather than suffer recurring blows to their self-esteem, overweight people may devalue the importance of dating or athletics. In sum, if stigmatized people are unable to effect change in the amount or nature of their negative outcomes, devaluing the dimension in which they receive those outcomes is a reasonable self-protective strategy.

Research by Claude Steele demonstrates that, despite being equally as academically qualified as White students, Black students chronically underachieve in school settings (Steele, 1992). They receive lower grades, drop out at higher rates, and graduate less often than do White students. Why? As Steele argues, Black students feel vulnerable in school. They realize that they stand to struggle in an educational system with teachers and student peers who see them in stereotypical terms: as less intelligent and motivated than White students. For many Black students, school achievement holds little promise as a basis for pride, improvement, and advancement. In response, Black students devalue academics in their self-concepts. By deciding that education and grades are not that important, Black students protect their self-esteem from chronic threat of being treated stereotypically in school. In an earlier chapter, I reviewed research that showed that when Black students took a test under the belief that it could not detect differences in intellectual ability, they performed equally to White students (Steele & Aronson, 1995).

Although the strategy of devaluing protects stigmatized students against the effects of chronic negative outcomes on the stigma-related dimension, it has a downside. It simplifies one's self-concept, leaving a stigmatized person fewer and more vulnerable dimensions or abilities on which to base his or her self-esteem. Second, devaluing tends to close off potential avenues of advancement or enrichment that contribute to life satisfaction. Black youth who drop out of school because they see little potential in education for developing their self-esteem have less education as a consequence.

Making Ingroup Comparisons

We often evaluate our own outcomes by what is expected or by what most other people are receiving. Even if they are not disadvantaged in absolute terms, stigmatized people realize that they are disadvantaged compared with others. A third self-protective strategy addresses the fact that chronic comparisons with the fortunes of nonstigmatized people have negative implications for the self-esteem of stigmatized individuals. Comparing one's outcomes and opportunities with those of similar others, such as members of one's stigmatized group, are likely to be less threatening and perhaps even beneficial. Hence, making ingroup comparisons on dimensions in which stigmatized people experience discrimination is protective of well-being.

There is ample evidence that all of us prefer to compare our abilities and outcomes with those of similar others (Ross, Eyman, & Kishchuk, 1986). We believe that people who are similar to us will give us the best information about our abilities and outcomes. Comparing ourselves with similar others rules out many of the possible reasons why we might be doing worse than someone else. The tendency for stigmatized individuals to compare themselves with other similarly stigmatized persons has been noted in blind people, the elderly, and women (Crosby, 1982; Rosow, 1974; Strauss, 1968).

Not all comparisons with ingroup and fellow stigmatized individuals may benefit self-esteem, according to research by Brenda Major and her colleagues. In one study of social comparisons by stigmatized individuals, researchers examined ingroup versus outgroup, as well as upward and downward, comparisons (Major, Sciacchitano, & Crocker, 1993). Upward comparisons involve exposure to those who are more advantaged or have performed better than oneself, whereas downward comparisons utilize those who are less advantaged or whose performance is worse than our own. Their results indicated that downward comparisons with ingroup members were more protective of participants' self-esteem than were upward comparisons. However, making downward comparisons with ingroup members was no more beneficial to self-esteem than was making downward comparisons with outgroup individuals.

Comparisons with nonstigmatized people are a constant reminder to stigmatized individuals that their attribute is associated with discrimination. However, things that are associated can, over time, be erroneously assumed to be causally related. Thus chronic outgroup comparisons may damage stigmatized persons' self-esteem in two ways: through the sting of being discriminated against and through the possibility that the discrimination may be deserved. One of the benefits of ingroup comparisons for stigmatized people is that such comparisons disassociate negative outcomes from one's stigmatizing attribute or status.

In summary, attributing negative outcomes to prejudice and either devaluing or comparing oneself with ingroup members on dimensions on which one (or one's group) fares poorly potentially protect a person's self-esteem and well-being from the negative implications of stigma. Unlike strategies for maximizing acceptance and opportunity, the self-protective strategies do not objectively improve the social circumstances of stigmatized people. Rather, they tend to be used defensively and in response to specific threatening outcomes.

Seeking Social Support

The positive influence of social support—being connected to other people who like us and help us in times of distress—on psychological well-being is well established (Wills, 1991). Other people can provide informational support by giving helpful advice and information, emotional support by empathizing with our hardships, or instrumental support by performing needed tasks on our behalf. Recall from Chapter 9 the research on well-being and social support among people who were diagnosed with AIDS (Crandall & Coleman, 1992). Compared with those who concealed their illness and received no social support from others, persons with AIDS who revealed their diagnosis to a small number of individuals reported greater levels of social support and well-being. Let's consider the impact of traditional social support and that which is available in the cybercommunity on stigmatized individuals' well-being.

ACTUAL SOCIAL SUPPORT   Karen Ruggiero and her colleagues did a study that examined how stigmatized individuals (in this case women) coped with discrimination when they believed there was social support available (Ruggiero, Taylor, & Lydon, 1997). They had 60 female university students take a test that was then evaluated by a male evaluator selected from a panel of eight male judges. The women were told that half of the judges discriminated against women; this communicated that there was a 50% chance their test would be evaluated by a prejudiced judge. All participants subsequently received a failing (D) grade on the test. After the bogus failure feedback, participants were afforded either informational or emotional support, both types of social support, or no social support at all. This was done by giving the women an opportunity to know how another participant had done on the test (informational support) or to talk to another person about the test (emotional support) or both. The women then rated how much their test failure was due to their ability or to discrimination.

The results revealed that when participants thought some type of social support was available compared with no support at all, they attributed their failure more to discrimination than to themselves. That is, the availability of either informational or emotional support reversed women's tendency to blame their own ability for a negative outcome and thereby discount the effect of discrimination. When both types of support were available, the effect was stronger. Women who could draw on informational and emotional support made the most "it's discrimination" attributions and the fewest "it's my fault" attributions.

Two lessons can be drawn from this study. First, having social support available is empowering to stigmatized people; it makes it less likely that stigmatized individuals will tolerate and rationalize the discrimination they face. Research reviewed earlier indicated that stigmatized people tend to minimize discrimination even when there is a 75% chance that they did experience it (Ruggiero & Taylor, 1995), perhaps because they are reluctant to react to interpersonal outcomes in ways that could alienate others. This research suggests that social support helps stigmatized people object to discrimination even when its likelihood is just 50%. Second, the participants in this study never actually received social support; they merely anticipated receiving it. So the availability of social support has positive effects even when other people are able and willing but not quite ready to lend support.

VIRTUAL SOCIAL SUPPORT   With the evolution of the Internet, chat rooms, and newsgroups, a new form of social support is available to promote the well-being of stigmatized individuals — *virtual* social groups. Participation in virtual social groups may be especially advantageous for stigmatized people, many of whom are denied acceptance in traditional social groups because of their identifiable discrediting mark (such as obesity or physical disability). However, people who have concealed stigmatizing marks (for example, gays and lesbians or alcoholics) may also benefit from the support of virtual groups for a different reason. As discussed earlier, although these individuals pass as normal in actual social contexts, the very strategy of passing combined with the difficulty of identifying other similarly stigmatized people may contribute to profound isolation and loneliness.

Researchers examined whether individuals with visible or concealed stigmas would be more likely to turn to virtual social support in the form of newsgroup participation (McKenna & Bargh, 1998). They selected newsgroups representing visible (soc.support.fat-acceptance, alt.support.stuttering, alt.baldspot, and alt.support.cerebral-palsy) and concealable (alt.drugs, alt.homosexual, alt.sex.bondage, and alt.sex.spanking) stigmatizing marks. Researchers analyzed the content of all the original posts in each newsgroup, as well as any follow-up posts that addressed the original post, for a 3-week period (totaling 1,888 posts). They measured how frequently an original poster reposted to the newsgroup after his or her original contribution and whether this participation in a virtual social group depended on the type of stigma (visible or hidden) and the group's response to the original post (positive or negative). The results showed that individuals with hidden stigmas posted almost twice as often to the newsgroups as people with conspicuous stigmas (5.5 and 2.8 posts per person, respectively). However, getting a positive rather than a negative reply to an original post did not affect the participation of people with visible stigmas but greatly increased the subsequent posts of individuals with hidden stigmas. In other words, stigmatized people who cannot easily avail themselves of actual support groups (those with hidden marks) turned to virtual groups more often than did people with visible stigmas.

In follow-up studies, Katelyn McKenna and John Bargh (1998) looked at whether virtual group participation led to increased self-esteem and decreased social isolation among stigmatized individuals. They surveyed about 150 participants in the three newsgroups related to concealed sexual stigmas (gay, bondage, and spanking-related groups). The results indicated that posters were significantly less socially isolated than "lurkers" (those who read but did not post to the group). Moreover, compared with lurkers, posters (those who participated in the newsgroup) placed greater importance on belonging to the group. The importance of the virtual group to posters' identity, in turn, predicted greater levels of self-acceptance, less estrangement from the dominant culture, and more instances of "coming out" to friends or family as a result of the newsgroup.

These innovative studies show that, like actual social groups, virtual groups provide social support to stigmatized people. Virtual social support, however, is more popular among and beneficial to people with hidden stigmas. This is likely due to the difficulty in locating similarly stigmatized people or groups in their actual social interactions and the resultant social isolation. Importantly, this research also shows that the benefits of virtual social support reach across the cyber-divide to one's actual social relations. That is, stigmatized people who participated in a relevant newsgroup were more likely to reveal their identity and confide in people outside of the virtual world.

A CASE STUDY IN STIGMA MANAGEMENT: COPING WITH THE STIGMA OF OVERWEIGHT

To complete our stigma "case study" begun in Chapter 9, let's consider how overweight people cope with their stigma. Two concerns about coping with the stigma of overweight confront overweight individuals. First, because others assume weight is controllable, overweight people must deal with others' blaming and punishing them for their own condition. Much research has established that overweight individuals are viewed less negatively if their weight is thought to be due to some uncontrollable factor (such as a glandular disorder) or if they can report a history of successful weight loss (DeJong, 1993; Rodin, Price, Sanchez, & McElligot, 1989). Second, because of the highly visible nature of (especially extreme) overweight, overweight people must cope with the impact of their stigma on interactions with others. Given these underlying dimensions of overweight stigma, several avenues of coping are open to overweight individuals.

Attributing Negative Outcomes to Prejudice

Researchers examined this mechanism of stigma management by having overweight and normal-weight participants express why they felt a confederate had behaved in a nasty manner toward them during a task involving compliance and incidental learning (Rodin & Slochower, 1974). Their findings indicated that, whereas normal-weight participants did not respond with any single explanation for the confederate's behavior, overweight participants overwhelmingly attributed the nasty behavior to their overweight condition. The authors posit that overweight individuals consistently use their weight to explain negative behavior toward them and that weight is a powerful cue for the obese in making judgments about their own and others' behavior.

As mentioned earlier, Jennifer Crocker and her colleagues examined explanations made by overweight women for their rejection for a date by a male peer (Crocker, Cornwell, & Major, 1993). The overweight participants attributed the rejection almost solely to their weight, whereas the normal-weight participants attributed the rejection to a wide variety of factors. Unlike studies involving women and African American persons who protected their self-esteem by attributing negative feedback to an evaluator's prejudice, this did not occur with overweight women. The overweight participants were unable to see the negative evaluation as reflecting poorly on the evaluator or to view him as prejudiced. Instead, they internalized the negative attitudes toward weight they perceived from their evaluator, showing increased depression and decreased self-esteem. This suggests that attributing negative feedback to an evaluator's prejudice does not serve a self-protective function for those suffering the stigma of overweight. Why?

One explanation centers on the fact that overweight is assumed to be a controllable condition and that overweight individuals themselves tend to agree with that assumption. If overweight persons believe that weight is controllable, they tend to see others' negative treatment of them as just and deserved. To examine the influence of belief in the controllability of overweight on reactions to negative experience, researchers had overweight and normal-weight women participate in a study they thought was about "dating relationships" (Amato, Crocker, & Major, 1995). As a basis for forming initial impressions of each other as possible dating partners, they exchanged personal information with a (fictional) male in the next room. While the female participants waited for their partner's response, they read (under the guise of an unrelated study) a "surgeon general's" report on obesity. For half of the participants the report characterized weight as controllable; for the other half the report described the uncontrollable nature of weight. After this the participants received either a negative ("I wouldn't be interested in dating you") or positive ("I would like to go out with you") response from the male coparticipant. The results indicated that, more than any other group, overweight women who were led to believe that weight is uncontrollable attributed their rejection by a male to his prejudice against overweight. These attributions, in turn, protected their self-esteem from the threat of being turned down by a prospective dating partner. This research suggests that attributing negative outcomes to others' prejudice can be an effective strategy for coping with the stigma of overweight, but only when overweight people reject society's stereotype about the controllability of overweight.

Devaluing Negative Outcome Dimensions

Devaluing a particular trait or ability on which a stigmatized person fares poorly is another strategy for stigma management. Overweight individuals may devalue traits such as thinness or physical attractiveness, placing a higher value instead on a characteristic on which they succeed, such as intelligence or social skills. Hebl and Heatherton (1998) found that Black women who are overweight often devalue mainstream White ideals, including the value placed on thinness. As this devaluing of thinness develops consensus, it should help destigmatize the condition of overweight.

Another aspect of devaluing involves a strategy of shifting to alternative goals when the original goal cannot be reached due to an actual or perceived intrusion by the stigmatizing condition (Miller & Myers, 1998). Shifting goals involves two components: first, making the decision to abandon the original, unattainable goal; and second, choosing an alternative goal. Often, to rationalize the abandonment of the initial goal, that goal will become selectively devalued by the individual, simultaneously making the failure to reach it less devastating and the new, replacement goal more enticing. In abandoning an original goal, the individual ceases behaviors directed toward achieving this goal and actively engages in behaviors directed toward achieving the new goal. For example, an overweight college student may abandon a goal of popularity and focus on an alternative goal, such as academics. He may then devalue the original goal, adopting a new belief that popularity is less important than academic success.

Strategic Self-Presentation

Overweight people may also cope with their stigma through presenting themselves to and interacting with others in strategic ways. One such strategy is termed "heading off" (Miller & Myers, 1998). "Heading off" involves offering a verbal or nonverbal signal of friendliness at the first sign that another person may be engaging in prejudice against overweight. For example, an overweight person may use humor, witty comebacks, or graciousness to deflect insensitive comments from prejudiced others about their weight. Research reviewed earlier suggests that some forms of strategic self-presentation improve the social outlook of overweight individuals (Blaine & Grahe, 1994). Recall that an overweight woman who presented herself in an application to college as someone who was interested in physical fitness rather than extracurricular activities prompted more acceptance and liking in her peers. This self-presentation also changed perceivers' beliefs about the controllability of weight, which we know is an important moderator of others' attitudes toward overweight individuals.

In general, the stigma management concerns of overweight people—perhaps especially women—revolve around addressing others' abiding (albeit inaccurate) belief that weight is controllable, as well as minimizing the negative impact of that belief on interactions with normal-weight people. Perhaps more than with other stigmatizing attributes, stigma management in overweight people also involves learning not to internalize the negative stereotype associated with obesity.

SUMMARY

Faced with chronic social rejection and discrimination and their negative effects on psychological well-being, stigmatized people may turn to a variety of stigma management strategies for the purposes of increasing their social opportunities and protecting their self-concepts and self-esteem. Although many stigma management strategies promote specific aspects of well-being and adjustment, their benefits must be reconciled with possible drawbacks in other areas of adjustment. Thus, for many stigmatized people protecting self-esteem may be associated with losses in social opportunity; likewise, improving acceptance may involve dealing with others' derogatory remarks or insulting actions.

KEY TERMS

stigma management   self-promotion
withdrawal   compensation
passing   self-protective strategies

FOR THOUGHT AND DISCUSSION

1. Can self-protective strategies (such as attributing negative outcomes to others' prejudice) be overused or perceived to be overused? What are some implications of their overuse for stigmatized people?

2. Reflect on some way that you have passed in a social situation, hiding from others some part of yourself. What was the experience like? How did it affect you?

3. Scientists have established that one's weight is largely predetermined and difficult to control. Could this information be used to lessen the stigma of overweight? How?

REFERENCES

Amato, M., Crocker, J., & Major, B. (1995, August). *Belief in the controllability of overweight as a moderator of coping with overweight stigma.* Paper presented at the annual conference of the American Psychological Association, Chicago, IL.

Blaine, B., & Grahe, J. (1994). [Self-presentational stigma management of overweight]. Unpublished raw data.

Cass, V. (1979). Homosexual identity formation: A theoretical model. *Journal of Homosexuality, 4,* 219–235.

Crandall, C., & Coleman, R. (1992). AIDS-related stigmatization and the disruption of social relationships. *Journal of Social and Personal Relationships, 9,* 163–177.

Crocker, J., Cornwell, B., & Major, B. (1993). The affective consequences of attributional ambiguity: The case of overweight women. *Journal of Personality and Social Psychology, 64,* 60–70.

Crocker, J., & Major, B. (1989). Social stigma and self-esteem: The self-protective properties of stigma. *Psychological Review, 96,* 608–630.

Crocker, J., Voelkl, K., Testa, M., & Major, B. (1991). Social stigma: The affective consequences of attributional ambiguity. *Journal of Personality and Social Psychology, 60,* 218–228.

Crosby, F. (1982). *Relative deprivation and the working woman.* New York: Oxford University Press.

DeJong, W. (1993). Obesity as a characterological stigma: The issue of responsibility and judgments of task performance. *Psychological Reports, 73,* 963–970.

Farina, A., Allen, J., & Saul, B. (1968). The role of the stigmatized person in affecting social relationships. *Journal of Personality, 36,* 169–182.

Frable, D., Blackstone, T., & Scherbaum, C. (1990). Marginal and mindful: Deviants in social interactions. *Journal of Personality and Social Psychology, 59,* 140–149.

Goffman, E. (1963). *Stigma: Notes on the management of spoiled identity.* New York: Simon & Schuster.

Hebl, M., & Heatherton, T. (1998). The stigma of obesity in women: The difference is Black and White. *Personality and Social Psychology Bulletin, 24,* 417–426.

Major, B., Sciacchitano, A., & Crocker, J. (1993). Ingroup versus out-group comparisons and self-esteem. *Personality and Social Psychology Bulletin, 19,* 711–721.

McKenna, K., & Bargh, J. (1998). Coming out in the age of the Internet: Identity "demarginalization" through virtual group participation. *Journal of Personality and Social Psychology, 75,* 681–694.

Miller, C., & Myers, A. (1998). Compensating for prejudice: How heavyweight people (and others) control outcomes despite prejudice. In J. Swim and C. Stangor (Eds.), *Prejudice: The target's perspective* (pp. 191–218). San Diego, CA: Academic Press.

Miranda, J., & Storms, M. (1989). Psychological adjustment of lesbians and gay men. *Journal of Counseling and Development, 68,* 41–45.

Rodin, M., Price, J., Sanchez, F., & McElligot, S. (1989). Derogation, exclusion, and unfair treatment of persons with social flaws: Controllability of stigma and the attribution of prejudice. *Personality and Social Psychology Bulletin, 15,* 439–451.

Rodin, J., & Slochower, J. (1974). Fat chance for a favor: Obese-normal differences in compliance and incidental learning. *Journal of Personality and Social Psychology, 29,* 557–565.

Rosow, I. (1974). *Socialization to old age.* Berkeley: University of California Press.

Ross, M., Eyman, A., & Kishchuk, N. (1986). Determinants of subjective well-being. In J. Olsen, C. Herman, & M. Zanna (Eds.), *Relative deprivation and social comparison: The Ontario symposium* (pp. 217–242). Hillsdale, NJ: Erlbaum.

Ruggiero, K., & Taylor, D. (1995). Coping with discrimination: How disadvantaged group members perceive the discrimination that confronts them. *Journal of Personality and Social Psychology, 68,* 826–838.

Ruggiero, K., & Taylor, D. (1997). Why minority group members perceive or do not perceive the discrimination that confronts them: The role of self-esteem and perceived control. *Journal of Personality and Social Psychology, 72,* 373–389.

Ruggiero, K., Taylor, D., & Lydon, J. (1997). How disadvantaged group members cope with discrimination when they perceive that social support is available. *Journal of Applied Social Psychology, 27,* 1581–1600.

Savin-Williams, R. (1990). *Gay and lesbian youth: Expressions of identity.* New York: Hemisphere.

Steele, C. (1992, April). Race and the schooling of Black Americans. *Atlantic Monthly,* 68–80.

Steele, C., & Aronson, J. (1995). Stereotype threat and the intellectual test performance of African Americans. *Journal of Personality and Social Psychology, 69,* 797–811.

Strauss, H. (1968). Reference group and social comparison among the totally blind. In H. H. Hyman & E. Singer (Eds.), *Readings in reference group theory and research* (pp. 222–237). New York: The Free Press.

Wills, T. (1991). Social support and interpersonal relationships. In M. S. Clark (Ed.), *Prosocial behavior* (pp. 265–289). Newbury Park, CA: Sage.

Undeserving but Preferred?

The Stigma of Affirmative Action

CHAPTER OBJECTIVE

To discuss the stigmatizing properties of "affirmative action" status and some of the consequences of affirmative action for the individual.

W e are now well aware that the experience of social difference is often as-sociated with widespread prejudice and discrimination. The experience of prejudice and discrimination is met with interventions at many levels. On a personal level, socially different or stigmatized individuals develop strategies for coping with prejudice and discrimination in their daily lives, as was discussed in Chapter 10. The United States government has also attempted to redress dis-crimination associated with stigma and minority status on an institutional level; most prominent among these interventions is **affirmative action.** Because af-firmative action is closely associated with minority and stigmatized groups, it is relevant to our study of the psychology of social difference. Further, many promi-nent scholars have referred to affirmative action as a stigmatizing status (Heilman, 1996; Nacoste, 1990; Steele, 1990).

The stigma attached to affirmative action is a relatively recent development and is related to how the meaning of affirmative action has changed (see Crosby & Cordova, 1996, for full discussion). Originally, affirmative action meant any positive act that would increase the likelihood that individuals of differing social categories would receive equal opportunity and treatment—in other words, equal opportunity. The "affirmative action principle" has been carried out in myriad ways. Laws and regulations were enacted to tailor affirmative action to changing social conditions, and guidelines and criteria were established to make employers and universities more accountable to the principle. The result of this evolution is that today affirmative action is perceived much differently than it was in 1965. Affirmative action has come to mean preferential treatment toward members of disadvantaged groups. Public perception of affirmative action often centers on the belief that affirmative action gives preference—in hiring and admissions—to people based on their race because minority individuals, for whatever reason, are not as qualified or prepared as majority-group applicants. This widespread belief has the potential to stigmatize affirmative action recipients.

In this chapter I consider three questions related to affirmative action and the individual. First, what do people believe about affirmative action programs and about those who receive affirmative action? Second, what influence does affirmative action have on the people who receive it or are eligible to receive it. And third, how do people cope with the stigma of affirmative action? Addressing the first two questions provides a framework for understanding the stigma associated with affirmative action. The first informs us about the stereotypes people hold about affirmative action recipients, and the second makes us aware of the experience of being or being perceived to be a recipient of affirmative action.

WHAT DO PEOPLE BELIEVE ABOUT AFFIRMATIVE ACTION?

Attitudes Toward Affirmative Action Recipients

INDIVIDUAL RECIPIENTS   Much research demonstrates that people who are or are described as recipients of affirmative action are perceived to have been treated preferentially and are seen as less competent by others (Heilman, Block, & Lucas, 1992; Kravitz & Platania, 1993). The belief that recipients of affirmative action, relative to other employees or students in similar work or academic contexts, have poorer qualifications, skills, and abilities is so pervasive that affirmative action has been called the "stigma of questionable competence" (Steele, 1990). Recall that to be stigmatized is to recognize that one has a mark or characteristic that activates in others a negative stereotype. The "mark" is the public knowledge or suspicion that one was hired or admitted through an affirmative action program. The stereotype consists of negative beliefs about one's (job- or school-related) ability, deservingness, and prospects for success.

The negative evaluations that accompany affirmative action status also depend on the person's record of accomplishment. Madeline Heilman and her colleagues had about 200 insurance company managers study folders that contained job performance, educational, and work background information about a recently hired (actually fictional) employee (Heilman, Block, & Stathatos, 1997). The job performance information was manipulated to indicate that the employee had achieved either clear or ambiguous success; in some cases no information was provided. Additionally, the employee was identified as a man, a woman, or a woman hired under an affirmative action program. The results showed that the managers evaluated the woman hired under affirmative action less positively than either of the other two employees, but only when her record was not clearly successful. In other words, when the employee's accomplishments were so-so or not available for review, the managers rated the woman receiving affirmative ac-

Affirmative action remains controversial. These people are protesting the repeal of affirmative action laws.

tion as less competent, deserving of a lower salary, and a recipient of more special treatment than the "normal" man and woman employees.

This study demonstrates that the stereotype of incompetence associated with the social category "affirmative action recipient" colored managers' interpretations of an employee's performance record (except when the record was obviously above reproach) and led to more negative evaluations of an affirmative action recipient than of a typical employee. As in Chapter 2, we see again here how stereotypic expectations for others' behavior lead us to perceive (and even cause!) the expected behavior. In this study the achievement records of employees who did and did not receive affirmative action were equalized, and the employee receiving affirmative action was still rated more negatively. In the real world, given the tendency for supervisors' stereotypes to recognize confirmatory evidence, affirmative action recipients would probably have to work much harder to achieve a performance record comparable with those of their majority-group coworkers.

SOCIAL GROUPS ASSOCIATED WITH AFFIRMATIVE ACTION Negative beliefs about affirmative action apply to groups of people as well as to individuals. In one study participants read a positive description of a new immigrant group to Canada (people from Suriname) that included references to Surinamers being "good job prospects," "active in many different kinds of jobs," and "contributing tax revenues" (Maio & Esses, 1998). In one condition the immigrant group was described as eligible for affirmative action programs; in the other condition no such status was mentioned. Participants who read the affirmative-action-eligible description viewed Surinamers as less competent and having poorer job skills and reported more negative overall attitudes toward them than participants to whom affirmative action was not mentioned. Also participants were less supportive of Surinamers' immigration and of immigration in general when the immigrant group was described as affirmative-action-eligible.

Three observations from this study are revealing. First, affirmative action eligibility alone was sufficient to prompt negative evaluations of the immigrant individuals. In a real-life scenario, many of these immigrants would not have been actual recipients of affirmative action; regardless, they would have already been stigmatized by their eligibility for the assistance. Second, the Surinamers were devalued by their affirmative action status even though the program was not set up with them in mind. Third, affirmative action status prompted more ethnocentric attitudes in the participants—a desire to restrict immigration of minority groups in general.

Taken together, these last two observations suggest that recipients of affirmative action may be scapegoats. When people are unhappy or frustrated by circumstances and cannot correct or control their situations themselves, research shows they often vent their hostilities against outgroup individuals who are believed to be contributing to or causing the stressful situation (Allport, 1954). This tendency to displace hostility onto target individuals is called **scapegoating**. Scapegoats tend to be members of relatively powerless social groups who cannot defend themselves against the unfair actions of the majority. Thus we may understand majority attitudes toward affirmative action recipients in scapegoating terms. Affirmative action may heighten majority-group members' fears that they are not receiving their fair share of resources and opportunities; these fears are then taken out on the blameless but also relatively powerless recipients of affirmative action in the form of prejudice and discrimination.

In summary, affirmative action is a social category associated with a negative stereotype. Prominent in the stereotype are general negative beliefs about the skill and competence of category members. As with all stereotypes, when the category "affirmative action status" is activated, it will guide one's behavior toward category members even if they are not actual recipients of affirmative action. Naturally, this category is most likely to be activated and the stereotype applied in the workplace or university.

Moderators of Attitudes Toward
Affirmative Action Recipients

SOCIAL CATEGORY   Researchers have found that women, Blacks, senior citizens, and disabled people are all rated more negatively when they are described as recipients of affirmative action than when they are not (Rioux & Penner, 1997; Turner, Pratkanis, & Hardaway, 1991). Although the stereotype of "affirmative action recipient" is negative, it is not used uniformly across all affirmative-action-eligible groups. In several studies Susan Clayton found that participants objected to people in particular social categories receiving affirmative action and were more strongly opposed to Blacks receiving it than to women (Clayton, 1992, 1996). Other research validates the finding that African Americans are accorded the most negative perceptions associated with affirmative action status. Audrey Murrell and her colleagues found that affirmative action programs that benefited Black individuals compared with members of other disadvantaged groups were least likely to be supported by others (Murrell, Dietz-Uhler, Dovidio, Gaertner, & Drout, 1994). These differential attitudes toward affirmative action recipients exist even though general attitudes toward minorities and women do not differ and even though people support affirmative action in principle (Clayton, 1992).

AFFIRMATIVE ACTION METHOD   Affirmative action is carried out in various ways, and attitudes toward people who receive (or who are believed to receive) affirmative action are dependent on the method of affirmative action. Research demonstrates that people approve of affirmative action plans in which merit is used to select recipients and disapprove of plans in which recipients are selected based on their social category (Heilman, 1996). For example, Russel Summers (1995) surveyed business school students and found that they preferred affirmative action programs that involved training programs to those that used differential hiring and promotion criteria or hiring quotas. These findings suggest that endorsement of some methods of affirmative action is inconsistent with American values of individualism and personal responsibility. In other words, negative attitudes toward affirmative action may reflect underlying beliefs that prosperity and opportunity should be earned and not bestowed. If this is accurate, we would expect much different reactions to affirmative action from Americans and from people from a less individualistic culture. Indeed, researchers compared the reactions of American and Japanese students to fictional scenarios of affirmative-action-based hiring of women (Ozawa, Crosby, & Crosby, 1996). Compared with the Americans, the Japanese respondents approved the practice more and rated it as more fair. The difference between American and Japanese attitudes toward affirmative action was not trivial—about 2 points on a 10-point scale. Although they differed greatly in their support for affirmative action, the American and Japanese participants valued fairness in hiring equally.

Explanations for Attitudes Toward Affirmative Action Recipients

Where do our attitudes toward affirmative action originate? Why do people hold negative attitudes about affirmative action recipients, particularly toward racial minority individuals who benefit from hiring quotas or are hired under a different (and presumably less stringent) set of standards? Alternatively, what predicts positive attitudes and support for affirmative action policies and recipients? Let's discuss some explanations for attitudes toward affirmative action, beginning with why people view affirmative action negatively and followed by why they view it positively.

SELF-INTEREST   Faye Crosby has identified three possible explanations for negative attitudes toward affirmative action: self-interest, prejudice, and concerns about justice (Crosby, 1994). The self-interest explanation states that disapproval of affirmative action and negative views of affirmative action recipients will be greatest among people who perceive that they lose valued resources such as jobs or income due to affirmative action programs. White men, as the most populous and privileged social group in the workforce, should have the most negative reactions to affirmative action. The research evidence on whether self-interest motivates anti-affirmative-action sentiment is mixed. Some researchers have found that only those employees who believe their job security will be threatened by affirmative action disapprove of it (Kluegel & Smith, 1983). Other studies have found the opposite. In one study researchers surveyed White students about their attitudes toward four different affirmative action policies that were allegedly to be implemented at their university either immediately or several years hence (Nosworthy, Lea, & Lindsay, 1995). One of the programs was described as including an easier set of academic standards for affirmative action students. If the students' self-interest (e.g., "It will be tougher for me to get As if they're giving them to affirmative action students") motivates their responses, disapproval of the affirmative action plan should be especially strong in the "immediate" condition—when the participants themselves could be affected by it. However, this did not happen. In fact, the students were generally supportive of the plans and reported that they would benefit both Black students and their own group. So, although self-interest plays a role in forming majority-group members' attitudes toward affirmative action, it is not the only explanation.

PREJUDICE   Prejudice can motivate negative attitudes toward affirmative action recipients. Much research has demonstrated what is intuitively clear: Negative feelings toward women and racial minority individuals is associated with opposition to affirmative action programs that would benefit individuals from those social groups (Murrell et al., 1994; Nosworthy et al., 1995; Tougas, Crosby, Joly, & Pelchat, 1995). What is less clear, however, is the direction of the relationship between prejudice and affirmative action. Does prejudice cause opposition to affirmative action or is the reverse more plausible—that opposition to affirmative action causes negative feelings toward those who receive it? We already know, for example, that affirmative action status (when manipulated by the researchers) prompted negative reactions among White Canadians to immigrants from Suriname and that those reactions extended to all Surinamers, not just those eligible for affirmative action (Maio & Esses, 1998). Apparently, the affirmative action status of a few group members can cause prejudicial reactions toward the group. Testing the reverse causal direction—whether generalized prejudice feelings prompt negative evaluations of affirmative action recipients—faces the methodological and ethical difficulties of manipulating others' prejudice. However, new models of implicit prejudice—such as the priming of negative stereotypes that operate below conscious awareness—may be useful in demonstrating this effect in future research.

JUSTICE BELIEFS In modern, symbolic forms of prejudice, negative feelings about people from minority social groups are disguised and expressed as opposition to policies that would assist those individuals. Opposition to affirmative action, then, can be defended on pure ideological grounds: that it violates important beliefs about fairness. For this reason peoples' beliefs about what is just and fair must be considered as an independent (of prejudicial feelings) cause of attitudes toward affirmative action.

In research discussed earlier, Glenn Nosworthy and his colleagues (1995) separated the components of symbolic prejudice by measuring participants' race prejudice and the extent to which they believed in a just world—a place where people generally get what they merit. The race-prejudice measure contained items such as, "The media tends to portray an unduly negative image of the black community" to minimize socially desirable responding. The results showed that both measures (independent of each other) were related to attitudes toward affirmative action, but the direction of the relationship depended on the type of affirmative action plan. When affirmative action was described as admission quotas for minority students, both prejudice and justice beliefs were associated with opposition. When, however, the plan involved an advertising campaign targeted to draw more minority student applications and admissions, racial prejudice predicted less and justice beliefs more support.

GUILT Not all of our attitudes toward affirmative action are negative. In a recent national poll, roughly 70% of the respondents supported equal opportunity initiatives ("In poll," 1997). Are these supportive attitudes rooted in genuine belief in the principle of affirmative action or in more selfish concerns? Janet Swim and Deborah Miller (1999) found that support for affirmative action was related to guilt about being White and thus being identified with a group that has been the agent of racial and ethnic discrimination. Over several studies that included adults of all ages and from varying backgrounds, Swim and her colleagues found that White guilt was associated with negative evaluations of one's (White) racial group, with greater awareness of the privileges of being White compared with Black, and with greater recognition that Blacks experience discrimination.

Could these factors, and not White guilt, explain Whites' support of affirmative action? No, because when the researchers took into account participants' guilt about being White, the relationship between White privilege and support for affirmative action disappeared. When White guilt was statistically accounted for, the relationship between recognition of Blacks' experience of discrimination and support for affirmative action also disappeared (Swim & Miller, 1999). So Whites' guilt about the advantages of being White and about being part of a discriminatory society appear to be an important explanation for positive, supportive attitudes toward affirmative action.

To sum up, these findings suggest that our attitudes toward affirmative action are not a simple extension of self-interest and prejudice; they also draw on deeply held cultural beliefs about what is fair, as well as on guilt about being both White and a benefactor of racial discrimination. Not surprisingly, attitudes toward affirmative action can vary widely according to who is receiving it and how it is being dispensed. The knowledge that Americans are deeply ambivalent about the practice and beneficiaries of affirmative action helps us appreciate why, over the years, the problems of discrimination in hiring and admissions have been difficult to correct.

WHAT ARE THE CONSEQUENCES OF AFFIRMATIVE ACTION?

In the prior section I discussed the psychology of affirmative action from the perspective of the majority-group observer or evaluator — the proverbial White male. This perspective and the research literature it comprises gives us some understanding of the stigma of affirmative action. Now let's take the perspective of the affirmative action recipient: What is the experience of receiving affirmative action? This perspective will help us identify some of the stigma management concerns of affirmative action recipients; in the final section of the chapter I discuss how people stigmatized by affirmative action might cope with their stigma.

Benefits

The primary benefit of affirmative action is that it provides a more level "playing field" for members of disadvantaged groups when they are competing with relatively more advantaged people for jobs, promotions, university admission, and scholarships. In principle, affirmative action assures that the collective discriminatory effect of having, for example, poorer day care, health care, educational facilities, teachers, and public libraries should not disqualify minority individuals from opportunities they would otherwise have had. Affirmative action has not been a panacea for racial discrimination in the workplace and in schools, as significant race and gender inequities still exist. For example, although men and women faculty members start their professional careers at the same level, men are tenured and promoted in greater proportion and earn higher salaries compared with women (Valian, 1998).

Despite these lingering inequities, there are many benefits of affirmative action for minority- and majority-group members alike. From the results of a survey of 45,000 students who attended elite colleges in the past 20 years, William Bowen and Derek Bok (1998) concluded that affirmative action was largely responsible for creating and maintaining the Black middle class by raising the trajectory of students' educational and career opportunities. According to a summary of the research done by the University of Michigan on the long-term effects of their affirmative action admissions, racial and ethnic diversity enhances learning for all students and makes it more likely that students will live and work in ethnically integrated contexts and have friends from other ethnic groups than their own (Holmes, 1999).

Costs

STEREOTYPE VULNERABILITY   Research on the psychological consequences of affirmative action status for its recipients has found several negative effects (reviewed by Heilman, 1994; Pratkanis & Turner, 1996). Primarily, preferential hiring imputes inferiority and vulnerability to people in work-related domains (Steele, 1990). Individuals who receive jobs or gain admittance to universities through affirmative action are, like many stigmatized people, faced with the problem of attributional ambiguity. That is, affirmative action recipients must determine if they came by their position because they were qualified or because of their social group membership. According to Madeline Heilman's (1994) research on women in the workplace, this ambiguity leads to uncertainty about their own abilities, to negative self-evaluations, to selecting less challenging tasks, and to avoiding nontraditional work roles.

The tendency for affirmative action recipients to devalue their abilities and underachieve at work or in school illustrates the concept of stereotype vulnerability discussed in previous chapters. All stigmatized individuals are vulnerable to "living down" to the stereotype others have of them. When recipients of affirmative action do so, they become "evidence" that affirmative action—or preferential hiring or admission—does not work. This reversal of fortunes is articulated by Shelby Steele (1990), who contends that the stigma of affirmative action creates more disadvantage in the workplace than affirmative action itself corrects. He argues that discrimination faced by stigmatized people in the workplace is largely a result of affirmative action recipients fulfilling the stereotypic expectations associated with their "role" and subtly communicated by their coworkers. In short, affirmative action may be fostering the very problems it was designed to eradicate.

Research data support the idea that affirmative action recipients live down to others' expectations of them. In one survey of Black U.S. government employees, respondents with White supervisors received less supervisory support and fewer professional development opportunities than Black employees with Black supervisors (Jeanquart-Barone, 1996). This study suggests that White compared with Black supervisors act out their affirmative action stereotype and, in doing so, erect obstacles to Black employees' achievement. The "poorer" achievement record of those same employees, in turn, becomes evidence that the stereotype about them is accurate.

Unfair treatment in the workplace or university may also come from other employees. Some studies suggest that when majority-group members are passed over for a job or promotion in favor of an affirmative action candidate, they develop more negative attitudes toward their work (Nacoste, 1990). Given that affirmative action hires are viewed as unfair and the employees underqualified, resentment among those within the company who are passed over may bolster prejudice and discrimination against affirmative action employees.

VICTIMIZATION AND DEPENDENCE   Two other potential costs associated with affirmative action bear mentioning (Steele, 1990). Although there is little direct research evidence with which to evaluate the ideas, they are consistent with research discussed earlier on the general effect of stigma on the self-concept. First, affirmative action thrusts the "victim" role into the self-concepts of minority-group members. This self-image is reflected in others' views of affirmative action recipients as benefiting from preferential and unmerited opportunity. Thus affirmative action holds the ability to shape the identity of minority-group individuals to reflect the notion that they have been victimized by a prejudiced society and are in need of special privilege.

Second, affirmative action fosters an illusion among disadvantaged groups that it can correct all past injustice and put everyone on equal footing. According to Steele (1990), this illusion is dangerous to affirmative action recipients because it peddles the notion that discrimination can be repaid and places minority-group members in a position of being dependent on majority groups for justice. However, the idea that discrimination can be corrected with a program likely extends from the just-world beliefs of majority-group members. In other words, in a "just" world, disadvantage and injustice are believed to be due to specific, correctable factors. In reality, injustice is due to a much more complex interaction of economic, social, and cultural forces and is, therefore, not likely to be eliminated through a single initiative.

HOW DO PEOPLE COPE WITH THE STIGMA OF AFFIRMATIVE ACTION?

Very little research has addressed how affirmative action recipients cope with the stigma of that status. We know from Chapter 10 that the coping strategies open to stigmatized individuals depend on the dimensions of the stigma itself. So let us discuss the underlying dimensions of the stigma of affirmative action and, based on this analysis, speculate on some potential strategies for coping with the stigma that is most often felt in the workplace or university classroom.

Charting the Dimensions of Affirmative Action Stigma

VISIBILITY   First, is affirmative action a visible or invisible status? It may be a visible mark for some. For example, those who are known to others as having received a "minority fellowship" to graduate school or an "empowerment grant" to expand their business may already be stigmatized by that status. Other members of disadvantaged groups are not so explicitly identified. In fact, minority em-

Minority employees must deal with coworkers' suspicions about whether they were hired under an affirmative action program or based on their merits.

ployees or students themselves may be unsure if quotas or preference had any bearing on their employment or admission to school.

However, whether one's affirmative action status is literally known or not may not matter. If minority individuals' coworkers or classmates perceive that preferential treatment exists, then the categorization of "affirmative action recipient" has already been made in their minds. Once this social categorization occurs, the stereotype associated with affirmative action recipients is activated, and the negative virtual identity of the affirmative action "recipient" is sealed. Recall the study by Maio and Esses (1998) in which they found that the mere future eligibility for affirmative action of an immigrant group lowered Canadians' ratings of the immigrant-group members. Furthermore, affirmative action categorizations very likely draw on case-specific factors, such as what other people were considered for the promotion or how long the position had been unfilled. In sum, the visibility of affirmative action status is difficult to determine. It is possible that many minority employees cope with being "known" to some coworkers, such as supervisors or personnel officers, and unknown to many other coworkers. If so, affirmative action recipients have the double burden of managing information surrounding their attribute and of coping with the tension their status imposes on social interactions.

CONTROLLABILITY Is affirmative action status perceived to be a controllable stigma? Recall from Chapter 9 that the social consequences of perceived controllability are clear: Stigmatized people who are believed to be responsible for causing or maintaining their stigma are disliked more, helped less, and blamed more for their own plight. The controllability of one's affirmative action status, however, is not so clearly established.

Most minority-group employees come by their affirmative action status quite innocently. Yet, from majority-group members' perspectives, there is an obvious measure of "controllability" in the preferential treatment minority job applicants or employees are afforded by affirmative action. However, the agents of control are not the affirmative action recipients but rather the policy makers who develop and the institutions that carry out affirmative action plans. Thus it is unclear if any attributions of controllability are imputed to affirmative action recipients by majority-group individuals.

As a result, one might speculate that affirmative action recipients, though technically regarded as innocent of their negative status by majority-group workers, may be scapegoats for the true, but essentially unassailable, agents of affirmative action—government legislators and policy makers. In general, affirmative action recipients fit the profile of a scapegoat: a low-status, disliked, and relatively powerless group whose members are blamed for a set of stressful and uncontrollable circumstances.

Strategies for Managing Affirmative Action Stigma

Given that affirmative action recipients are believed to be less qualified and competent than other, majority-group individuals who might have been offered the job or promotion, compensating for this assumption likely comes to the fore for people with affirmative action stigma. Recall from Chapter 10 that compensation is a stigma management strategy in which stigmatized people present to others behavior that contradicts the assumptions being made about them. For people stigmatized by affirmative action status, this would involve demonstrating such competence through one's work, which would eliminate questions about one's deservingness for the position. An illustration may help communicate this stigma management strategy. As a graduate student, I had a Hispanic friend, a fellow student who had received a minority fellowship. Although she possessed similar academic qualifications to the other graduate students, she was concerned that her "minority scholarship" status would lead others to assume that she was less qualified and deserving of her place in the graduate program. This vulnerability compelled her to work harder to dispel others' possible beliefs about her.

Individuals who are stigmatized by their affirmative action status must also exhibit the mindfulness that is characteristic of other stigmatized individuals. In order to cope with others' assumptions of lower competence and undeservingness, affirmative action recipients must be alive to the subtleties of their own productivity and conduct at work or school, lest they confirm the inadequacy others believe about them. This analysis of strategies for coping with affirmative action stigma suggests that people with affirmative action stigma may become victims of the stereotype held about them. That is, they must work harder than others to show that they are equally qualified and deserving of their position at work or in school.

SUMMARY

Because many minority or stigmatized individuals experience chronic discrimination and disadvantage, they are more likely to be recipients of affirmative action. However, assumptions of incompetence and of benefiting from preferential treatment stigmatize affirmative action recipients, making them vulnerable in the workplace and classroom. Affirmative action stigma is a particularly vexing status because, unlike other stigmatizing conditions, its dimensions are ambiguous. Affirmative action recipients may be unsure with whom they are discredited and with whom discreditable. As a result, stigma management strategies are less clear and perhaps more burdensome.

KEY TERMS

affirmative action
scapegoating

FOR THOUGHT AND DISCUSSION

1. Imagine being a student at your school on a "minority scholarship" or having been admitted under a special "equal opportunity" program. How would this status, if at all, affect how you approach your schoolwork? Interact with others? Think about yourself?

2. How might the fundamental ambivalence White Americans have toward affirmative action affect how it is implemented and how it works?

REFERENCES

Allport, G. (1954). *The nature of prejudice.* Reading, MA: Addison-Wesley.

Bowen, W., & Bok, D. (1998). *The shape of the river: Long term consequences of considering race in college and university admissions.* Princeton, NJ: Princeton University Press.

Clayton, S. (1992). Remedies for discrimination: Race, sex, and affirmative action. *Behavioral Sciences and the Law, 10,* 245–257.

Clayton, S. (1996). Reactions to social categorization: Evaluating one argument against affirmative action. *Journal of Applied Social Psychology, 26,* 1472–1493.

Crosby, F. (1994). Understanding affirmative action. *Basic and Applied Social Psychology, 15,* 13–41.

Crosby, F., & Cordova, D. (1996). Words worth of wisdom: Toward an understanding of affirmative action. *Journal of Social Issues, 52,* 33–49.

Heilman, M. (1994). Affirmative action: Some unintended consequences for working women. In B. Staw & L. Cummings (Eds.), *Research in organizational behavior* (pp. 125–169). Greenwich, CT: JAI Press.

Heilman, M. (1996). Affirmative action's contradictory consequences. *Journal of Social Issues, 52,* 105–109.

Heilman, M., Block, C., & Lucas, A. (1992). Presumed innocent? Stigmatization and affirmative action efforts. *Journal of Applied Psychology, 77,* 536–544.

Heilman, M., Block, C., & Stathatos, P. (1997). The affirmative action stigma of incompetence: Effects of performance information ambiguity. *Academy of Management Journal, 40,* 603–625.

Holmes, S. A. (1999, May 11). A new turn in defense of affirmative action. *New York Times,* pp. 1, 20.

In poll, Americans reject means but not ends of racial diversity. (1997, December 14). *New York Times,* pp. 1, 32.

Jeanquart-Barone, S. (1996). Implications of racial diversity in the supervisor–subordinate relationship. *Journal of Applied Social Psychology, 26,* 935–944.

Kluegel, J., & Smith, E. (1983). Affirmative action attitudes: Effect of self-interest, racial affect, and stratification beliefs on Whites' views. *Social Forces, 61,* 797–824.

Kravitz, D., & Platania, J. (1993). Attitudes and beliefs about affirmative actions: Effects of target and of respondent sex and ethnicity. *Journal of Applied Psychology, 78,* 928–938.

Maio, G., & Esses, V. (1998). The social consequences of affirmative action: Deleterious effects on perceptions of groups. *Personality and Social Psychology Bulletin, 24,* 65–74.

Murrell, A., Dietz-Uhler, B., Dovidio, J., Gaertner, S., & Drout, C. (1994). Aversive racism and resistance to affirmative action: Perceptions of justice are not necessarily color blind. *Basic and Applied Social Psychology, 15,* 71–86.

Nacoste, R. (1990). Sources of stigma: Analyzing the psychology of affirmative action. *Law and Policy, 12,* 175–195.

Nosworthy, G., Lea, J., & Lindsay, R. (1995). Opposition to affirmative action: Racial affect and traditional value predictors across four programs. *Journal of Applied Social Psychology, 25,* 314–337.

Ozawa, K., Crosby, M., & Crosby, F. (1996). Individualism and resistance to affirmative action: A comparison of Japanese and American samples. *Journal of Applied Social Psychology, 26,* 1138–1152.

Pratkanis, A., & Turner, M. (1996). The proactive removal of discriminatory barriers: Affirmative action as effective help. *Journal of Social Issues, 52,* 111–132.

Rioux, S., & Penner, L. (1997, August). *Aversive racism, aversive sexism, and reactions to affirmative action programs.* Paper presented at the annual conference of the American Psychological Association, Chicago, IL.

Steele, S. (1990). *The content of our character: A new vision of race in America.* New York: HarperCollins.

Summers, R. (1995). Attitudes toward different methods of affirmative action. *Journal of Applied Social Psychology, 25,* 1090–1104.

Swim, J., & Miller, D. (1999). White guilt: Its antecedents and consequences for attitudes toward affirmative action. *Personality and Social Psychology Bulletin, 25,* 500–514.

Tougas, F., Crosby, F., Joly, S., & Pelchat, D. (1995). Men's attitudes toward affirmative action: Justice and intergroup relations at the cross-roads. *Social Justice Research, 8,* 57–71.

Turner, M., Pratkanis, A., & Hardaway, T. (1991). Sex differences in reactions to preferential selection: Towards a model of preferential selection as help. *Journal of Social Behavior and Personality, 6,* 797–814.

Valian, V. (1998, September–October). Sex, schemas, and success: What's keeping women back? *Academe, 84,* 50–55.

Making the Most of Our Diversity

CHAPTER OBJECTIVE

To review the dual principles guiding the psychology of diversity and to suggest some responses for promoting social justice.

I n this, the closing chapter of our study of the psychology of diversity, we would do well to review the principles that connected the chapters and topics in this book. First, the diverse social contexts in which we live, work, and study are, in part, our own creation. When we enter a social situation, things change: People who are socially different from ourselves become more different, people who are typical members of a social category become atypical, and people who behave independently now act out our expectations for them. Second, the social contexts in which we think and act help create us. When we enter a socially diverse setting, we can change: once a worthy individual and now discredited, once a multifaceted person and now one-dimensional, once a competent person and now incompetent. The psychology of diversity, then, is a story of the individual thread in a colorful and textured fabric of social difference. The fabric is made poorer without the individual thread, and the individual thread seems lost apart from the fabric.

Over the past chapters we have learned that we often do not respond well to the social differences we encounter. For example, we found that our information-processing tendencies produce attitudes and judgments of others that are inaccurate and often negative. Our natural concern for saving cognitive resources and our subsequent reliance on social categories lead us to conclude that we are more different from others than we really are. The same concern—efficiency—drives our overreliance on atypical social group members to inform our stereotypes. Similarly, our emotional needs lead us to respond rather negatively to socially different people: Our natural need for a sense of personal worthiness drives competition with, and discrimination against, socially different others, and our concern with self-esteem leads us to derogate those who don't believe as we do.

It is clear that, left to their natural tendencies, our cognitive capabilities and emotional impulses get in the way of contact and productive interaction with socially different people. But are these outcomes inevitable, or can we develop greater acceptance and understanding of socially different others? In the last pages of this book, let's consider some ways that we as individuals can promote acceptance of socially different individuals. I have tried to keep this study of the psychology of diversity value-free. That is, we have not concerned ourselves with what responses to diversity should occur but rather with what does occur. What should occur with regard to behavior toward socially different others in any given community is left to the citizens of that community, along with their government and civic representatives, to decide. If, however, the diversity of our social contexts is partly constructed, then what *can* occur is a reconstruction of sorts. With that distinction, I offer some steps for reclaiming and cultivating acceptance, equality, and goodwill between people from different social or cultural groups.

PRACTICE PERSPECTIVE TAKING

The eminent psychiatrist and writer Scott Peck (1994) has observed that many of the ills of modern society, including problems associated with perceiving social differences, stem from a general lack of civility among people. Civility is more than mere politeness or courtesy; it is an active consideration of others in one's actions and thoughts. The psychological foundation of civility is perspective taking, the act of perceiving the circumstances and perspective of someone else.

Many of the outcomes associated with prejudice and stereotyping arise because we make dispositional inferences about others. That is, others' actions tend to be taken as evidence of their inherent, stable qualities. As discussed in Chapter 2, when applied to inferences about group members this tendency is called the ultimate attribution error. According to this fallacy, African American students generally do worse than White students at school because they are "less intelligent," and women are less likely than men to hold managerial positions because they are "less assertive." As we should now appreciate, these stereotypical and prejudicial positions are supported by an ignorance of the impact of situations on the behavior of Blacks in school and of women at work.

The explanations for this fundamental bias in understanding others' behavior are several. The situations that influence other people's behavior are notoriously hard to see (Gilbert & Malone, 1995). Furthermore, once imagined, we "see" others' circumstances primarily from our own rather than their perspective. Nevertheless, researchers have established that when we are asked to imagine and explain the situations in which other people act, we commit the fundamental attribution error less often (Krull, 1993). Although the "practice" of perspective taking may seem onerous, it actually demands no more of our attention or memory than does social perception, which is focused on drawing dispositional inferences. So perspective taking has the potential to soften the prejudice and stereotypes we hold toward outgroup members, and it does not further burden our cognitive capacities.

To practice perspective taking in terms of the preceding example would be to ask yourself, What other things could cause women not to hold managerial positions to the same extent that men do? By viewing things from the woman's perspective, perhaps drawing on the life demands of other women you know as an aid, you would be more apt to come up with some possible alternative explanations. For example, it could dawn on you that women may not be offered managerial jobs or that they may have more life demands than men in general, with child care or domestic responsibilities. Although these possible explanations may not be factually correct, just realizing they are possible is sufficient to soften one's dispositional attributions toward women in the workplace.

Perspective taking would also lessen the burden of stigma experienced by outgroup individuals. Recall that stigma is the recognition of being known by others in more negative and simplistic terms than one knows oneself. To the extent that this disparity (others' views of you compared with your own views of yourself) is supported by the fundamental attribution error, perspective taking would undercut this support and result in others holding fairer and less stereotypical views of people with stigmatizing attributes.

Christian Crandall's research (Crandall, 1994; Crandall & Biernat, 1990) shows that prejudice against overweight people is driven by beliefs about the controllability of weight and the perceived irresponsibility of eating too much or exercising too little. Taking the perspective of the overweight, however, involves considering the idea that weight is largely uncontrollable and that overweight is not a simple matter of gluttony or laziness. Indeed, when Crandall (1994) had his study participants take the perspective of the overweight by thinking about the uncontrollability of weight, they were more accepting of fat people than were participants who did not engage in perspective taking. More generally, perspective taking means making some effort to know stigmatized people as multidimensional rather than unidimensional individuals. This can be done by being open to aspects of stigmatized people—such as talents, interests, past experiences, or social affiliations—that are unrelated to their stigmatizing attribute. Perspective taking, then, will not only lessen our prejudices but will also help destigmatize those whose perspective we are taking. To appreciate that an individual who happens to be fat has little control over his or her weight and also has many other qualities reduces the discrepancy between his or her virtual (at least where one perceiver is concerned) and actual identities, thus lessening the stigma he or she experiences.

PRACTICE CROSS-CATEGORIZATION

Although social categorization helps us manage the complexity of our social contexts, social categories also impose differences on the world that are exaggerated and overemphasized. Once established, ingroups and outgroups are never equal.

We always attach more significance to our social groups than to others' groups. Thus prejudice is a direct result of social categorization and our needs for positive ingroup feelings.

Imagine that you attend a soccer game between your school, City College, and the crosstown rival, State College. Among the fans there will be a clear and simple social categorization, with no love lost between the groups. At the game, however, you run into several old friends from high school who are now students at State College. How will this cross-categorization affect your dislike of "State Collegers"? Anthropologists who study primitive societies have observed that crosscutting social ties lessens the prejudice between neighboring tribes and clans (LeVine & Campbell, 1972). The effect of cross-categorization has been demonstrated in controlled research settings too (see Brown, 1995, for review). These studies show a clear pattern: When members of opposing groups share another category membership, their original hostility is reduced or eliminated.

Although it is well known that cross-categorization reduces feelings of prejudice, how does it work? Many explanations for the beneficial effects of cross-categorization have been tested and found to have empirical support. To determine which model best explains the effect, researchers summarized a large number of cross-categorization studies through the process of meta-analysis — examining evidence for an idea across many studies rather than within a single study (Migdal, Hewstone, & Mullen, 1997). They concluded that the best, but not the only, explanation for cross-categorization effects is the idea that cross-categorization reduces the perceived differences between one's own and another's social group while increasing the perceived differences among the members of one's own group. In other words, when we cross-categorize ourselves with a member of a disliked or avoided outgroup, "they" become (or, actually, are perceived to be) less different from "us." Additionally, the act of cross-categorization is a reminder that you and your fellow ingroup members share group memberships with other people, and this leads to the perception that "we" are not as similar to each other as once believed. Both outcomes can help explain why cross-categorization undercuts prejudice. Prejudice is more difficult to maintain against people with whom we share some similarity. Likewise, when they are perceived to be more variable, our ingroups become a less fertile breeding ground for prejudice because we sense less agreement among the members of our own group about who "they" are and how we should act toward "them."

The principle of cross-categorization is apparent in other prejudice-reduction scenarios. It is well known that cooperative interaction among members of opposing groups reduces prejudice between them, but how? Uniting with others under a common goal or identity forms a new group. It is difficult to maintain negative feelings toward people from a "disliked" group when you realize they are also members of "your" group. So cross-categorization has the potential to lessen prejudice felt toward members of outgroups and, subsequently, the stigma felt by members of those groups.

To cross-categorize ourselves and those who populate our social world is not to ignore the ways in which we are socially different from each other. Nor does

Working together on projects with people from different social groups helps us to cross-categorize them and to balance our thoughts about people who are socially different from us.

cross-categorization require us to give up our social allegiances. Ingroup pride is an important contributor to psychological well-being. Only when ingroup pride is dependent on how we "stack up" against individuals from another group does it contribute to dislike and derogation of outgroup members. Cross-categorization, then, encourages us to balance our thoughts about socially different people so that our differences do not completely overshadow our similarities.

EXPOSURE TO PEOPLE WHO ARE SOCIALLY DIFFERENT

Perspective taking and cross-categorization are steps individuals can implement to learn to respond to social diversity in ways that promote acceptance, goodwill, and social justice. Each of these practices is cognitive and involves changing the way we perceive our social world. Granted, perspective taking and cross-categorization require some effort, as does any relearning of old habits. Together, these practices will help us view our social contexts as less divided and stratified, and the inferences we do make about socially different people will be more informed and open to revision. The third recommendation follows naturally from the first two and involves action.

Physical segregation—keeping with our own kind—is a natural human tendency. From an evolutionary perspective, to remain physically close to one's kin or tribe members meant safety and survival. Today, our social clustering is not for safety or survival. More important, associating with our own kind is often a response to perceived rather than actual differences. However, physically mixing with socially different people has the potential to reduce prejudices and stereotypical beliefs even if there is no actual interaction. Interaction with outgroup members, of course, increases that potential.

Physical separation between groups of people helps maintain stereotypes and negative feelings. When we are separate from socially different others, we have little chance to form impressions of them beyond the stereotypical notions we associate with their social category. When we are separate from others, our judgments of them are likely to be overinformed by the odd, memorable, and negative case. Moreover, separation from others makes us generally uncertain about them, as we are not sure who "they" are, what "they" are up to, and if we are getting our fair share of things. Such uncertainty is fertile ground for suspiciousness and defensiveness. To sum up, the physical division of our social contexts into ingroups and outgroups contributes to ignorance about, suspicion of, and hostility toward people from other social groups.

Our well-learned patterns of physical segregation and avoidance, however, can be unlearned. As we know from research on the contact hypothesis (Chapter 4), personal and cooperative interaction with people from outgroups will help reduce our negative attitudes and stereotypic beliefs about them, especially if we perceive that an individual is a typical member of his or her group. New research also suggests that the contact hypothesis can have beneficial indirect effects. Stephen Wright and his colleagues had participants take a bogus test that was diagnostic of an important individual difference variable (Wright, Aron, McLaughlin-Volpe, & Ropp, 1997). Allegedly on the basis of the test, participants were assigned a group membership (coded either "green" or "blue") and given a correspondingly colored T-shirt to wear throughout the study. Participants then watched an interaction through a one-way mirror between a "green" group member and a "blue" group member. They were told that these interactions were to be either between close friends (who happened to be in the same study by chance), neutral strangers, or disliked strangers (who ostensibly had a tense negative relationship outside of the study). After observing the interaction, participants rated their fellow group member and the outgroup member of the pair. The ratings of participants reflected ingroup bias, such that ingroup members were rated more positively than outgroup members, but only when the interactions were between neutral or disliked strangers. When they observed an interaction between friends from opposing groups, participants' ratings did not reflect the typical ingroup-biased pattern. Rather, they liked both groups equally.

This research shows that the effect of contact with outgroup individuals on softening prejudice and stereotypes need not depend on firsthand experience. Merely observing an interaction between members of opposing groups when those people seemed friendly with each other led to positive evaluations of both people. This research has important implications for the role of television in breaking down stereotypes and prejudice. Specifically, this research suggests that cross-group interactions (interactions between Black and White characters, for example) that are portrayed in a way that implies the individuals have some prior friendly relations will be beneficial in reducing viewers' negative attitudes toward the outgroup character. It is not certain, however, that these attitudes toward TV characters would generalize to the same group members in the real world.

In sum, exposure to socially different others can accomplish several things. First, it allows us to see and interact with typical members of groups with which we are unfamiliar. By this means stereotypical beliefs are challenged and hopefully revised. Second, exposure to socially different others may preempt the need for stereotypes altogether, as we will see others less as group members and more as individuals. Third, by becoming more familiar with outgroup individuals, we may find that we share common interests or experiences with them, and these commonalities can serve as a basis for a shared group membership. Fourth and finally, acting is believing, according to a strong tradition of psychological theory and research (Bem, 1972; Festinger, 1957). The more we associate with socially different others, the more we realize that our acceptance of them, which may have started out as strained and superficial, has become genuine.

SUMMARY

Our study of the psychology of diversity has given us some intellectual insight into what role the individual plays in prejudice, stereotyping, and discrimination, as well as a new appreciation of the experience of prejudice. The dynamic of this psychology is that the individual both forms and is formed by the social difference surrounding him or her. Given this psychology, the social problems associated with living in diverse communities are also at least partially solvable by individuals. In this chapter I have briefly discussed several steps that, when practiced, will change the way individuals perceive and understand the social differences around them.

FOR THOUGHT AND DISCUSSION

1. In what ways do you go out of your way to associate with your own kind or to avoid associating with people who are socially different (such as where you shop, eat, or sit in the classroom)? What effect might this have on your perceptions of both ingroup and outgroup members?

2. Think about someone about whom you hold some prejudice, such as a disabled, overweight, or gay person. Make a list of the ways that you typically think about that individual. Now try taking the perspective of that individual by imagining being him or her, living in his or her circumstances. Write down the thoughts and images that come to mind as you imagine yourself in this person's place and discuss the effects of this perspective taking with someone.

REFERENCES

Bem, D. (1972). Self-perception theory. In L. Berkowitz (Ed.), *Advances in experimental social psychology* (Vol. 6, pp. 1–62). New York: Academic Press.

Brown, R. (1995). *Prejudice: Its social psychology.* Oxford, England: Blackwell.

Crandall, C. (1994). Prejudice against fat people: Ideology and self-interest. *Journal of Personality and Social Psychology, 66,* 882–894.

Crandall, C., & Biernat, M. (1990). The ideology of anti-fat attitudes. *Journal of Applied Social Psychology, 20,* 227–243.

Festinger, L. (1957). *A theory of cognitive dissonance.* Stanford, CA: Stanford University Press.

Gilbert, D. T., & Malone, P. S. (1995). The correspondence bias. *Psychological Bulletin, 117,* 21–38.

Krull, D. (1993). Does the grist change the mill? The effect of the perceiver's inferential goal on the process of social inference. *Personality and Social Psychology Bulletin, 19,* 340–348.

LeVine, R., & Campbell, D. (1972). *Ethnocentrism: Theories of conflict, ethnic attitudes and group behavior.* New York: Wiley.

Migdal, M., Hewstone, M., & Mullen, B. (1997). The effects of crossed categorizations on intergroup evaluations: A meta-analysis. *British Journal of Social Psychology, 37,* 303–324.

Peck, M. S. (1994). *A world waiting to be reborn: Civility rediscovered.* New York: Bantam Books.

Wright, S., Aron, A., McLaughlin-Volpe, T., & Ropp, S. (1997). The extended contact effect: Knowledge of cross-group friendships and prejudice. *Journal of Personality and Social Psychology, 73,* 73–90.

APPENDIX OF WEB RESOURCES

CHAPTER 1

http://www.inform.umd.edu/EdRes/Topic/Diversity/

From the University of Maryland, a fine site of links and resources, including a dictionary of diversity-related terms.

http://alabanza.com/kabacoff/Inter-Links/diversity.html

A site of diversity resources on the Internet, including those specific to ethnicity, gender, sexual orientation, and disability.

CHAPTER 6

http://www.pbs.org/adultlearning/als/race/

A fascinating site on racial/ethnic diversity in education. Check out the Campus Diversity Initiative National Poll results on attitudes toward ethnic diversity in education.

CHAPTER 7

http://www.cme.org/cme/cta/bib-viol.html

A list of resources for doing research on the influence of TV violence on children.

http://www.nielsenmedia.com/

The Nielsen site is a great place to browse to learn about who is watching what.

http://Othello.localaccess.com/hardebeck/

A provocative anti-TV site.

http://sooth.com/a/johnson.html

A physician's report on the effects of TV on children's physiological and cognitive development.

CHAPTERS 8–10

http://www.nmha.org/newsroom/stigma

A site promoting public awareness of the negative images of the mentally ill. Check out the "stigma alert."

http://www.telerama.com/~brooklyn/stigma.htm

An article by a mentally disabled individual on using humor to cope with the stigma of mental illness.

http://www.openthedoors.com/index_2.htm

A site promoting public awareness of and efforts to destigmatize schizophrenia.

http://www.telusplanet.net/public/bshiell/links.htm

Site for the Fat Acceptance Newsletter; information and links related to the stigma of overweight.

http://naafa.org/

Official site of the National Association to Advance Fat Acceptance.

http://www.laureate.com/nedointro.html

> *The National Eating Disorders Organization site. Follow the "Steps toward recovery" link for some suggestions for thinking critically about portrayals of women's weight and appearance in the media.*

http://nch.ari.net/wwwhome.html

> *A site of information and resources about homelessness; the "Facts About Homelessness" section is interesting.*

http://www.affa-sc.org/

> *The Alliance for Full Acceptance site stays abreast of news relevant to gay prejudice and homophobia.*

http://psychology.ucdavis.edu/rainbow/default.html

> *A super site of research and information about sexual orientation, prejudice against gays, and AIDS stigma.*

http://www.messiah.edu/hpages/facstaff/chase/h/index.htm

> *For a much different perspective on prejudice against gays, this site organizes conservative Christian resources about homosexuality and AIDS. The link to Exodus International is worth following.*

http://hatewatch.org/frames.html

> *A guide site to racism and bigotry on the Web. Follow the "Online Bigotry" link to a list of bigotry sites organized by social group and national origin. Follow the "Bigotry Software" link to a chilling list of downloadable games promoting prejudice and hatred.*

http://www.glaad.org/glaad/electronic/hate.html

> *Another guide site to "hate" websites — this one focuses on sites that promote hatred of, and prejudice against, gay individuals.*

CHAPTER 11

http://humanitas.ucsb.edu/projects/aa/aa.html

> *A must-see site for students; articles, analysis, and research materials on both sides of the affirmative action debate.*

http://www.auaa.org

> *A good "news and views" site on affirmative action.*

http://www.ceousa.org

> *A site devoted to conservative opinion and analysis on affirmative action.*

GLOSSARY

actor–observer effect The tendency for us to explain our own actions in situational terms, whereas others explain our actions in dispositional terms

actual identity The "you" you know yourself to be; a component, with virtual identity, in the experience of stigma

affirmative action A government-mandated principle in hiring and admissions that originally meant equal opportunity but that has come to stand for preferential treatment for minority groups

ambivalence The presence of both positive and negative reactions to stigmatized individuals

compensation An effort to manage the negative consequences of stigma in which stigmatized people present to others behavior that contradicts the assumptions held about their abilities or character

contact hypothesis The idea that physical contact with a member of a negatively stereotyped group reduces the negative beliefs and feelings we hold about that individual and improves our attitudes and feelings toward the group as a whole

courtesy stigma Stigma that is experienced indirectly, based on one's association with a stigmatized individual

cultural stereotypes Beliefs about a social group that are specific to a nation, culture, or society

ethnicity A social category that is based on non-physical qualities such as one's national origin, culture, or language

evolutionary psychology A way of explaining behavior by describing how it perpetuates the genes of the individuals who display that behavior

gender bias The tendency to value men and masculine traits over women and feminine traits

gender stereotypes Attributes, abilities, and beliefs commonly associated with males and females

illusory correlation The co-occurrence of an unusual behavior and a distinctive social category, leading to an erroneous belief that the two things are related

ingroup bias The tendency to evaluate people in one's own group more favorably than people in a comparison outgroup

just-world theory The belief that people have a general need to see the world—and the people and events in it—as reasonable, orderly, and just. In a just world, people get what they deserve

linguistic intergroup bias The tendency to describe the expected or typical actions of outgroup members in abstract (or relatively unchanging, dispositional) terms, while using concrete (or specific, situation-bound) terms to describe their unexpected or atypical actions

master status attribute An attribute that organizes and subordinates all of an individual's other abilities and qualities

mindfulness Being vigilant in social situations and adopting the perspective of one's interaction partners

modern prejudice Expressions of prejudice that are subtle, easily justified, and difficult to detect and that have evolved with changing societal norms about prejudice

outgroup homogeneity effect The tendency to think of outgroups as a collective of similar individuals and ingroups as a collective of relatively unique individuals

passing A stigma management strategy that involves concealing or minimizing one's stigmatizing attribute or condition from others for the purposes of appearing nonstigmatized

prejudice Unjustified negative feelings toward or judgment of an individual based on his or her social group identity

race A social category that is based primarily on skin color and associated physical qualities

racism Negative attitudes and behavior toward individuals based on their racial or ethnic group membership

realistic group conflict The tendency to evaluate socially different others negatively when we are in competition with them for some valued resource

scapegoating The tendency for majority-group individuals who are frustrated by negative and uncontrollable circumstances to displace their hostility onto members of relatively powerless social groups

self-fulfilling prophecy Our expectations for an individual's personality or behavior that cause the person to act in ways that confirm our expectations

self-promotion A stigma management strategy by which stigmatized people demonstrate to other people that they are skilled and competent in multiple domains

self-protective strategies Cognitive stigma management strategies in which stigmatized people think about their stigma and the experiences associated with it in ways that are beneficial to self-esteem and well-being

social categorization Forming mental groups of people who have the same social characteristic; thinking about people as members of social groups rather than as individuals

social identity theory The idea that our identity derives from our social categories and group memberships and that we want these social affiliations to be as positive as possible

social portrayals A term referring to the traits, behaviors, and roles associated with the people who appear on television

social representations A term referring to the social world that is represented on television: who does and doesn't appear on the small screen

social stigma The experience of being socially discredited or flawed by a personal trait or characteristic

stereotype A set of characteristics and beliefs about the members of a social group that tend to be inaccurate and overgeneralized to individual group members

stereotype threat The anxiety and vulnerability caused by students' recognition that others' stereotypes about their group are obstacles to both academic achievement and the self-esteem derived from success in school

stigma controllability Refers to who or what caused or is responsible for the stigmatizing attribute, status, or condition or to what extent it could have been prevented

stigma management Individual efforts to cope with the negative social and psychological implications of stigma

stigma peril The danger associated with a stigmatizing condition by others

stigma visibility How apparent a stigmatizing attribute, status, or condition is to others and how difficult it is to conceal from others

subtyping Modifying a stereotype of a group by reclassifying group members into more specific subgroups

terror management theory The idea that our identity and self-esteem derive from cultural worldviews that serve to protect us from existential anxiety

ultimate attribution error The tendency to cite inner, dispositional causes when we explain the actions of outgroups or outgroup members and situational, circumstantial factors to explain our own or our group members' actions

virtual identity The "you" other people believe you to be; a component, with actual identity, in the experience of stigma

withdrawal A stigma management strategy in which stigmatized people avoid others who treat them stereotypically

PHOTO CREDITS

INDEX